GOD, HARLEM U.S.A.

GOD, HARLEM U.S.A.

THE FATHER DIVINE STORY

JILL WATTS

University of California Press

Berkeley · Los Angeles · Oxford

University of California Press
Berkeley and Los Angeles, California

University of California Press, Ltd.
Oxford, England

© 1992 by
The Regents of the University of California

Library of Congress Cataloging-in-Publication Data

Watts, Jill.
   God, Harlem U.S.A. : the Father Divine story / Jill
Watts.
      p.   cm.
   Includes bibliographical references and index.
   ISBN 0-520-07455-6 (alk. paper)
      1. Father Divine.   2. Peace Mission Movement.
3. Afro-American clergy—Biography.   I. Title.
BX7350.W38   1992
299'.93—dc20
[B]   91-21662
                                                           CIP

Printed in the United States of America
1   2   3   4   5   6   7   8   9

To Tom, Doris, and Rebecca Watts,
and to the memory of
my grandfather Edward M. Hohlfeld

Contents

Preface

In 1983 in a master's seminar, I was assigned to do a paper on the African-American minister Father Divine. At the time, what I knew about Father Divine was based on vague memories from an undergraduate history course: Father Divine claimed to be God and founded an aberrational cult that grew to prominence in the ghettos of the northeastern United States during the 1930s. His appeal, I had read, rested basically on the free meals he supplied to his black parishioners and the emotional impact of his sermons. He had complete control over his followers, forcing them to break family ties, practice celibacy, and surrender their savings to his ministry. Although he had garnered much criticism, Father Divine's popularity boomed throughout the 1930s. I remember one impressive story of a letter addressed to GOD, HARLEM, U.S.A. The postman delivered it promptly to Father Divine.

My early research into the secondary literature produced between 1936 and 1954 confirmed many of these common assumptions surrounding Father Divine. But as I read further, I discovered *God Comes to America* by Kenneth Burnham, a sociologist. Burnham offered the first book-length scholarly analysis of Father Divine and treated his ministry with objectivity and respect. Quoting liberally from Father Divine's sermons, Burnham acknowledged their theological content but chose to focus his analysis on Father Divine's charismatic leadership. I was impressed because he took the minister so seriously when most other accounts were cynical and disparaging.[1]

Among the active extensions of Father Divine's Peace Mission listed in the appendix of Burnham's book is the Circle Mission Church in South Central Los Angeles. I visited the church on several Sundays but never found anyone there. I tried calling on the phone, and finally one Thursday morning someone answered, "Peace." I was startled, but then I recalled that Father Divine's followers adhered to strict language requirements, including the substitution of "peace" for "hello." Thus began my first contact with members of the Peace Mission movement, whom I have found to be honest, witty, and warm.[2]

The members of Father Divine's church generously shared their experiences and literature with me. I found that many of my assumptions concerning Father Divine's ministry were inaccurate. His Peace Mission movement during the 1930s spread nationwide and attracted many white followers. His disciples appear to have had a degree of authority regarding the direction of the organization, and it became obvious that followers joined the movement voluntarily and could leave freely.

I came to reject the characterization of the movement as a *cult*. The anticult movement of the 1970s has sapped the term of scholastic meaning, reducing it to a slur. Since American society has historically relegated many African-American religious movements to marginal status, the label robs credibility from the creation and development of black theological alternatives.[3] My research proved to me that Father Divine and his followers had been misrepresented and underestimated. I resolved to do my dissertation on Father Divine and correctly place him in historical perspective.

This book, an outgrowth of my dissertation, traces the life and ministry of Father Divine. I view Father Divine foremost as a religious leader and his Peace Mission movement as primarily a religious movement. He clearly taught his disciples to believe that he was God, and the movement adopted idiosyncratic rules of syntax and capitalization to reinforce this concept. Father Divine's appeal rested on his theology, a unique blending of several popular American religious traditions. My work has been strongly influenced by two early religious scholars, Charles Braden and Clarence Howell, who in the 1930s and 1940s contended that Father Divine drew heavily from the proto–New Age ideology New Thought. Based on the power of positive thinking, New Thought promised practitioners health, prosperity, and salvation. Father Divine adopted these tenets and encouraged followers to "channel" his spirit for material and spiritual success. During a time of racial strife and economic upheaval, he offered Americans a theological shield to ward off the demons of dislocation.[4]

In the early stages of my research, I had a brief scare. In 1983 I discovered an advertisement for a recently published book by Robert Weisbrot, *Father Divine and the Struggle for Racial Equality*. I feared my Father Divine project had come to an end but found that Weisbrot's focus was different from mine. Weisbrot opened his work with an examination of Father Divine's early life as a sharecropper's son in the Deep South. Suffering under segregation and discrimination, Father Divine developed into a social critic with a commitment to eradicating racism from American society and establishing equality. After moving to Harlem, Father Divine pursued antidiscrimination campaigns and initiated social-welfare programs. Weisbrot maintained that Father Divine was one of the first ministers to reintroduce social relief and political activism to the black church. He defined Father Divine as a civil-rights leader whose campaigns were precursors to the civil-rights struggles of the 1950s and 1960s.[5]

The following pages affirm many of Weisbrot's conclusions but depart from his study on fundamental levels. My research has shown that Father Divine did not grow up in the Deep South. Although he refused to acknowledge any family ties, the U.S. Census confirms one identity attributed to him by early acquaintances—George Baker, a Baltimore gardener born in an African-American ghetto in a small Maryland town. While blacks in Maryland endured racism, Father Divine matured in an atmosphere where African Americans maintained limited rights commonly denied to blacks in the lower South.[6]

Furthermore, I argue that Father Divine's importance rested on his religious leadership, and I believe that those social, political, and economic programs that Weisbrot concentrates on may be understood only in the light of Father Divine's theological orientation. A thorough examination of his theology clarifies the motivations for and meanings of secular projects undertaken by the Peace Mission movement. Thus, it becomes apparent that Father Divine was initially a reluctant social leader who based his secular programs on his version of New Thought ideology. For instance, he believed that poverty resulted from negative thinking, and he did not offer welfare to the poor. Instead, he focused on job training and offered his disciples a spiritual reorientation toward positive thinking.

His attitude toward racism was similar. Like some postmodernists today, Father Divine insisted that race did not exist but was a product of the mind. Negative thinking had created race, an artificial categorization that perpetuated oppression and inequality. Hence, Father Divine, who demanded that followers abandon negative language, extended that ban to racial labels. He also castigated those who identified themselves as black, contending that they were manifesting the derogatory qualities that society had assigned to African Americans.[7]

Reasoning that African Americans brought racism upon themselves, Father Divine demanded that they assume much of the burden of battling discrimination. Therefore, while on the surface many of his campaigns resembled those of the later civil-rights movement, the underlying philosophies of the two movements were radically different. Civil-rights leaders not only agitated for equality but attempted to compel the country to accept racial differences. Father Divine based his campaigns on racial denial and did not challenge, but to an extent supported, many of the accepted white assumptions concerning black inferiority. My inquiry into the life of Father Divine has shown as a whole that the African-American clergy was never very sympathetic to the minister and found his methods unreasonable.

One of the problems in researching Father Divine is that both he and his followers were and continue to be "ahistorical." He denied all family ties, and similarly Peace Mission members divulge little about their past. But Father Divine and Peace Mission leaders have maintained a policy of openness with the public, granting interviews to journalists and scholars. The result has been the appearance of numerous unflattering pieces on the preacher and his congregations. One by Sara Harris, *Father Divine: Holy Husband,* contended that even though Father Divine condemned carnal relations, he enjoyed a series of mistresses. Harris asserted that his sensuality drew the women, who composed most of his following, and compared female disciples' behavior during worship service with that of women during sexual intercourse. Harris's interpretation offended Father Divine, and in 1953 he placed a curse on her: "All those who carry the article of that book, they shall be cut off, This is Judgment Day! . . . Now she is cursed! Naturally she is cursed! I mean I curse her. I in the name of Almighty God! . . . and you have declared I am God. . . . I curse her without end—until the world shall never end."[8] Similarly, none of the other works on Father Divine met with his approval, for he insisted that it was impossible and inappropriate to write his biography. "Man cannot define GOD and cannot write a true history of him," he told one prospective author.[9]

While we must be sensitive to the Peace Mission movement's perspective, a biographical history of Father Divine makes his life's work and Peace Mission activities more intelligible and meaningful. Furthermore, it broadens our understanding of a long-ignored facet of American history—the intellectual history of working-class African Americans. A product of a black ghetto, Father Divine reflected some of the ideological traditions of blue-collar African Americans. Lower-income blacks studied and debated his teachings, and their participation in his movement reveals much about their worldview. But Father Divine's importance goes beyond the African-American experience, for his life was touched by trends in American culture, and his story reflects many of the historical issues that have dominated modern American society. In the following pages I use the tools of social and intellectual history to probe the life of Father Divine and provide a balanced account of his movement. I hope that such an approach will furnish a methodology and impetus for the study of similar figures and groups whose full historical importance lies dormant, waiting to be recovered.

Acknowledgments

This biography of Father Divine would not be what it is without the people mentioned in these acknowledgments. I thank Mrs. M. J. Divine and the followers of Father Divine for their assistance. Mrs. Divine has spent much time in person, on the phone, and by letter patiently answering my questions. She invited me to her Woodmont estate and provided me access to her collection of Peace Mission publications. I am grateful for her generosity and hospitality. Other members of the Peace Mission movement who devoted time to discussing Father Divine were Lavere Belstrom, Edna Mae Claybrooke, and Heavenly Rest. But of all the followers, I thank most Hezekiah Craig and Eli Diana, who have spent long hours talking with me about Father Divine. I realize that my study will fall short of their expectations, but I hope that its positive intentions are clear.

I also owe a great debt to the citizens of Rockville, Maryland. The librarians at the Rockville Public Library, and Mary Gordon Malloy and Jane Sween of the Montgomery County Historical Society, were most helpful in introducing me to the history of their community. I especially thank Willie Mae Carey and her family, who took me into their home and whose kindness and hospitality I will never forget.

I have had good and solid advice from my mentors, Richard Weiss, Alexander Saxton, Daniel Howe, and Edward Reynolds. Richard Yarborough's careful readings have been most beneficial and encouraging. Margaret Washington Creel guided my career as a graduate student at the University of California, Los Angeles, and I am grateful for her time, friendship, and direction.

Others to whom I owe thanks include the archivists and the librarians at the University of California, Los Angeles (especially Sharon Huling, Oscar Sims, and Simon Eliot); the staff at UCLA's Film and Television Archives; George Corey, formerly of the *New*

York Times; Cathy Gaskin and Terry Latour of the McCain Graduate Library at the University of Southern Mississippi; Eva Slezak of Baltimore's Pratt Library; the staff at the Maryland Archives in Annapolis, Maryland; the archivists at the Schomburg Library in New York; and Barbara Bair and Robert Hill, editors of the Marcus Garvey papers at UCLA. Dace Taub, of the Special Collections Division at the University of Southern California, was especially helpful in locating photos. Richard Newman, of the New York Public Library, offered important insights, sent me numerous materials on Father Divine, and was a wonderful friend.

My research on Father Divine was funded by fellowships from the Center for Afro-American Studies and the Department of History at UCLA. I owe much thanks to the staff of UCLA's history department for their kindness and friendship. Funding was also provided by Weber State University.

Many friends and colleagues have seen me through this process, and they also deserve mention: Susan Baker, Diana Brooking, Ernesto Chavez, Michael Fitzgerald, Mark Kleinman, Cindy King, Monte Kugal, Judy Kutulus, Jonathan McLeod, Susan Neil, Ray Prado, Peggy Pascoe, Amanda Podnay, Emilia Puma, Ellen Slatkin, Sonja Sonnenburg, and Nan Yamane. I would like to express my deep appreciation to Sheila Levine and Amy Klatzkin of the University of California Press. Ms. Levine has been wonderful to work with, and her guidance has been excellent. Finally I thank my parents, Thomas and Doris Watts, and my sister, Rebecca Watts, for their love, support, and inspiration.

According to the Flesh

But if I would bear record of myself according
to the flesh, it would only be a material or literary record. It would not really be practical or
essential for the good of mankind. . . . Man,
consciously, has in himself and in his history
the records of every material thing in history
of man and the history of the earth, and it
proves nothing, in a way, towards salvation in
my opinion.

New York News, August 20, 1932

Before the 1870s, Rockville was a quiet, modest village tucked among
the rolling hills and dense woods of Montgomery County, Maryland. But after the Civil War, land developers saw an opportunity
to make a profit and began promoting the town as "Peerless Rockville," an undiscovered treasure for "homeseekers and investors"
searching for "health, wealth, and comfort." In 1873, the Baltimore
and Ohio Railroad established a regular route through Rockville,
and by 1880, the town was in the midst of a housing boom. Sixteen
miles up the Potomac River from Washington, D.C., Rockville, with
its mild temperatures and cool breezes, offered a summertime refuge from the sweltering heat and humidity of the nation's capital.
Rockville quickly became a popular resort town and lured the elite
of Washington society, who fled from mugginess, mosquitoes, and
malaria to the elegant homes and quaint cottages in the growing
but still serene little town.[1]

Yet not everyone in Rockville enjoyed the pleasures of prosperity and leisure. At the northern edge of town was a black ghetto
known as Monkey Run. White vacationers and residents of Rockville maintained an awkward relationship with the black population. Although they treated African Americans with contempt,
whites were thoroughly dependent on the inhabitants of Monkey

Run to work in their homes, on their farms, and in their businesses. Six days a week, black men, women, and children trudged up a gentle slope to work in white neighborhoods. Except for the police, who monitored the ghetto from the courthouse bell tower, white residents paid little attention to the lives of those who lived in Monkey Run.[2]

However, in May 1897 the local white newspaper took notice of the death of Nancy Baker, a resident of Monkey Run. The paper reported that when Nancy Baker passed away, she was five feet tall and weighed 480 pounds. Her body lay in her home for almost two days as a local carpenter rushed to build a coffin large enough to accommodate her. On the day of her funeral, the coffin could not be removed until the door of her home had been cut away. Ten pallbearers carried Nancy Baker to her final resting place in a black Rockville cemetery. She left behind a husband and several children, including a teenage son, George Baker, Jr., who would become the evangelist Father Divine.[3]

Nancy Baker's life had never been easy. She was born into slavery in the 1840s in Gaithersburg, an agricultural hamlet about five miles from Rockville.[4] Slavery in Maryland differed from that in other parts of the South. The need for slaves had lessened as Maryland farmers abandoned tobacco to cultivate grains and produce. While many planters sold their slaves to buyers from the lower South, others manumitted them. By 1850, over 45 percent of Maryland's African-American population was free. But Nancy was not so fortunate. Actually, the decline of slavery had detrimental effects on those like Nancy who remained enslaved in Maryland. They were separated from relatives and friends who had been sold away or freed and isolated from the support network that had developed among large slave populations.[5]

Under these conditions, Nancy grew to adulthood. She spent her early life on Mount Pleasant, a 180-acre plantation owned by Lemuel Clements and located just outside Gaithersburg. Local residents considered Mount Pleasant, with its two-story brick manor house high on a knoll, one of the finest estates in the area. A devout Catholic, Clements probably followed the church's requirements concerning the treatment of slaves and saw that all, including Nancy, were baptized and catechized. But Clements, like other Catholic masters, regarded blacks with animosity and treated his slaves callously. In 1859, Clements participated in an unsuccessful campaign to expel free blacks from the state. Like other masters, he had no reservations about separating slaves from their families and friends, and sold Nancy away from the community that nurtured her to another Catholic slaveholder, Henry B. Waring.[6]

A longtime resident of Montgomery County, Henry Waring lived only a few miles from Mount Pleasant. In the late eighteenth century the Warings, prosperous tobacco planters and merchants, owned many slaves, but by 1864, Henry Waring had only nine slaves. As the Warings' only female slave, Nancy assumed the responsibilities of a house servant—cooking, cleaning, and caring for the master's and the slaves' children. Nancy's hours began before breakfast and lasted long past dinner. Expected to attend to any household or family emergency, she often worked late into the night. In constant contact with the master and his family, she bore the brunt of white racism and lived in danger of physical and sexual abuse. Improper clothing and inadequate nutrition contributed to the severity of her life. To add to her hardships, in 1860 she gave birth to her first child, Annie, who by the time she was four had been separated from her mother, possibly sold to another master.[7]

Nancy's slave community rarely accepted its subordinate status and devised a variety of covert and overt protests. One of the most powerful means of slave resistance was religion. Nancy lived in an intensely spiritual society whose flexible character embraced a variety of religious traditions and molded them into a doctrine that challenged slavery. The major organizational basis of the slave community, religion attracted enthusiastic participation by most slaves. Hidden from the master, religious practices and institutions evolved that affirmed black independence and defied the white superstructure. Combining teachings from European Christianity with African religious traditions, slaves fashioned their own syncretic belief system. Drawing from African roots, slave religion fused the sacred with the profane and maintained that spiritual forces actively controlled the material world. Moreover, as in Africa, everyone in the community played an active role in religious celebrations, and without a doubt, Nancy worshiped with her brothers and sisters in bondage when she could. These clandestine devotionals were held in safe private places—the woods or slave cabins. Worship began with a song of praise and continued with biblically inspired sermons, witnessing, singing, and dancing. The rituals and theology affirmed community solidarity and disseminated messages of hope and strength to those under white oppression.[8]

But like many other slaves, Nancy worshiped in two religious spheres, for her Catholic masters demanded that she attend their church. The Warings had built a small brick chapel on their farm that in the early 1800s served as the principal place of worship for local Catholics. Since she worked in the Waring home, she received further exposure to Catholicism. Frequent visits from parish priests, whom the Warings entertained and lodged, increased her familiarity with Catholicism. As a house servant caring for the slaveowner's offspring, Nancy must have internalized some Catholic values, for she was expected to uphold Catholic standards for the master's children.[9]

In 1861, life on the Waring farm changed quickly for everyone, especially Nancy. With the outbreak of the Civil War came confusion and chaos. Although the presence of the U.S. military ensured Maryland's loyalty to the Union, the white residents of Montgomery County were staunch Confederate sympathizers who clung to the institution of slavery. In spite of their efforts, the war dealt a final blow to slavery in Maryland, and on November 1, 1864, the state assembly outlawed slavery. As the war came to an end, Nancy joined other former slaves as they asserted their independence and searched for their families and friends. Nancy left her master and selected the surname Smith. Reunited with Annie, she settled in Rockville with a newborn daughter, Margaret. In July 1866, Nancy bore another daughter, Delia, and to support her family, secured a position as a domestic in one of Rockville's white homes. Since housing for blacks in Rockville was scarce and rents high, several families usually crowded into a single home. On her meager wages Nancy Smith found lodging for her young family in a small cabin with twenty-seven other people.[10]

During the transitional years of Reconstruction, life changed quickly for Nancy Smith and her family. Once old enough, Annie, Margaret, and Delia went to work in white homes but unlike their mother, had an opportunity to gain some education through the local Freedmen's School. Their home life changed significantly in the 1870s when Nancy Smith married George Baker, a newcomer to Rockville. Born in Maryland in the 1840s, George Baker's exact origins remain a mystery, but some claim that he migrated from Prince George's County, which borders Montgomery on the southeast. He began supporting his family as a farm laborer, a skill he probably acquired while a slave on a Maryland plantation. George moved his new family into a small home on Middle Lane owned by a fellow field hand, Luther Snowden. There, in May 1879, Nancy gave birth to her first son and named him George after his father.[11]

George Baker, Jr., was born at the beginning of a new era for black Americans. By 1876, the U.S. government had terminated all Reconstruction assistance to former slaves. Without federal support, blacks independently continued their struggle to establish and protect their rights as American citizens. But Maryland remained unique among southern states, and the experience of African Americans there during the post-Reconstruction years differed from that in other parts of the South. Although black Marylanders suffered segregation and discrimination, the state's distinctive economic, political, and social atmosphere offered them limited opportunities unavailable in other southern states. As the young George discovered, Maryland society both carried on the traditional repression of the South and offered the restricted freedoms of the North. Thus George Baker, Jr.'s beliefs and actions as an adult did not develop exclusively from a background of oppression but also derived from his maturation in an African-American community that maintained a heritage of economic activity, political participation, and social activism.[12]

In 1879, Luther Snowden was the only black landowner within Rockville's city limits, but over the course of the next twenty years, whites sold small parcels of land along Middle Lane to African Americans. As the population swelled with constant new arrivals from the country, Monkey Run was born. On Middle Lane poor blacks could purchase inexpensive lots and live close to their jobs as domestics and laborers. By the late nineteenth century, landowning among blacks in the city was common. Rockville banks willingly made loans to blacks who lacked the resources to buy land. Such lenient policies not only expanded black landholding but also increased African-American indebtedness. Many blacks developed a distrust of banks, which controlled them through financing and by shortchanging their accounts. Bound to their small homes by bankers' mortgages and loans, Rockville blacks resorted to taking in boarders to bolster insufficient family incomes.[13]

George Baker, Jr., spent his childhood in a small cabin full of people who barely subsisted on limited wages. In 1880, the Snowden household had fourteen occupants: Luther, his wife, his two teenage daughters, a young married couple, a bachelor, and the Baker family, which now included a new baby, Milford. Young George's standard of living did not differ significantly from that of his slave ancestors. Clad in hand-me-downs or inexpensive clothes, he went barefoot for most of the year. Like his enslaved forefathers and foremothers, he grew up on a diet of cornmeal, pork fat, red herring, and hominy. Disease spread quickly among the impoverished residents of Monkey Run, and the life expectancy of blacks in Montgomery County was well below national and state levels.[14]

Eventually Nancy Baker's obesity rendered her incapable of working. Although most African-American children were hired out to supplement their families' earnings, the loss of Nancy's income probably drove young George into the work force at an early age. George followed his father, who had begun taking odd jobs around town, which probably included doing yard work for whites. For blacks the hours were long, the work hard, and the pay low. But young George, who brought home about twenty-five cents a day, made an important contribution to the Baker family.[15]

Although the employment situation of African-American Marylanders was in many ways similar to that in other southern communities, the opportunities for landholding differentiated the black experience in post-Reconstruction Maryland. Farther south, blacks found themselves increasingly drawn into sharecropping. However, in Maryland, whites, compelled by indebtedness and a desperate need for laborers, willingly sold land to African Americans. Whites parceled out just enough property to inhibit African Americans from moving away, restricting lot sizes so that blacks were unable to support their families off the land; to make a living, black landowners had to work for whites. But throughout Maryland, black landholding was common, and even the few sharecroppers eventually made enough money to purchase small farms.[16]

Black Marylanders bought land whenever and wherever it was available, from urban centers to rural districts. Small farms owned by African Americans sprang up throughout the countryside. Some blacks purchased adjoining lots and established cooperative farming communities. As a child and young man, George observed the efficiency of these collective enterprises, for many were close to his Rockville home. These farms illuminated the changing state of African-American attitudes toward land and labor. Immersed in Western culture and values, black Americans trying to compete in the American economy adopted the individualism of the Euramerican economic tradition. Families in black farming communities maintained separate plots and retained individual profits. Yet blacks did not completely abandon their African heritage; following the African communal tradition, they shared labor and equipment. African Americans saw landowning as an assertion of their independence and often sacrificed much to become landowners. Joseph Sutton, a contemporary of George's from Talbot County, Maryland, explained: "It was very important to own land. To have a home to go to. . . . It was right hard on them the wages they had working."[17]

Landholding was also a reality in the Baker family, and by 1886, the senior George Baker had saved and borrowed enough money to purchase a ninety-by-seventy-foot lot on Middle Lane. On the plot Baker built a small home for his family. Growing up in a home owned by his father exposed young George to the ideals of independence and status associated with the ownership of land. In an age when most African Americans in the South could never hope to own land, for George it was simply part of everyday life.[18]

Landholding was not the only freedom maintained by black Marylanders. George matured in a community that proudly guarded its constitutional rights and fully participated in the electoral process. In 1870, with the ratification of the Fifteenth Amendment, African-American men in Maryland won the right to vote. By the 1890s, when most southern states had passed legislation disenfranchising blacks, African Americans in Maryland had fought successfully to retain their rights. Welcomed into the Republican party, whose victories depended on African-American votes, black males had some say in political affairs. African Americans were appointed to governmental posts and called to jury duty. But even though the Republicans campaigned to protect black suffrage, they denied African Americans leadership positions in the party and resisted nominating them for elective office. Nevertheless, because

African Americans identified the Republicans with Lincoln and believed that the party addressed at least some of their interests, they continued to support Republican candidates.[19]

Although Maryland blacks fended off threats of disfranchisement, they suffered under the severe segregation enforced by Jim Crow laws passed in the late nineteenth century. Young George lived in a world where strongly entrenched legal and social barriers separated blacks from whites. Even though Republicans supported African-American suffrage, the party abandoned its black constituency on issues of segregation and discrimination. Theaters confined blacks to the galleries, and white restaurants and hotels refused to serve them. Interracial marriages were illegal. Strict social and legal codes prohibited blacks from residing in white neighborhoods unless they worked as live-in help. Racism confined young George to a ghetto whose name, Monkey Run, invoked the image of caged primates in a zoo.[20]

The ugliness of the white racism George encountered was often manifested in shocking acts of violence. Throughout his early life, he heard of lynchings in Maryland, and several took place close to Rockville. In Rockville local authorities made no effort to prosecute members of lynch mobs. The *Montgomery County Sentinel* labeled these vigilantes "respectable, conscientious men" and warned the black population that "when the wolf comes and carries off our lambs we must hunt him with dog and gun and shoot him down in his tracks."[21]

Any black male could be targeted by a lynch mob acting on rumors and false information. Punishment was usually meted out to blacks who challenged white authority or deviated from the rigid social code. The loss of a family member not only created emotional pain but also increased economic hardships. Each lynching symbolically asserted that the law did not protect blacks and did not bind whites. But the African-American community in Maryland that nurtured George Baker, Jr., did not passively submit to white violence. Lynchings prompted black citizens to organize committees to agitate for legal protection, one group vowing to take "whatever precaution necessary to prevent similar occurrences."[22]

On occasion, black frustration with white oppression exploded into violence. Some Montgomery County African Americans were not afraid to match force with force. In several cases when white men whipped blacks who had allegedly insulted white women, Montgomery County blacks retaliated with fierce retribution. At a Montgomery County religious revival, a bloody confrontation broke out when members of the African-American community intervened in the unwarranted arrest of a black man. Nine years old at the time of this clash, George surely heard of the incident, which must have generated much discussion among the residents of Monkey Run. Reared in a community that militantly rejected white oppression, he observed the methods employed by blacks challenging the injustices in American society.[23]

Following a pattern initiated by those in slavery, George's community asserted independence through the evolution and maintenance of separate cultural practices and institutions. Such features, collectively based, fostered black solidarity and served as a release of tension. In Rockville, leisure activities usually included the entire neighborhood. Sunday was the only day off for most African Americans, so on Saturday night Rockville came alive. By sundown, Middle Lane was filled with people from the city and surrounding areas, some shooting craps, drinking, and playing cards, and others just sitting on their porches and talking. "Cakewalks," dances popular since slavery, drew large crowds. Some people threw parties or had picnics, and others flocked to concerts given by Rockville's black brass band.[24]

Excessive drinking was common at social gatherings and was not confined to the black population. Temperance fever ran high throughout the county, and in April 1881 antialcohol activists pushed through legislation prohibiting the production and sale of alcohol in Montgomery County. But temperance advocates, including African-American clergymen, continued their campaign against alcohol, and Montgomery County "drys" organized integrated rallies. White teetotalers attempted to organize an African-American temperance union in the county. Despite these efforts, blacks in Rockville violated prohibition, continuing to manufacture bootleg liquor and run speakeasies in their homes. Local authorities prosecuted Luther Snowden several times for selling whiskey.[25]

Growing up in the Snowden household where Middle Lane residents came to drink and buy whiskey, George witnessed the debilitating effects of alcohol abuse. He watched as his friends and family, who lived on subsistence wages, spent their earnings and became addicted to alcohol. For inhabitants of Monkey Run, alcohol offered an escape from their confinement in a slum surrounded by a society that offered little hope for a better future. George, like most young people, searched for direction in his life and found inspiration from the temperance advocates.

The black public schools also shaped George during these formative years. His attendance was probably sporadic, but he learned basic skills and became an avid reader. Young George attended a segregated public school on the outskirts of town that was supplied with desks and books discarded by white schools. The expenditures for black schools were considerably less than those for white schools, but despite inequitable resources, black schools were well patronized, with an absentee rate slightly lower than that in white schools. Terms in black schools ran six weeks shorter than in white schools because, education officials explained, abbreviated semesters gave the black "children time to learn to work."[26]

The African-American community considered education a tool for liberation. But most whites supported only occupational education, dedicated to producing farmhands, day laborers, or domestics. Schools partially satisfied African-American demands without threatening the white community. Crowded into a one-room schoolhouse with students of all ages and abilities, George learned reading and mathematics. However, following the Freedmen School model, the curriculum in black schools was designed to freeze African Americans into a position that would benefit and not endanger the hierarchical structure of American society. Christianity, patriotism, and the work ethic provided the foundation of black education, and textbooks bombarded African-American students with Victorian standards. Lessons emphasized punctuality, cleanliness, temperance, and hard work; tardy or disorderly students were whipped. Young George's instructors also taught the philosophy of "self-help," based on the notion that blacks had to improve their position independently through self-reliance and vocational training. Self-help ideology also promoted the American ideal that through hard work all Americans, including blacks, could climb the ladder of success. According to this philosophy, African

Americans bore the obligation for their own advancement. Educators anticipated that self-help would produce black citizens anxious to assume positions as subordinate laborers in the southern economy. But many black teachers and their students, including George, refined self-help ideology into a radical doctrine of racial uplift.[27]

However, it was religion, the core of African-American society, that most strongly influenced the development of young George. Nancy Baker raised her children in Rockville's Jerusalem Methodist Church, formed in 1867 after white Rockville Methodists abandoned the church over a dispute with the national leadership, who supported African-American civil rights. Black members continued to worship in the church, although they were relegated by the Methodist bureaucracy to the basement. In an attempt to free themselves from white restrictions, the black Methodists founded their own church in a building across the street and joined the Washington Mission Conference for Negroes of the Methodist Church. The conference assigned a white bishop to oversee the new church and a black pastor to supervise the congregation. In George's congregation church activities encompassed all aspects of life. He spent his Sundays in church school and worship services, his weeknights at prayer meetings and Bible study. The church closely coordinated social life, organizing picnics, dinners, and camp meetings. Inevitably, the intense spirituality and religious dedication of the African-American community left a deep impression on George.[28]

Perhaps most inspiring to his developing mind was the inclusiveness of the Methodist ministry. For Methodists, spirituality came from the heart, not from laborious study. The church did not require formal clerical training and selected as preachers African-American members who demonstrated inspirational speaking ability. This denomination promised black communicants opportunities for leadership and some degree of self-determination. The church provided George with a loving community, and through his participation in worship services and Sunday school, he won acceptance and respect. His life was filled with the insecurities of poverty and the sting of racism, compounded by ridicule because of his petite size, for even as an adult, he stood only five feet two inches. In the church George discovered an arena that furnished him with admiration and power.[29]

But George was not influenced only by Methodism. In Maryland a history of religious tolerance permitted a variety of churches to flourish and exposed Marylanders to a wide selection of religious traditions. Through his mother he became familiar with Catholicism. As an adult, he expressed admiration for celibate nuns and priests endeavoring to draw nearer to God. Further, he undoubtedly came into contact with Quakerism, for the Society of Friends thrived in and around Montgomery County and historically had a strong allegiance to the black community. But at the root of his early religious experiences was black religion, the combination of traditional African religion and Christianity passed down through generations of African-American slaves. Black religion provided young George with specific rituals, theological tenets, and a legacy of syncretism. As a young man, he sifted through different faiths and creeds, developing his personal spiritual convictions from a conglomeration of religious teachings.[30]

Family and personal relations also molded George. Nancy's obesity undoubtedly embarrassed and created tension in the family. George struggled to adulthood in his small home, watching obesity slowly overcome his mother. When she died, the *Montgomery County Sentinel* reported that "she was without a doubt the largest woman in the county, if not the state," memorializing Nancy as a curiosity.[31]

One day not long after his mother died George vanished from Rockville. He fled the poverty and agony of Monkey Run, leaving behind relatives and friends puzzled over his disappearance. He rejected destitution, his obese mother, his struggling family, and the white racism that promised to imprison him in Monkey Run for life.

The George Baker who disappeared from Rockville was a religious man who, confronted by the alcoholism, crime, and poverty of Middle Lane, had chosen to live a temperate, righteous, and Christian life. With fresh memories of his obese mother as a reminder of the suffering caused by destitution and white domination, George sought a new life free of these woes. His departure marked the beginning of a search for a new identity and a spiritual quest for existential truths. Reflecting on his experiences several years later, he declared to his congregation, "Cast all mortal tendencies, personal ideas and fancies out of your consciousness and consequently out of your system and you will feel light. You feel like a new creature. It is such a wonderful blessing to know that when you deny yourself . . . Christ is there . . . waiting to arise."[32]

2

Nothing but GOD

I went into My Body and drove out the spirit
of speculation and the sellers of doves and the
moneychangers. I drove them *out*. I would not
have those mortal spirits that came down to
ME in MY Body. . . . I drove out every last one
of those d—v—ls and would have nothing but
GOD. I would have starved in the streets rather
than indulge them.

First spoken September 30, 1931

In 1899 a twenty-year-old gardener named George Baker wandered into Baltimore's busy streets searching for a new home and a new church.[1] Baltimore was only fifty-seven miles from Rockville, but in many ways the distance between Maryland's largest city and Baker's childhood home was much greater. Baltimore's sidewalks were filled with people, its streets clogged with traffic, its air filled with the stench of garbage and smoke. Immigrants from all over the world poured into the city. Goods and foodstuffs flowed in and out of its ports. Factories pumped out products sold at home and abroad. Urban dwellers lived in overcrowded buildings packed tightly along the streets. In this bustling industrial center no one cared who Baker was, where he came from, or where he was going. Here he could free himself from his past and independently shape his identity.[2]

On his arrival in Baltimore, Baker joined hundreds of other black migrants who hoped to find a better life in the sprawling metropolis. In Baltimore's large African-American community, Baker met people of African heritage from other parts of the country and the globe. Baker's new contacts exposed him to new ideologies and gave him broader insight into the effects of white oppression. Most of the black migrants came from small southern farming communities where racism and limited mobility stifled their prospects. Although blacks in Baltimore also struggled with restricted job options and bigotry, the thriving economy of the city provided more opportunities than their hometowns. Joseph Sutton recalled that "many people went to Baltimore. There wasn't work enough here for 'em all."[3]

African Americans who journeyed to Baltimore with high hopes quickly realized that hardships abounded even in the city. Unskilled and semiskilled blacks encountered a society that excluded them on two sides. First, in the black community, there was a marked division between the middle class and the working class. African-American leaders—doctors, politicians, and ministers—lived in three-story row houses along Druid Hill Avenue, which W. E. B. Du Bois described as "one of the best colored streets in the world." Successful and ambitious, black middle-class Baltimorians carved out a separate community and were fiercely proud of their neighborhood. Inspired by the Progressive movement, middle-class African-American homeowners organized the Colored Law and Order League and attempted to combat crime and vice in black lower-income neighborhoods. On the whole, the black middle class viewed poorer blacks patronizingly and through economic segregation excluded the less affluent blacks from their neighborhoods and social institutions.[4]

In addition, Baker had to contend with vicious, sometimes violent white racism. Legally and socially restricted by whites, African Americans daily withstood a barrage of contempt and degradation. No black Baltimorian was exempt from the sting of racism, and even well-respected African Americans became targets of abuse. In downtown Baltimore, a white police officer once accosted world lightweight champion Joe Gans as he waited for a streetcar, shouting, "Nigger, what are you doing sitting there?" Gans, who would later become a follower of Father Divine, explained that he was waiting for a car. The policeman yelled, "Get up, nigger! Stand up when you talk to me." The officer then pulled out his nightstick and beat the boxing champion.[5]

But police brutality was just one of many insults borne by black Baltimorians. Baltimore operated on inflexible codes of residential segregation, and housing discrimination affected all African Americans, regardless of class. Strict segregation confined the black middle class to Druid Hill Avenue and the black poor to the city's most undesirable housing. Most recent black arrivals made their homes in "Pigtown," a shantytown along the city's docks. As the name suggests, the living conditions were grossly inadequate, as "country" blacks crowded together in makeshift structures among weeds, refuse, and stagnant water.[6]

Most black migrants moved out of Pigtown as soon as possible but found they were restricted to a labyrinth of alleys in the southwestern district of downtown Baltimore. Hidden behind white homes and businesses, slums developed in the buildings that lined these ten-foot-wide corridors. In the alleys, African Americans made their homes in rented tenements, tents, or hastily constructed dwellings. Life in the inner-city black ghettos did not differ greatly from that in Pigtown, the alley homes dark, choked with stale air, and dilapidated. And the black population continued to swell, forcing larger numbers of people to share single rooms in small dwellings.[7]

Baker had known substandard living conditions while growing up in Monkey Run, but they did not match the destitution produced by urban poverty and overcrowding. In 1905, one charity group estimated that 81,000 blacks, about one-third of Maryland's black population, lived in Baltimore's slums. Repeated outbreaks of tuberculosis and other infectious diseases swept through the densely populated and unsanitary ghetto. To worsen the situation, the influx of black immigrants in the late nineteenth and early twentieth century created a job crunch. Unable to find work, many blacks resorted to panhandling or crime. And as in Rockville, many turned to alcohol. In his study of Baltimore, Booker T. Washington noted that a seven-by-two-block section of the black ghetto contained forty-two saloons. Gamblers and prostitutes operated openly in the alleys, and the children of working parents roamed the streets.[8]

Baker had journeyed to Baltimore to escape ghetto life, but those neighborhoods open to him appeared even worse than Rockville's Monkey Run. Shocked by the indigence and despair, Baker attempted to distance himself from the inner city and by a unique stroke of luck secured lodging on the property of an elderly white businessman, William Ortwine. Ortwine owned a home on Garrison Avenue on the outskirts of Baltimore, a solidly middle-class exclusively white neighborhood. The only blacks in the area were live-in household help, with the exception of Baker, the self-employed gardener.[9]

Baker roomed in the servants' quarters, sharing a home with the Ortwines' coachman, maid, and their families. Although the situation was not ideal, it was better than the tenements and shanties of Baltimore's slums. The homes in the area were spacious and brightly painted, with large yards that promised Baker steady work. Symbolically, by moving into a comfortable and respectable white community, Baker challenged the restrictiveness of white society and rejected the poverty of his past. This was his first attempt to move upward and withdraw from his past, a goal he pursued throughout his life.[10]

With scythe and shears, Baker scoured the neighborhood around Ortwine's home, offering his gardening services for fifty cents a day. He carefully conserved his money, for he knew the job market was fickle for blacks. Like other African Americans, he suffered through long periods of unemployment and was forced to seek other jobs.[11] Sometimes, when gardening slowed down, Baker found work along Baltimore's waterfront.

Since the days of slavery, African Americans had worked on the docks, but during the early twentieth century, the expansion of commercial traffic through Baltimore heightened the demand for black stevedores. It was hard work, the most dangerous and grueling tasks going to seasonal African-American workers. "You can go down to the stevedores' docks and see the men working down in the ships in the heat of summertime when it is so hot that people are falling down in the restaurants under the fans," Baker would later recall. "But, those men down in the hold, they have no other way to earn their bread and they work down there digging out sulphur, sometimes twenty feet from the hatchhole where not a breath of air could get to them, and they are shoveling that sulphur and pig iron, etc., under pressure, with the boss up there shouting at them to hurry." Drawn by economic uncertainty into new occupations, Baker tasted life in the urban labor force.[12]

While working on the waterfront, Baker encountered the union movement for the first time. In general, whites denied blacks union membership, and racial tensions flared when companies employed African-American strikebreakers. Many blacks, including Baker, came to despise unions. But interaction with the African-American union movement compounded Baker's aversion to organized labor. A large and active union had developed among African-American dock workers, but the organization represented only full-time, permanent longshoremen. In addition, the union demanded membership dues, which most temporarily employed stevedores could not afford. With no fear of union intervention, white water-front employers freely exploited nonunion blacks, making them work long hours for low pay. The black union's refusal to protect short-term workers garnered their animosity. Baker, like other black workers, came to see the union movement as cliquish, self-interested, and ineffective.[13]

Despite the dramatic differences between Rockville and Baltimore, especially in black employment opportunities, Baker discovered some familiar traditions in the big city. Like Rockville, Baltimore possessed an active and assertive African-American electorate. As in Montgomery County, Republicans in Baltimore relied on black votes to stay in power, and the party became a watchdog for black suffrage. Although the party deserted its African-American constituency on desegregation and equal rights, Baltimore's numerous African-American voters ensured the election of blacks to city government. As early as 1890, the city council had a black member, a trend that continued into the early twentieth century.

During this period, a political machine led by an African-American boss dominated black politics and controlled the distribution of appointive governmental posts. Several elected officials were influential black pastors who fought for civil rights for their community. Baltimore's elections tutored Baker in the nuances of machine politics, the advantages of voting in consolidated blocks, and the power furnished by politics to men of the cloth. Yet politics did not preoccupy Baker during these early stages of his ministerial career, perhaps because in Maryland African-American males considered voting more a hard-won tradition than a constitutional right that had been consistently denied.[14]

While turn-of-the-century Baltimore yielded some liberties, blacks still found themselves denied many of the basic rights promised to all Americans. Struggling for equality, black Baltimorians engaged in various forms of dissent. Many joined the national dispute between Booker T. Washington, who advocated self-help and accommodation, and W. E. B. Du Bois, who called for integration and immediate equality. While both leaders generated national movements for racial uplift, most resistance to racism still originated from the black church. During the early twentieth century, the church remained the center of African-American life and to working-class blacks like Baker, the most accessible channel for black protest. Although the diversity of African-American churches in America at the time indicates that there was no monolithic "black church," the institutions were united by one factor—they originated from the struggle against white oppression. But between 1900 and 1930, as Baker reached his spiritual maturity, the mainstream black church underwent a significant change. External and internal forces began to erode the churches' claim as the primary agency of black radicalism. Denominations like the Presbyterians, Methodists, Baptists, African Methodist Episcopalians (AME), and African Methodist Episcopalian Zionists were unable to stay current with the needs of the African-American community and found their power slipping away.[15]

Much of the decline resulted from the static organization and focus of black institutional churches. Most mainstream denominations maintained rigid church hierarchies and in many cases began requiring formal training as a prerequisite for the ministry. Furthermore, the leadership of these churches neglected to address the issues confronting a community becoming increasingly urbanized. Like other sectors of American society coming to terms with the rise of the city, African-American churches clung to their agrarian roots. The ministers of these churches employed revivalism and preached sermons heavily laden with moralism and ephemeral promises of satisfaction in the afterlife. Ignorant and in many cases unprepared to keep up with the demands of the thousands of African-American migrants who flooded into the cities, the black church neglected to provide social relief to the urban poor. In some cases, this was financially impossible since many black churches operated on limited budgets. But in other cases, African-American ministers were simply too caught up with the internal politics of their denominations and the daily operations of their churches to become involved in social activism. While the mere existence of a separate and independent black institution symbolized African-

American protest, the mainstream black church shrank from its liberating potential and glided along a seemingly safe and conservative route.[16]

The major denominations also suffered from class tensions that created sharp divisions among churches and within congregations. Black middle-class Baltimorians predominantly attended Methodist, Episcopal, Presbyterian, AME, AME Zion, and established Baptist churches. Many bourgeois African Americans attempted to distance themselves from the poorer sectors of the community, and often lower-income blacks felt uncomfortable in congregations dominated by educated, affluent African Americans. A religious alternative for working-class blacks evolved—the storefront church. In urban centers across the country, African Americans joined together and organized congregations, most independent, owing no allegiance to nationally established denominations. Other new sects had ties to Spiritualists, Baptists, Holiness orders, and African Methodist Episcopal churches. Working-class African Americans selected their own leaders and organized churches in rented rooms or buildings. Some groups created their own religious rituals and beliefs; others adhered to more traditional practices. Many who worshiped in storefront churches were recent arrivals from the rural South who found the mainstream churches stifling and unwelcoming. Through their independent churches, African-American newcomers attempted to restore, to a degree, familiar patterns in their religious life.[17]

Independent storefront churches were also a component in the black migrants' search for a new identity. Most major denominations maintained churches in the poorer black neighborhoods. If migrants had wished solely to simulate past religious experiences, they would have sought out their previous religious affiliations. But many recent arrivals, like George Baker, bypassed familiar churches for storefronts. Exhausted by rigid and irrelevant church discipline and the exclusionary church hierarchy they encountered in many of the major denominations, some blacks found that storefront churches more effectively addressed their needs. Threatened by the popularity, spontaneity, and proliferation of new faiths, the established denominations charged that storefronts were disorderly and misguided. However, the opposition of mainstream churches did little to inhibit the growth of storefronts, which continued to multiply, driven by the African-American desire for independence and the quest for self-redefinition.[18]

The black storefront churches of Baltimore nurtured Baker, guiding his spiritual development and intensifying his religious commitment. The loose organization of storefronts provided him with leadership training and allowed him to refine his evangelistic skills. He taught Sunday-school classes and occasionally preached, becoming a powerful and inspiring orator. As his devotion grew, he became increasingly committed to bringing others to God, so that they could share in the peace of mind and comfort provided by pure religiosity.

Baker frugally saved his money, and in 1902, when William Ortwine moved to downtown Baltimore, he set out on an evangelical campaign to preach and teach in the South. It was a brave move for the young black itinerant, for the trip was undoubtedly both challenging and dangerous, but he succeeded in bringing at least one soul to God before he returned to Baltimore. One day, outside an Alabama coal mine, he preached to miners as they passed by on their way to and from work. Most of the men simply ignored the small balding, bearded evangelist. But Baker's sermon attracted the attention of one miner, Isaac King, who befriended the evangelist and took him home.[19] In later years, King would recall that he was electrified by the originality of Baker's message, which he claimed had remained unchanged since the first time he heard it.

By this time, Baker had blended several religious ideologies and had begun to formulate his own theology. Drawing elements from Methodism, Catholicism, the black church, and storefront traditions, he produced a foundation that potentially had broad appeal to people from diverse religious backgrounds. But during his early years in Baltimore he had also become immersed in a religious ideology called New Thought, and by adopting and adapting components of this doctrine, he created a unique and attractive theology.

A precursor of the New Age ideology of the twentieth century, New Thought evolved in New England in the 1840s from the teachings of Phineas Quimby, a hypnotist and inventor. Believing that thought controlled health, he advocated healing illnesses through positive thinking. Later, students of Quimby, including

Mary Baker Eddy, added a spiritual component to his ideology and argued that a link between God and humankind made mental healing possible. Christian adherents to New Thought reasoned that since God created men and women, his spirit existed within all people. They concluded that illness resulted from sin and was contrary to God. New Thought disciples believed that tuning in to God's inner-dwelling presence and achieving oneness with his spirit restored health and well-being.[20]

As New Thought spread, some disciples added the Protestant work ethic and contended that mind-power also brought financial and material rewards. Hard work and positive thinking promised success and fortune. Other students discovered Eastern mysticism and metaphysics, and incorporated the principles of reincarnation and celibacy into their versions of New Thought. Basically, all variants of New Thought shared three major assumptions: that God existed in all people, that the channeling of God's spirit eradicated problems, and that unity with God guaranteed salvation.[21]

Although New Thought organizations were exclusively white, by the early twentieth century, the ideology had attracted a fair number of African-American followers. It is unclear precisely when the African-American community discovered New Thought, but its first contact with the mind-power ideology may date to Reconstruction. Essentially a guide to self-improvement, New Thought could have inspired the development of the Freedmen Schools' philosophy of black self-help. Many of the teachers were educated in New England during the evolution of New Thought, and Yankee educators may have incorporated variations of New Thought into the curriculum of African-American schools.[22] By the turn of the century, New Thought had become integrated into many facets of American society, and numerous New Thought and metaphysical societies appeared. New Thought lecturers traversed the states; disciples organized international conventions; publications espousing it circulated around the country. New Thought ideology even crept into the novels of the period. These teachings became so prevalent in American popular culture that African Americans could hardly have escaped their influence.[23]

As an adult, Baker read religious literature voraciously and must have discovered New Thought through literary channels. His first readings may have included Mary Baker Eddy's *Science and Mind* and the works of mental healer Emma Leonora Excell Lynn. But during these early years he was most profoundly influenced by the works of the Unity School of Christianity. Founded by a real-estate agent and former Christian Scientist, Charles Fillmore, the Unity School first met in 1889.[24] By 1900, Unity had opened a headquarters in Kansas City, Missouri, and begun to expand its operations. Fillmore and his followers published newspapers, a children's periodical, and several books that the school distributed nationally. The school offered spiritual assistance to anyone in need through "Silent Unity," a nightly meeting at which Unity members meditated on prayer requests received by mail. Over the next few years Unity would continue to grow, establishing branches across America. Unity's success and popularity created a stir in religious circles, and Baker closely monitored Fillmore's progress. Later he would publicly express admiration for Unity's founder and its achievements.[25]

New Thought provided the foundation for Fillmore's teachings and functioned as the core of Unity School ideology. According to Fillmore, God was an "impersonal" deity, not confined to any single entity or being. God, whom he often referred to as Father-Mother-God, existed in all things, including people. Expounding the traditional New Thought line, Unity's founder argued that the mind was a powerful instrument that shaped human destiny. While sin, sickness, and misfortune resulted from negative thinking, awareness of God's internal presence and the power of positive thought allowed men and women to overcome adversity and actualize their desires. But Fillmore took New Thought one step further, contending that positive thinking brought mortals close to divinity. He insisted that people could attain a status similar to that of Jesus Christ through efficient channeling of God's spirit. In turn, these sons and daughters of God would bring heaven, which was simply a state of mind, to earth. Once a disciple became at one with God, a new body was generated assuring a devoted practitioner immortality. Fillmore encouraged his followers to abstain from sex, except to reproduce, since he believed that intercourse weakened the body, potentially leading to death. But for those devoted souls not lucky enough to achieve eternal life, reincarnation offered another chance.[26]

Fillmore's theology carried significant social components. He envisioned Unity as a challenge to the leaders of the traditional church, who, he argued, impeded humankind's spiritual progress out of their obsession with power and authority. Therefore, Unity lacked hierarchy, for every member was identically blessed and had equal access to God's power.

Fillmore's teachings maintained a strong capitalistic tone, and he encouraged followers to strive for prosperity, purchase property, and refuse to buy on credit. Even though affluence was the natural outcome of hard work and pure faith, Fillmore cautioned disciples not to become enslaved to money. But he saw no righteousness in poverty. In his opinion, God's kingdom held sufficient riches for all people, and poverty, a product of negative thinking, was an indication of a dangerous estrangement from God's presence. Negative thoughts not only bred economic destitution but caused the travails of humankind. According to Fillmore, most Americans suffered from unhappiness, indigence, sickness, and death because they perpetuated the "Race Mind," a legacy of negative attitudes and beliefs inherited from their ancestors. Fillmore's theology of mind-power offered people a new direction and promised to revitalize American society.[27]

For Baker, much of the attractiveness of Unity School theology rested in its implications. Fillmore's brand of New Thought provided a formula for the acceptance and inclusion of African Americans without altering or threatening the structure of American society. Exercising mind-power and oneness with God, anyone, regardless of race, had the potential to achieve spiritual and social equality. Blacks possessed just as much divinity as whites and, by applying mind-power, could overcome oppression and reap the benefits of American enterprise. Positive thinking allowed African Americans to assert control over their destiny and to combat their feelings of powerlessness in white America. If it was the Race Mind that held blacks in bondage, then by following Fillmore's guidelines, African Americans could conquer white oppression. The solution to racism was quite clear; it rested on a spiritual cleansing of the American mind.

In 1906, Baker embarked on another missionary trek, this time to California, a land dubbed by mind-power enthusiasts "the natural home of New Thought." He arrived in Los Angeles and visited his old friend Isaac King, who had settled in the city. The two traveled to San Francisco to see the damage caused by the recent earthquake and then returned to Los Angeles. Undoubtedly the religious climate of Los Angeles impressed the twenty-seven-year-old evangelist. New Thought had strong adherents in the city, and disciples opened a "Metaphysical Library," published books and periodicals, and frequently sponsored lectures. Although racial segregation in Los Angeles prevented Baker from attending the meetings of white New Thought organizations, he had the opportunity to obtain New Thought literature and seek out white positive-thinking proponents who made their homes in California.[28]

But Los Angeles produced another religious alternative that stimulated much excitement nationally and internationally. In April 1906, the same month as the San Francisco earthquake, thousands flocked to services, known as the Azusa Street Revival, conducted by an African-American minister, William Seymour. What drew people to Los Angeles was the vast number of worshipers demonstrating the ultimate communion with God—speaking in tongues. Glossolalia was not a new phenomenon, but before the Azusa Street Revival it had not been accepted as a significant religious experience. Seymour advanced the notion that the act was a gift from God and with conversion and baptism completed the sanctification of the individual. Regarded by many as the father of modern American Pentecostalism, Seymour attracted both blacks and whites to a humble building on Azusa Street. Seymour's large integrated congregation often spilled into the streets, and constant shouting, singing, and crying could be heard for blocks. Many on their way to worship found themselves overcome by God's spirit and fell into trances on the sidewalks of downtown Los Angeles.

Driven by religious curiosity, Baker attended the revival. He too was overpowered and joined in the "speaking in tongues in Los Angeles in nineteen six."[29] This was a major turning point in his life. While he spoke in tongues, he felt a stirring, and suddenly, as he later explained, "the HOLY GHOST . . . came into expression."[30] Baker believed that he had reached a state of ultimate spiritual purification, a condition Fillmore described as the "consciousness of himself as a spiritual being, knowing himself to be the Christ of God, he is I AM, and ready to recreate the world."[31] God had disposed of the mortal George Baker, given him a divine identity, and revealed to him that his mission was to "spread [God's message] throughout this country." His visit to the West Coast had triggered a spiritual transformation that shattered his ties to the past, but his realization of God's inner presence was just the beginning of his spiritual metamorphosis. It would take a little more time and a lot of meditation before Baker completely formulated his new spiritual identity and solidified his teachings.[32]

He returned to Baltimore with a fuller understanding of mind-power and a deeper commitment to bringing salvation to humankind. He secured lodgings with the laundress and "female evangelist" Harriette "Anna" Snowden, who lived with her two grandchildren in a rented home on Fairmount Avenue in southeastern Baltimore. The neighborhood was predominantly black but contained a number of white residents, most of whom were eastern European Jewish immigrants who had established a synagogue and a Hebrew School in the vicinity.[33]

Shortly after moving into Harriette Snowden's row house, Baker joined a Baptist storefront located nearby on Eden Street. A former day laborer, Thomas Henderson, had organized the church around 1904. Baker took over a Sunday-school class and occasionally addressed Wednesday-night prayer meetings. The congregation enjoyed his dynamic sermons, and he quickly became one of the church's most popular members.[34]

One Sunday morning in 1907 a stranger wandered into the Eden Street Church and during the worship service rose to address the throng. A hush fell over the congregation as they strained to hear the soft-spoken visitor. His remarks, taken from a biblical text, did not seem out of the ordinary—not until he paused, spread his arms, and shouted, "I am the Father Eternal." The congregation, appalled by his claim, threw him out bodily. Intrigued, Baker helped the man to his feet. The newcomer introduced himself as Samuel Morris and assured Baker that this was not the first church that had expelled him.[35]

Baker learned that Morris hailed from Allegheny City, Pennsylvania, where he had worked in the steel mills and as a teamster. Morris, who had occasionally preached in the black churches of Allegheny City, was a fervent student of the Bible. He claimed that one night as he read he had been regenerated by a verse that read, "Know ye not that ye are the temple of God, and that the spirit of God dwelleth in you?" These words shook Morris, who believed that the passage implied that since God dwelled within him, he was God. That night Morris dreamed of men drowning and heard a voice that commanded him to "go to Baltimore and save them." The next morning, Morris left his wife and children, and on foot, without any money, he set out for Baltimore. Along the way, he preached in African-American churches but did not reveal that he was "the Father Eternal" until he reached Baltimore. Once he arrived at his destination, Morris attended every church he could find in an effort to spread his message, but his teachings had been uniformly shunned until he discovered the sympathetic Baker.[36]

Morris moved into Snowden's home and began teaching the residents a religious philosophy centering on the notion that he transcended mortality and was a human incarnation of God. According to Morris, before long, the entire household had accepted his divinity. Morris and Baker adopted new names and New Thought ranks to symbolize their spiritual regeneration: Morris, Father Jehovia, God in the Fathership degree; Baker, the Messenger, God in the Sonship degree. Baker's new name signified another critical step in his spiritual metamorphosis and separation from his roots. By 1907, the Messenger believed that he was the son of God and that his destiny was to spread God's word to the ignorant and unredeemed.[37]

Father Jehovia, the Messenger, and Harriette Snowden conducted worship services in their home several evenings each week. The devotionals functioned as a forum for the dissemination of Father Jehovia's teachings, and they drew between ten and twenty people. The mild-mannered Father Jehovia opened the meeting with a barely audible sermon, raising his voice only at the end when he exclaimed, "I am the Father Eternal!" Then Morris quietly took his seat, and the Messenger delivered a stirring message indirectly asserting that Father Jehovia was God.[38]

One evening a newcomer, Reverend Bishop Saint John the Vine, dropped in to worship with the Fairmount Avenue residents. Formerly John A. Hickerson of Alexandria, Virginia, the Bishop was a cook and sailor who in port served as a minister in a Baptist church. As a seaman, the Bishop visited many places and investigated churches. Before stumbling upon the Fairmount Avenue devotionals, he had worshiped in Pentecostal and Holiness churches, and during a stay in New England may have come into contact with

New Thought. By 1905, the Bishop had relocated in Baltimore, where in the city directory he listed his occupation as teacher. Since the Bishop was illiterate, he must have been alluding to his role as a religious instructor who taught his pupils his original theology, which incorporated several components characteristic of New Thought.[39]

The Bishop later adamantly insisted that his teachings were not derived from New Thought but inherited from his Ethiopian ancestors. Although records indicate that his mother was born in Virginia, he claimed that she was Abyssinian and had taught him to speak fluent Hebrew. The Bishop's identification with Abyssinia evolved out of his immersion in "Ethiopianism," an ideology popular with African Americans since the late eighteenth century.

Ethiopianism was based on the belief that the Bible designated Ethiopia as the cradle of civilization and Ethiopians as the only true Jews. Disciples contended that all blacks were descended from Ethiopian Jews and that Jesus Christ was African. Since blacks were God's "chosen people," followers believed that God would redeem all people of African heritage and return them to their homeland, Ethiopia. The philosophy also contained an element of mind-power, for many adherents of Ethiopianism subscribed to mental healing and believed that material circumstances could be altered though God's power. Such notions closely paralleled tenets of New Thought and may have also provided a bridge for the ideological compatibility between the Bishop and the leaders of the Fairmount Avenue ministry.[40]

In the home on Fairmount Avenue the Bishop discovered others practicing a religion compatible with his own convictions, and he immediately moved in. Flamboyant and engaging, the Bishop was a valuable addition to Fairmount Avenue devotionals. Bearded, attired in flowing robes and turban, he appeared much like the Rastafarian priests of later years, presenting a striking figure. His sermons began with faint mumbling, which became louder as he ran the length of the room, jumped high, and landed, shouting. The spectacle drew a few more worshipers to weeknight rituals. According to Father Jehovia, the Bishop also accepted his divinity and, like the Messenger, assumed the "sonship degree" in their sect.[41]

Although Father Jehovia's name implied that a hierarchy evolved within the triumvirate, the relationship may have been more egalitarian than his recollections indicated. Since all three men discovered the internal-God philosophy independently, they probably believed that each had equal access to the highest spiritual plane. The Messenger and the Bishop most likely considered Father Jehovia a spiritual master who had achieved oneness with God through his purity and faith. But the Messenger and the Bishop, both inspirational speakers and creative thinkers, played important roles in the Fairmount Avenue sect. Although both provided charisma and direction to the group, it was the Messenger who was the organizational power behind the Fairmount Avenue ministry. His home became its base of operation, and as a dedicated student of New Thought literature, he tutored his colleagues in the ideology and the specific terminology of mind-power philosophy. Under the Messenger's guidance, the little sect persevered and occasionally gained a convert.[42]

Initially the ministerial alliance ran smoothly, and the three shared religious enlightenment and engaged in friendly theological debates. They continued to work during the day and worship together in the evenings. The Fairmount Avenue services disseminated the varied theologies of the Messenger, Father Jehovia, and the Bishop and further spread New Thought ideology in the black community. The meetings, like those held in black churches throughout history, operated as a forum for intellectual discussion. The tradition of audience participation transformed meetings in black churches into dialogues among the congregants. The openness of black sects like the Fairmount Avenue ministry advanced the creation of theological alternatives. Since the worshipers were black, working-class, and often illiterate, historians and scholars have ignored or denied the intellectual component of African-American religion. But in many ways the devotionals led by Father Jehovia, the Messenger, and the Bishop resembled the lectures and discussion groups organized by white apostles of New Thought who have been clearly considered intellectual.[43]

During one meeting in 1910, the Messenger sang to his congregation:

> Well, I don't want no sorrow in my heart.
> I don't want no sorrow in my heart.
> For if you are sorrowful, I am sorrowful too.
> And if you are joyful, I am rejoicing too.

The composition represented his dedication to the power of positive thought and his determination to banish sadness from his memories. The 1910 census revealed that the Messenger had almost finalized his break with the past. Under the name Anderson K. Baker, the Messenger gave the census taker an incorrect birthdate and birthplace. He further obscured his parentage by listing his parents' birthplaces as Virginia.[44]

Providing the census taker with inaccurate data was not only a rejection of his parents and Monkey Run but an important step in eliminating his mortal ties and magnifying God's internal spirit. Since coming to Baltimore in 1899, the Messenger had evolved into an enthusiastic promoter of his interpretation of New Thought. He had blended New Thought with Methodism, a little Catholicism, Pentecostalism, and African-American storefront theology, and had devised a syncretic belief system. Truly a positive thinker, he found beneficial attributes in all religious traditions: "I have been coming into contact with the different religions from years back. Personally . . . I find there is something good in all of them. I endeavor to be as a honeybee to get the good out of every seed or flower."[45] During these years in Baltimore, the Messenger theologically matured and developed. The young evangelist redirected his life, symbolically swept away his sorrows, and endeavored to help others find spiritual fulfillment.

Before long, the soft-spoken Father Jehovia found himself increasingly overshadowed by the captivating sermonizing of his associates. The Bishop had begun to question Father Jehovia's monopoly on divinity, contending that the Bible implied that God was equally present in all people. The two frequently quibbled over the interpretation of the biblical verse "Whosoever shall confess that Jesus is the Son of God, God dwelleth in him and he is God." At first the Messenger distanced himself from the squabbling, but finally he entered the battle and announced he would take neither side. He rejected both Father Jehovia's claim to divinity and the Bishop's assertion that everyone was God. The Messenger declared that he himself was the only true and pure expression of God's spirit. His pronouncement shattered the ministerial partnership, and in 1912 the Fairmount Avenue triumvirate collapsed.[46]

3

Carrying the Message

House to house, house to house, house to
    house canvas
Carrying the Message everywhere I go.
House to house, house to house, house to
    house canvas
Carrying the Message everywhere I go.
                    World Echo, March 3, 1934

Not too long after the disintegration of the Fairmount Avenue ministerial alliance, the Messenger observed from the window of his home an incident that inspired him to reassess his ministry:

Right after the Jim Crow law came out in the South, at about the same time, there were thousands of people going up and down the streets of Baltimore, Washington, Chicago, New York and all of the larger cities of this country begging. The zeal of MY courage was stirred and as they passed by my door . . . in Baltimore . . . they would walk up and down the streets and in every block they would sing an old song that had been composed by "Stanley" or someone before that time . . . they would sing an old death song and they would pass their hats around in this block and then they would walk up in the next block and sing a song in that block and pass the hats around to the windows all around.[1]

From his window, the Messenger compared reality with his theological expectations. He witnessed a hungering not only for food but for spiritual substance. The experience forced him to formulate three specific objectives that would guide his ministry for the rest of his life.[2]

First, he resolved to prove that the "Gospel can be preached without money and without price." The poor marching through Baltimore's streets were not merely panhandling migrants. In the Messenger's vocabulary, "beggars" were synonymous with street-corner preachers. He considered God's word a gift to all people and regarded those who solicited contributions in God's name as opportunists and thieves. He not only criticized itinerants who accepted money but also attacked the established churches' practice of tithing. Following the example of Jesus Christ, who urged disciples to reject materialism, he refused all monetary donations to his missionary work, believing that sacrificing the collection plate and trusting that God would provide drew him closer to spiritual purity.[3]

Second, he claimed, the vision of poor southern migrants displaced from their homes by economic hardship and Jim Crow segregation "stirred me to my depths." The oppression of blacks in other parts of the South contrasted with the life of limited freedoms he had known in Maryland. The difference alerted him to both the inequalities and the opportunities in America. Ignoring the segregation that flourished in his home state, he chose to "go South and break down the wall or partition of Jim Crow if it costs my life."[4]

Third, he interpreted the migrants' "old death songs" as evidence of their spiritual desperation and need for his theological guidance.[5] The songs sung by the destitute on the sidewalks of Baltimore were hymns composed by white Protestants like the Anglican Arthur P. Stanley. The Messenger labeled these "death songs" because they promoted the belief that after death, heaven promised a happier and eternal life. Inspired by Fillmore, he rejected the concept of an afterlife and embraced the notion that unity with God's internal spirit ensured eternal life on earth. People did not have to wait for happiness, for heaven was on earth, and even mundane activities functioned as a part of God's kingdom. He framed his teachings to guarantee eternal life, assure salvation, and promise social, economic, and political progress.[6]

His itinerant zeal unleashed, the Messenger left Baltimore in 1912 and traveled south, preaching his doctrine of heaven on earth, calling for racial harmony, and refusing monetary contributions to his ministry: "I took no money with ME, no clothes and would not depend on anything of that kind." As an itinerant, he subsisted solely on southern hospitality. Accepting food and lodging from his new acquaintances did not contradict his theological convictions. He reasoned that all good came from God's spirit, and such generosity demonstrated God's power and love. Since most of the people who welcomed him into their homes were poor, their benevolence appeared to him as an encouraging testimony of God's great ability to provide.[7]

Traveling through the cities and towns of the South, he evangelized anywhere he found an audience. He spoke in black churches and exhorted crowds from street corners, but his favorite rostrum was in the relaxed atmosphere of a private home. In several southern residences, he organized services that resembled the devotionals held in his Fairmount Avenue home. By the time he began his vagabond ministry in 1912, his worship services included preaching, singing, and a ritualized banquet that symbolized Holy Communion.[8]

At each Holy Communion banquet, he attempted to recreate Christ's last supper and reinforce his own role as a savior of humankind. As a testimony to God's supremacy and abundance, he encouraged participants to furnish large amounts of their finest fare. Although he aimed for extravagance at these banquets, the quality of the meals depended on the resources of the celebrants, and he gladly served any dish the congregation provided. He opened services with a hymn and, as the congregation sang, blessed each dish by inserting a serving spoon or fork. He passed the platters around, then served the beverages. After filling his own plate, he listened as worshipers sang and testified. During the meal, the Messenger rose and delivered an electrifying sermon. At the conclusion of his message, the congregation continued singing, testifying, and dancing, sometimes late into the night.

The Holy Communion banquets were memorable events. A woman visiting the Messenger in New York twenty-five years later recalled: "You came to Americus, Georgia, and there you had meetings. Banquets were served just as you are serving today, and people were singing and shouting and praising and worshipping you."[9] Many of those drawn to the Messenger's banquet table suffered from improper nutrition and found both relief and hope during these Holy Communion services. The Messenger's worship services symbolically challenged the impoverishment and destitution foisted on blacks by America and demonstrated that the evangelist's powerful philosophy had the potential to improve the lives of oppressed African Americans.

The Messenger and his teachings were not always warmly received. Some ministers who initially welcomed the evangelist angrily challenged him after hearing his message. "[I] was preaching in a church at the invitation of the pastor and MY message got a little too hot for him. It was more than he wanted his people to have, so he stopped me and wanted to know whether I was ordained and who sent ME out to preach and if I had any diplomas, saying, 'If you weren't sent out, you can't preach.' "[10] Conflict between the Messenger and clergymen often resulted in serious consequences. In 1913, a clash with ministers in Savannah landed him on a Georgia chain gang for sixty days. While he served his term, several Georgia prison inspectors were injured in an automobile accident. He believed that the community's rejection of God's word had caused the mishap. As a reminder of the occasion, he carried a newspaper clipping about the accident, and in the margin he noted, "Be sure your sins will find you out."[11]

After his release from prison camp, he returned to the itinerant circuit and in early 1914 arrived in a small southern town, Valdosta, Georgia. Invited to preach one Sunday at the black Holiness Church, he contended that "God's second appearance on earth was in a form of Jew and that now he comes in the form of a negro. He told them that he was going to bring the world to an end before long and that those who do not believe on him will be lost. He declared that he would take his spirit out of those who are not faithful." Stunned by the evangelist's brazen pronouncements, the congregation ejected him from the pulpit and banished him from their church.[12]

His sermon did appeal to several worshipers, who invited him to speak in their homes. Within a few weeks, the itinerant built a large following composed exclusively of black women. He moved into a follower's home that, like his Fairmount Avenue residence, became his headquarters. Each night, women from the black community crowded into the dwelling to worship and hear his message. Some left their homes and moved in with him. By early February, his congregation had significantly multiplied and captured the attention of the local white newspaper, which ran a story entitled "Negro Claims to Be God."[13]

The black women of Valdosta discovered that his theology directly addressed their restricted position in America. These women lived in a community that burdened them with numerous responsibilities but furnished few freedoms. In addition to housekeeping and childrearing, most African-American women took full-time jobs to support their families. Accorded the lowest status in southern society, black women found solace in religion and were traditionally the African-American churches' most supportive participants.[14] For these women, the Messenger's teachings reinforced their religious convictions and liberated them from oppressive roles. This African-American god inspired pride, improved the self-image of black women, and gave them the impetus to take control of their lives.

Within his fold the Messenger created an alternative lifestyle and community. Worshiping and living together as a collective unit challenged gender roles and freed women from their responsibilities as wives and mothers. Influenced by Fillmore and Eastern philosophy, he demanded that his followers practice celibacy. Childbearing was a constant threat to the health of black women, and celibacy freed them from the fear of childbirth as well as from the consuming tasks of the home.

The Messenger's teachings contained liberating potential for women. His earliest recorded comments indicate that he rejected gender distinctions, attributing them to categorizations conjured up by the mind: "those who call themselves women" and "so-called men." He eschewed gender indentification even for himself, often claiming that he was father and mother, sister and brother, to his children and only appeared "to be another man." But he acknowledged that even though gender was artificial, he had benefited from popular attitudes toward it. He attributed his appeal to women to their socialization in American culture, believing that since women were forced from childhood to defer to male authority, they easily transferred their submission from men to God.[15]

Radicalized, his female disciples began to rebel against their traditional roles. After worshiping with him, one woman returned home and began beating her husband. In turn, the man battered his wife with a stick until she was severely bruised and warned her that "he would maul her into the ground if she did not give . . . [the Messenger] up."[16] The Messenger discouraged violence, but he tapped into women's rage and provided them with the inspiration they needed to openly challenge their prescribed status.

His presence drastically upset the organization of the African-American community and particularly threatened the black men of

Valdosta. More black women became involved in his flock, forcing black men to assume responsibility for household duties and child-care. According to the men, many families suffered from the loss of the women's contribution to the family income. At the insistence of the Messenger, many women terminated sexual relations with their husbands, which increased the men's hostility toward the small but handsome preacher. Led by several African-American minis-ters, the black men of Valdosta complained to local authorities that the Messenger had placed curses on community leaders and that "their wives and mothers were bereft of reason and that if some-thing wasn't done the whole community would be crazed." Ten-sion continued to mount, and finally the black men of Valdosta filed lunacy charges against him.[17]

On the morning of February 6, 1914, Valdosta's chief of police arrived at the Messenger's home and attempted to arrest the con-troversial evangelist. According to the chief, when he entered the residence, the Messenger "began to jump up and almost go to the ceiling." Quickly his female followers surrounded their leader, forming a human barricade. The frustrated officer called for help and with the assistance of several black men took him into cus-tody.[18]

The women menacingly followed the chief and his prisoner to the city jail. When the officer booked the Messenger, he asked for the evangelist's true name, and a female disciple shouted, "He ain't named nothing but God." Throughout the day, followers contin-ued to gather outside the jail, and the authorities feared trouble. However, with the exception of two women whom the police jailed for hysterical public behavior, the crowd remained orderly. The court assigned a local lawyer to defend him and set a trial date.[19]

Incarceration did not impede him but actually promoted his ministry. Pandemonium and chaos reigned as he preached from his cell and received a flood of visitors. While in jail, he attracted more disciples and won support from the surrounding commu-nity. His new followers included a number of whites, who, a guard commented, "seemed to be as wild over him as the negroes." Given the atmosphere of intense racial hatred, the addition of white fol-lowers from a small town in the Deep South was an amazing feat. Those whites attracted to his teachings had previously subscribed to similar religious ideologies. Many whites who visited the jail spoke in tongues, and others were students of New Thought. At the jail, his proselytes organized makeshift services during which he delivered sermons and black and white congregants sang, witnessed, and worshiped together.[20]

J. R. Moseley, a Georgia peach farmer and minister, was one of the whites who called on the Messenger at the jail. A New Thought devotee, Moseley engaged him in a discussion of the principles of the ideology and asked him if he had refused to give his name and the details of his life in an effort to amplify God's internal spirit. "You understand me better than anyone else," the Messenger responded. Impressed by the evangelist's sincerity and dedication, Moseley offered financial assistance. The Messenger refused Moseley's money but asked for some bread to share with his fellow inmates.[21] Shortly afterward, Moseley contacted an old college friend and one of Valdosta's most respected lawyers, J. B. Copeland, who reviewed the case, decided that the Messenger had been "railroaded," and agreed to represent the minister free of charge.[22]

On February 27, the Messenger was tried for lunacy in the Valdosta court. The primary complainants and the prosecution's chief witnesses—Dr. Stafford, a medical doctor and pastor of the Holiness Church, and the Reverend White, a black Methodist minister—took the stand first. Both testified that the Messenger preached an irrational and dangerous message, and contended that his assertions of divinity were proof of his insanity.[23]

During the cross-examination, Copeland first questioned Dr. Stafford. He asked the minister for his opinion on glossolalia; Stafford contended that he believed God's spirit induced speaking in tongues. When Copeland inquired if Stafford considered those who rejected speaking in tongues insane, the Holiness minister replied that such people were "spiritually blind" and "slightly crazy" but not insane. Next Copeland questioned Reverend White, who testified that speaking in tongues sounded "like beating pans." The Methodist minister claimed that anyone who believed that speaking in tongues was a manifestation of the Holy Spirit was not exactly insane but definitely of "unsound mind." The conflicting testimony drew laughter from courtroom spectators, and by the time Copeland finished questioning the prosecution's witnesses, each had questioned the rationality of the other's religious convictions. Copeland argued to the jury that since the soundness of religious convictions was relative, the Messenger could not be convicted of lunacy.[24]

Although hilarity reigned during Copeland's questioning, the atmosphere in the courtroom grew serious as the prosecution presented a string of witnesses, all male, who testified that the evangelist exercised a strange control over the black women of the community. The newspapers estimated that by the end of February, half the African-American female population of Valdosta had become followers. The courtroom listened to tales of women who neglected their jobs, husbands, and children, and gave all their money to the preacher.[25]

Finally, the Messenger, who had sat quietly and calmly throughout the proceedings, took the stand. Wearing a cutaway coat and immaculately groomed, he presented a striking and dignified figure. During the questioning, he insisted that he was known only as a "Messenger of God" and under pressure declared that he had come from New Jersey. Challenged to prove his divinity by performing a miracle, he explained that he did not produce miracles, but that they were generated "by the spirit that works in him." He insisted that faith fueled miracles and since the courtroom observers lacked faith, such phenomena were impossible.[26]

Throughout the questioning, which was at times cynical and condescending, he remained confident and composed. Despite the efforts of the prosecution to belittle him, he testified convincingly and defended his theology with Scripture. He impressed many, including the reporter from the *Valdosta Daily Times*, who declared that the evangelist's teachings were based on "clear" reasoning.[27] Reflecting on the trial several years later, J. B. Copeland recalled, "I remember that there was about the man, an unmistakable quiet power that manifested itself to anyone who came in contact with him."[28]

Despite his persuasiveness, the jury found the Messenger guilty of insanity after a short deliberation. But excluding his "maniacal" religious beliefs, the panel concluded that he was mentally sound and therefore did not merit institutionalization. The judge released him and requested that he leave Valdosta. The court's decision outraged the male members of the African-American community, who complained that the sentence was too lenient. They argued that he would resume his activities and that many of the black women of Valdosta would end up in the state mental hospital. African-American leaders threatened to "take the law into their own hands" if the court refused to take action against the preacher.[29]

Despite opposition from the African-American community, the authorities released him from jail. Immediately the black men of Valdosta filed a vagrancy warrant against him, forcing the chief of police to rearrest the evangelist. Until this point, whites in the town appeared undisturbed by the controversy surrounding the Messenger. His unconventional claims muted his pleas for civil rights. Most whites perceived the evangelist as harmless and dismissed the uproar as a problem for the black community. But the attempt by black men to undermine the decision of a white judge and jury, combined with J. B. Copeland's support for the preacher, attracted sympathy from some of Valdosta's most powerful white residents. The *Valdosta Daily Times* argued that the Messenger could not be declared a transient since the black women of the town provided him with food and lodging. Several local lawyers charged that the arrest violated a Georgia law that prohibited the detention of the mentally ill on vagrancy charges. The feud continued bitterly until Copeland arranged a compromise between the factions. In exchange for his release, the Messenger promised to leave Valdosta immediately and never return.[30]

Exiled from Valdosta, he traveled to Lakeside, Georgia, hoping to thank his friend J. R. Moseley. Unable to find Moseley, he left an invitation to Sunday devotionals. When Moseley arrived, he found three of the Messenger's followers—Michael, Gabriel, and one heavyset woman—engaged in concentrated worship. The disciples informed Moseley that he had just missed the Messenger, who had gone for a walk.[31]

Some months later Moseley received word that the Messenger had been involved in another squabble and had been sent to the state sanatorium. Moseley contacted the asylum's supervisor and had him discharged. Shortly afterward, he journeyed to Moseley's home in Macon and thanked the peach farmer for his help and support. The two ministers spent several hours in theological discussion, and the bond of respect and admiration grew stronger between them. That afternoon Moseley took him to the depot, and the evangelist boarded a train for Americus, Georgia, regretfully bidding him good-bye. Even though a deep friendship formed between the two men, the barrier of racism separated them. "He had the HOLY GHOST and he wanted Me to be with them," the Messenger later recalled, "but he was afraid to take Me back on his farm because he felt like his brother might lynch Me. But yet he was more with ME—was absolutely ONE with Me." [32]

In Americus, he reunited with a small cadre of disciples who had forsaken family and friends and dedicated themselves to him and his teachings. These fiercely devoted believers followed him as he roamed the country relying on the kindness of strangers:

> When I was travelling as an Individual and as an Evangelist from place to place, not taking any money and when I would get to some towns and we would be holding a meeting or a series of lectures, the different ones would say, "YOU can stay right here, YOU and YOUR FOLLOWERS, as long as you want and if you will send some one over to the house we will send YOU something to eat." And I would say to those who went over, get only enough for this meal. Don't let them give you anything for the next one.

Typically, when the group arrived in a new town, the Messenger canvassed local churches, requesting an opportunity to speak. He also promoted his theology with spontaneous street-corner worship services. If the townsfolk proved receptive, he and his followers stayed as long as a month. The disciples took jobs to pay for food, housing, and transportation, and he preached, served banquets, met with ministers, and organized the group's itinerary. The disciples did not resent supporting their leader, for he worked long hours teaching his formula for eternal life and salvation. The disciples labored cheerfully, believing that all material goods and wealth were derived from God and therefore belonged rightfully to the Messenger. [33]

These were difficult times for the Messenger and his faithful followers, and during the lean years the entire band, including their leader, suffered and sacrificed. The radical tone of his teachings often placed him in danger's way. Even in the relatively receptive environment of Americus, he encountered hostility and barely escaped a lynch mob. According to his recollections, he encountered lynch mobs in many parts of the South and had "sacrificed this body thirty-two times or once for each year I was on earth before, to bring this consciousness to the hearts of men." Followers testified that in one town a group of white men captured him and hanged him until he was clearly dead. The next morning, on their way to work, the members of the mob discovered him preaching along the roadside. The disciples proudly claimed that the scars crisscrossing the back of his head resulted from numerous unsuccessful attempts to lynch the evangelist.[34]

The critical social underpinnings of the Messenger's philosophy placed him in jeopardy and made him a target for lynching. But it seems improbable that a black man in the South would have escaped an angry lynch mob. Since he saw his mission as a defiance of American racism and southern lynchings, he may have interpreted racist attacks on his ministry as symbolic lynchings. Certainly he and his devotees endured prejudice and confronted frightening racial violence, but with memories of the lynchings in Montgomery County, Maryland, he willingly risked his life to fight this brutality. The perils of his mission strengthened the commitment of the evangelist and his flock, and forged a strong bond among members of the group.

He did not confine his evangelizing to the South and soon added major northern cities to his circuit. In late 1914, he arrived in New York and located his former colleague, Reverend Bishop Saint John the Vine, who had organized a church in Harlem, the Church of the Living God, the Pillar and Ground of Truth, that had attracted a sizable and growing congregation. One Sunday, the Messenger slipped into one of the Bishop's services and found the Bishop still frisking about in robes and a turban, proclaiming that God's spirit existed equally in all people. The Messenger observed that the congregation appeared joyful and that they enthusiastically praised God in testimony and song.[35]

But before long, the Bishop spotted the Messenger in the crowd. Angrily he reproached his former associate: "He came up to ME saying 'I am as much GOD as YOU are, I am as much GOD as YOU are.' I said, 'I did not say anything about your not being as much GOD as I.' I hadn't said a word about it." The Messenger seized the opportunity to promote his teachings before the Bishop's disciples. According to the Messenger, under his influence, all members of the Church of the Living God abandoned the Bishop and joined the Messenger's band. Since the Bishop's church continued to thrive, the Messenger probably added only a few of the Bishop's proselytes to his fold.[36]

Leaving New York City, the Messenger continued to wander around the nation trailed by his devout apostles, his quest to spread his teachings broadening his sensitivity and knowledge. In later years he incorporated many of his experiences in the South into his sermons. He often related to audiences one incident that involved a woman hospitalized for religious fanaticism. He attempted to convince her husband that she was perfectly sound and pleaded for her release. But the husband transferred the woman to an insane asylum. When the Messenger learned of this, he reprimanded the husband and threatened to "shake the town." The man ignored him, and

> that night a tremendous storm came up, of rain and thunder, but no lightning, something no one had ever seen before, and it flooded everything. [The Messenger] said He heard it reported that the rain was hot and burned the trees. The husband had gone to bed and locked the door of his room, but it came open, and continued to open every time until at last . . . [the Messenger] appeared to him and told him to get his wife.

The man capitulated and with the help of the Messenger, persuaded the institution to discharge his wife.[37]

To nonfollowers the tale of the institutionalized woman seems unbelievable, but the story probably contains some elements of truth. During his travels, he probably encountered a woman hospitalized for unusual religious beliefs. It is conceivable that he confronted the subject's husband, that a severe storm blew through the town, and that the Messenger, his followers, and the woman's husband interpreted the downpour as a sign of God's displeasure. But on one level, the accuracy of the story in unimportant, for his followers accepted the tale as true and the parable established his commitment to religious freedom and women's rights. The tale spoke of the needs and interests of women drawn to his teachings. Women had no recourse if their husbands declared them insane. His support for the institutionalized woman not only legitimized her religious beliefs but asserted that a woman could be right and her husband wrong. Furthermore, the tale advanced religious liberty and assured followers of God's protection. His journey around the country had influenced his teachings, and increasingly he was evolving into an articulate advocate of women's rights and religious freedom.

In 1917, after five exhausting years on the circuit, he decided to establish a permanent base in New York City. At thirty-eight, he remained energetic but was weary of the constant travel and yearned for a more stable home. During the course of his journeys, he had collected between six and twelve disciples, and they may have become cumbersome as he moved from town to town. After depositing his flock in New York, he continued to make occasional trips to the South and returned home with a few new converts, but his following remained relatively small. The size of his congregation did not concern him, for he concentrated on gathering the most faithful and believed that eventually the flock would grow. Wonderful things were in store for his followers.

In 1917, he declared to his dedicated congregation that

> HE was preparing and others were preparing for a "Vanishing City" in which ten million people would leave this globe and go to other planets. They would be the purest of the pure in heart and the event would take place in the year 2525. HE said HE would allow such a development to come forth in aerial transportation long before that time, that when the time came the ten million people would be easily accommodated. HE said, "Many here now are preparing for a trip to Venus and Mars that you know so little about. Don't you want to go? For this cause came I into the Flesh and all will be fulfilled."

In New York he gathered "the purest of the pure" and organized a colony that he hoped would serve as a twentieth-century "city on the hill," a spiritual example to the world.[38]

His relocation in New York was part of a larger trend. In 1917, African-American migration to major metropolitan areas escalated. The war industry created numerous job opportunities and lured many black southern migrants to the city. Most black newcomers settled in Harlem, which emerged as the nation's largest and most famous African-American community. Harlem provided a glamorous alternative to the country life southern migrants had known in their hometowns. The dance halls, casinos, and nightclubs bewitched newcomers. But despite the booming war industry and the glitter of Harlem, the vast majority of blacks in Harlem lived in destitution. Employers demanded long hours and paid black workers low wages, and there was little time for diversion. The Messenger found New York's black neighborhoods little different from Monkey Run. In New York, as in his hometown, blacks contended with substandard housing, malnutrition, overcrowding, crime, poverty, and addiction. If anything, New York, like Baltimore, was worse, for poverty was on a far larger scale than in Rockville and was spreading rapidly.[39]

In the city, he encountered a religious community feverishly expanding. As the migrant population grew, new religious sects continued to appear throughout the African-American community. In his opinion, New York City was overrun by false prophets, who endangered citizens with their self-serving ministries. According to the Messenger, passersby who refused to contribute to street-corner evangelists often found that the preachers got "off . . . their . . . stools, and they would take [them] and break your head with [them]."[40] Repulsed by these religious hustlers, he became determined to end their "soliciting and begging on the streets of New York City."[41]

To protect his flock from the temptations of street-corner preachers and Harlem's highlife, he isolated his entourage in a rented apartment in Brooklyn where more affluent and conservative blacks made their homes, and he instituted a strict moral code that required abstinence from sex, smoking, profanity, drugs, and alcohol. He assigned men and women to separate rooms and permitted the sexes to interact only on business or religious matters. The flock welcomed only newcomers who agreed to abide by the rigid rules. Those residing in his Brooklyn home viewed themselves as integral components of God's redemption of humankind. He transformed the Brooklyn apartment into a spiritual center where each evening the faithful gathered and worshiped God with a generous Holy Communion banquet.[42]

The Brooklyn apartment operated as a collective and ran efficiently under his guidance. Several members of the household attended solely to domestic chores. He assumed the role of an employment agent and placed his other followers in domestic positions or blue-collar jobs. The flock pooled their wages to pay household expenses that the Messenger, through clever business practices, cut to the minimum. He clothed his followers in high-quality secondhand garments altered by one of the disciples. Each meal served in the household was substantial and balanced, but the food was selected from local markets featuring bargain prices. Through his careful budgeting and communal organization, the household slowly began to build up its savings.[43]

The Messenger's collective primarily contained women who, like the women of Valdosta, found the evangelist's teachings socially and spiritually appealing. In the Brooklyn commune, he put his teachings into operation. He organized the home on the basis of democracy; each member, regardless of sex, had equal status and equal say in household decisions. Furthermore, the home provided women displaced by personal or economic hardship with a refuge where he furnished not only food, clothes, and shelter but also gainful employment. According to his teachings, anyone in contact with God's spirit, regardless of race or sex, transcended social or economic limitations and could achieve material success.[44]

The Messenger's theological formula for economic advancement and social welfare also lured a few men into his flock. Of the identifiable male disciples, most were unskilled day laborers previously active in the black church. He promised black men liberation from poverty and racism through religion, a powerful channel that these men respected. As a role model, he inspired dignity and a sense of self-worth. Primed with newfound self-confidence and his teachings, his disciples, men and women, began their fight for a place within the American system and a share of its vast economic rewards.[45]

Joseph Gabriel, a square-shouldered day laborer from the South, was one of the earliest male apostles drawn to the Messenger's spiritual and social beliefs. Probably one of the disciples Moseley met in Lakeside and deeply dedicated to Christianity, Gabriel had joined the ministry and led a small church in his hometown. Ordinarily a soft-spoken man, he came alive before a congregation and delivered fiery, emotional sermons. According to Gabriel, the Messenger first appeared to him in the 1880s but quickly vanished. Then one day in 1914 as Gabriel smoothed wet cement, the evangelist materialized at his side and walked through the fresh cement. Initially dismayed, Gabriel examined the cement and discovered that it remained without a single footprint. He invited the Messenger to preach to his congregation. After hearing the itinerant's message, Gabriel abandoned his ministerial post to assist the Messenger in his crusade. By the time they reached Brooklyn, Gabriel had become one of his most trusted disciples.[46]

But of all the Messenger's disciples, the most important was the stately, heavyset Peninniah. As his most dedicated follower, Peninniah successfully cut her ties to the past, and her name, age, and birthplace remain obscure. Like the Messenger, Peninniah attended a black Methodist church. Later she left Methodism and became a devout member of Joseph Gabriel's congregation, a highly valued parishioner who remained active despite crippling attacks of rheumatism. By the time the Messenger arrived in town, Peninniah's disease had advanced, and she was unable to walk. Her pleas for help brought the Messenger to her side, and he healed her immediately. Captivated, she deserted her family and friends, and joined his flock.[47]

Peninniah followed the Messenger as he traveled from town to town, and she too was probably among the followers Moseley encountered in Lakeside. She became an instrumental follower, witnessing in churches and on street corners, recounting her astonishing recovery. Before congregations, she sang of her conversion and newfound faith:

> I heard a Voice saying come up higher;
> I'll show you the things that will surely come to pass;
> I heard a voice saying, come up higher,
> The Mystery of the Seven Seals. . . .
> I heard a few names in Sardis
> Which have not defiled their Garments;
> And they shall walk with Me in white.[48]

In Peninniah's interpretation, the Messenger fulfilled the prophecies of the Book of Revelation. For her, the millennium had come. The Messenger had revealed the mysteries of the Lord and promised eternal salvation.

While the small band of pilgrims roamed around the country, the bond between Peninniah and the Messenger grew stronger, and the two were married. But Peninniah marked her wedding date as June 6, 1882, a date that probably denoted her first religious experience. According to the Messenger, the marriage was purely spiritual and never physically consummated, the union representing God's love for and intimate bonding to humankind.[49]

Several factors compelled him to select Peninniah for his wife. Though she was portly and several years older than the Messenger, Peninniah was attractive, a regal presence. She provided a respectable female representative for his mission, and her healthy, well-fed appearance testified to his great ability to provide and heal.

She probably drew many of the sick and infirm into the fold. Furthermore, Peninniah offered him a degree of protection. As a bachelor, his appeal to women provoked rumors and innuendo. Traveling and living with a group predominantly of single women was acceptable only for a married man accompanied by his wife. Peninniah also furnished a safeguard against advances by self-interested female followers. As a married man, the Messenger more gracefully repelled the offers from such followers.

But it was mainly Peninniah's total dedication to his teachings and goals that brought the couple together. She thoroughly understood his theology and upheld his expectations. He remarked: "Hold everything from an impersonal standpoint of view. Do not see it as a personal thing, then it can never leave you. I told . . . [Peninniah] . . . years ago that I could never leave her if she held ME in an impersonal point of view, and she has looked upon ME in that way. She has never beheld me as a person and I never approach her as a person." Peninniah worshiped the Messenger, and he held her steadfast allegiance in high esteem. She was the foundation of his movement, and he provided her with direction and meaning. Together the couple shared a relationship filled with mutual respect, fierce devotion, and love.[50]

Warm and gracious, Peninniah won the hearts of all followers. They looked to her for guidance and consolation during rough times. By the time he and his followers settled in Brooklyn, the band had evolved symbolically into a family unit. Disciples honored the Messenger and Peninniah by calling them Father and Mother, and the couple referred to the followers as their children.[51]

Within his Brooklyn colony, he reconstructed familial relationships and provided his followers with the ideal substitute family. Before joining his flock, many disciples had suffered through divorces, abuse, and homes wrecked by social and economic hardships. The Brooklyn colony was a happy alternative, a financially sound and stable family guided by a stern but loving father and a compassionate and dependable mother. As children, the followers relinquished a certain degree of control over their lives but gained security and tranquillity.

But the Messenger's Brooklyn home was more than a relief shelter. The commune functioned as a rehabilitation center where the sick and poor found occupational therapy and training. He inspired the household with positive thinking, industry, and self-help, teaching his disciples how to survive and prosper in the American system. His theology gave his followers the power to change their lives and helped them to pull out of the downward spiral that had trapped most black Americans.

Settling in Brooklyn transformed the Messenger's life. The management of the colony forced him to cut back on travel. Business affairs dominated more of his time as he attempted to keep his household constantly employed. To deal more effectively with the public, he adopted an unusual but more acceptable name—Reverend Major Jealous Divine. This new name encapsulated many of his teachings and his struggle for equality: both *reverend*, an ecclesiastical title, and *major*, a military rank, commanded respect and deference. He selected *jealous* from Exodus 34:14: "For thou shalt worship no other god. For the Lord whose name is Jealous, is a jealous God"—reminding his followers of his expectation of total commitment. The surname Divine further supported and reinforced his claim that he was God. While his business associates came to know him as Reverend Divine, his followers affectionately addressed him as Father Divine. "God is here on earth today," sang his disciples. "Father Divine is his name."[52]

4

In This Dining Room

So I Am glad to say that charity, or love, be-
gins at home and spreads abroad, we are
going to manifest this mighty love right here
in this dining room and from here we are
going to manifest this Truth from shore to
shore and from land to land, and it all comes
about through those who are willing to sacrifice.

Spoken November 16, 1931

On a crisp February morning in 1919, throngs of black and white
New Yorkers lined Fifth Avenue and cheered the Fifteenth Regiment of New York's National Guard as they marched proudly home
to Harlem. During World War I the fighting men of the Fifteenth,
an all-black regiment, had heroically defended America on the bat-
tlefields of Europe. For the black community, the regiment's march
signified more than a homecoming; it heralded the birth of a cultural awakening and revitalized political militancy known as the
Harlem Renaissance. The black soldiers of the Fifteenth represented the germination of a new self-confidence in the community.

Political leaders like Cyril Briggs, A. Philip Randolph, and
W. E. B. Du Bois represented the growth of a new consciousness
and a renewed direct struggle against white oppression. Black literature, art, and music flourished and manifested a heightened
self-respect and racial awareness. The outpouring of creativity attracted many whites, who actively participated in the Renaissance.
With some white assistance, black writers like Langston Hughes
and Countee Cullen and black musicians like Louis Armstrong and
Ethel Waters rose to national prominence. Beginning on that February morning in 1919 and continuing throughout the 1920s, a
whirlwind of self-discovery and creativity engulfed Harlem's residents.[1]

The Renaissance was not confined to Harlem's African-American middle class; the wave of racial pride and assertiveness flowed through black working-class communities in all parts of the United States. Some artistic avenues, like entertainment, welcomed poorer blacks. But a lack of education, time, and money thwarted working-class efforts to produce literature and other works of art. Despite the constraints, working-class blacks did develop and participate in much of the Renaissance, especially in politics and religion. In some cases, black working-class Americans dominated certain facets of the Harlem Renaissance.[2]

Marcus Garvey's Universal Negro Improvement Association (UNIA), one of the most popular components of the Harlem Renaissance, drew support from blue-collar African Americans. Born in Jamaica, Garvey was influenced by Booker T. Washington and in 1917 brought the UNIA to Harlem. A separatist, Garvey contended that blacks could free themselves from white oppression by harnessing the forces of capitalism and returning to their ancestral homeland, Africa. His philosophy, which maintained that God and Jesus Christ were black, boosted pride and self-confidence.

The UNIA held massive parades that included bands, motorcades carrying UNIA officers, and marching legions of smartly uniformed men and women. Members published newspapers and opened chapters in cities around the world. Garvey also established a shipping firm, the Black Star Line, and sold shares to African Americans across the country. He encouraged his followers to open and buy only from black businesses. The UNIA's goal of economic opportunity for African Americans attracted many supporters in the African-American community, especially poorer blacks, who were encouraged by Garvey's philosophy and invested enthusiastically in UNIA projects. In fact, one of Garvey's zealous supporters was an illiterate working-class preacher known as Reverend Bishop Saint John the Vine.[3]

But most members of the black working class discovered that the church provided the most accessible forum for their celebration of African-American culture and pride. During the Harlem Renaissance, schisms deepened within the black religious community. The migrants drawn to the cities during World War I brought a wealth of competing ideologies. Furthermore, literacy in black America had increased remarkably. In 1900, only 55.5 percent of nonwhite Americans could read; by 1920, the proportion had risen to 77 percent. The circulation of new ideas advanced the growth of literacy, producing an ideological explosion and a proliferation of new religious sects.[4]

New sects increased not only in number but also in variety. Between 1919 and 1930, at least eight factions of African Americans claiming to be descendants of Ethiopian Jews appeared in Harlem. Some of these groups, like the Commandment Keepers Congregation of the Living God, led by Rabbi Wentworth A. Matthews, sought to mold Orthodox Judaism into a black activist theology. Others, like Elder Warien K. Roberson's Temple of the Gospel of the Kingdom, blended some Judaic rituals and beliefs with elements of New Thought. Islam also found followers among Harlem's black population. Some joined the Moorish Science Temple, organized by Prophet Noble Drew Ali, who rejected Christianity and claimed that Islam was the true religion of people of African descent.[5]

Despite the proliferation of groups rejecting Christianity, most new sects remained rooted in Christian teachings. By far the most popular was the World Gospel Feast, a traveling devotional program of gospel music featuring the black evangelist George Wilson Becton with his choir and orchestra. But the majority of the new Christian sects were the simple storefronts that modestly celebrated the Renaissance with their self-created and independent theologies.[6]

Undoubtedly Father Divine considered many aspects of the Harlem Renaissance destructive and immoral. Alarmed by the worldliness of the Renaissance, Father Divine discouraged followers from associating with members of the black community. He stayed on the fringe of the Renaissance and participated only through his attempt to spread his theology among Harlem's residents. Although its contributions were limited during this phase, Father Divine's small sect represented a faction of the working-class component of the Renaissance and would eventually benefit from the expansion of cultural pride and black assertiveness.

Not far from vibrant Harlem lay the sleepy village of Sayville in Suffolk County, Long Island. In many ways Sayville, a summer retreat from the heat and congestion of New York City, resembled Father Divine's hometown. While the city broiled, well-to-do urbanites swarmed into the seaside resort to enjoy the cool breezes of the Atlantic Ocean. At summer's end, vacationers deserted the village, leaving Sayville's permanent residents to savor the seclusion of their quiet hamlet.[7]

Sayville was a close-knit and relatively homogeneous community of white middle-class shopkeepers, artisans, and retirees. During the off-season the village was usually tranquil, but in 1917 a dispute between two German-American residents shattered that serenity. Fearing the increase of anti-German sentiment during World War I, Edward Felgenhauer changed his surname to Fellows. A German-born neighbor began to taunt Fellows, accusing him of cowardice. A squabble ensued and continued after the war was over. In the fall of 1919, Fellows, exhausted and exasperated by constant quarreling, put his house up for sale. Reportedly, Fellows, seeking revenge, advertised for a "colored" buyer. Father Divine seized the opportunity, paid Fellows $700 in cash, and secured a mortgage for $2,500. On October 27, 1919, Father and Mother Divine signed the deed for the property at 72 Macon Street and became Sayville's first African-American homeowners.[8]

Father Divine's claim that he "went out to Sayville with the mind to hide as a person from the world of religion and all civilization" suggests that in one sense his relocation was almost a retirement from evangelism.[9] But his activities indicate that he had no intention of retreating from the original goals he had decided upon in Baltimore. His self-imposed exile in Sayville represented an active quest for religious purification and a new stage in his proselytizing tactics. Essentially, Father Divine's move to Sayville was a logical extension of his missionary impulse.[10]

Sayville furnished the perfect environment for the promotion of Father Divine's teachings and the actualization of his objectives. The isolation of this resort town seventy miles from New York City gave Father Divine more control over his disciples. In Brooklyn, Father Divine not only competed against worldly seductions like sex, alcohol, and drugs, but also, according to sociologist Kenneth Burnham, fought off other religious sects' attempts to steal his disciples.[11] By distancing his disciples from other religious orders, familiar surroundings, and previous companions, Father Divine eliminated many of the temptations luring away converts and increased his followers' allegiance to and dependence on him.

In addition to practical considerations, his relocation in Sayville carried symbolic connotations. After seven years of preaching without pay or monetary compensation, the acquisition of the Macon Street home demonstrated to the faithful his link to divinity and his remarkable ability to provide for his flock. Father Divine had not only supplied a fine house but also led his congregation into a respectable and exclusively white middle-class neighborhood. Before the autumn of 1919, less than a dozen blacks lived in Sayville, and Father Divine's arrival represented his continuing attempt to "break down the wall of segregation." In that year, Father and Mother Divine moved into the white neighborhood with nine followers and embarked on a quiet campaign against racism.[12]

Since his early days in Baltimore, Father Divine had avoided living in African-American ghettos, and his relocation in Sayville was a rebellion against his roots. From the perspective of his bleak childhood in Monkey Run, his Long Island home signified a great personal victory. Through pious self-help and positive thinking, he had escaped from the slums and purchased a comfortable house in a resort town similar to Rockville. He hoped to take advantage of the amenities that he had been denied as a youth. In many ways, moving to Sayville was like a triumphant homecoming for the now middle-aged, hardworking minister.

The resort location was advantageous, for Sayville provided Father Divine's spiritual children with excellent employment opportunities. A few disciples commuted to work in New York City, but most found jobs in or around Sayville. Many members of New York City's elite maintained second homes on Long Island, and the unreliability of domestics who commuted from the city forced them to rely on live-in help. Father Divine shrewdly forecast their willingness to hire from a local labor pool. Soon after his arrival, Father Divine placed advertisements for his free Busy Bee Employment agency in a local newspaper and was quickly swamped with responses from local residents. Many white employers dispensed with live-in help, hired Father Divine's followers, and drastically cut household expenses.[13]

For Father and Mother Divine and their spiritual children, the transition from the Brooklyn apartment to the Long Island home went smoothly. Macon Street's new residents repaired, scrubbed, and painted their home. Father Divine cleared the property, hauled away piles of trash that Fellows had accumulated, relandscaped the lot, and surrounded the house with neatly manicured lawns and colorful gardens. He stocked the home with all the modern conveniences and purchased first-rate furniture. Soon after moving in, Father Divine bought an automobile, the ultimate symbol of twenties success. On Long Island, Father Divine and his disciples enjoyed a greatly improved standard of living and impressed the neighbors with their industry and apparent prosperity.[14]

In Sayville, Father Divine and his followers became even more determined to share their material blessings with the needy. His impoverished childhood and the generous support he received from the poor while he was an itinerant compelled him to offer assistance to the destitute. Additionally, Father Divine calculated that those in desperate need made the most faithful recruits. He christened his new project the Refuge Home for the Poor Only and opened his doors to the indigent who promised to abide by his rules and work for their support. Occasionally, homeless individuals and families found their way to his Sayville address. A few discovered solace in his teachings, and dedicated their lives to the sect, but most stayed only until they found jobs and then abandoned the Long Island cloister.[15]

Although the household had a high turnover rate, Father Divine and his followers appeared to be respectable, dignified, cooperative citizens. All residents of 72 Macon Street were neatly groomed, well dressed, polite, and exceptionally honest. Each day the entire household rose early and left promptly for work. If Reverend Divine was not busily placing followers in jobs, he could be found doing chores around the house, tending his chickens and ducks, or working in his gardens. Occasionally he offered ministerial counseling and entertained guests. All callers were invited to dine and worship with the residents. The entire flock spent each evening and every Sunday in devotionals. Sometimes in the stillness at dusk, the Macon Street neighbors could hear the household singing softly. But fearing rejection by the white community, Father Divine and his followers cultivated a pious image and maintained a low profile.[16]

The sudden appearance of a black household in the midst of a white residential area probably infuriated many of Father Divine's neighbors. In 1919, as he relocated on Long Island, race riots broke out in many of the major cities in the United States. The resurgence of intense racism continued throughout the twenties and extended even into the small community of Sayville. After World War I, the Ku Klux Klan underwent a revival, and membership boomed all over the country, including Suffolk County. In 1923, the Long Island Klan burned a fifteen-foot cross in Sayville's village square. A year later, the KKK's Suffolk County leader, a Methodist minister, boasted that the local Klan contained over six thousand members. It was impossible for Father and Mother Divine and their household to escape discrimination and segregation in a town so easily drawn to the KKK.[17]

One warm summer day, Father and Mother Divine packed blankets, towels, and snacks, and started out for the beach. At the shore, he attempted to rent a cabana, and what had begun as a merry outing turned into an ugly scene. The attendant refused to wait on the couple and informed them that all blacks were barred from the beach. Father Divine claimed he retorted, "Well, if I can't swim, no one else will either" and headed home. According to his recollections, within a week a tarlike substance filled the ocean, and "they looked for some tar ship which might have been wrecked but they never found out what it was, and that year there was no bathing at that beach. Some went into the water at the first, but they got all stuck up with tar and it wouldn't come off."[18]

The accuracy of his account is not as important as the underlying feelings it expresses. This clash with white racism insulted and angered him. In this tale, whites emerged from the sea with black skin, their fate self-inflicted through negative thinking. In turn, they experienced firsthand the agonies of American racism.

While some whites in Sayville were blatantly hostile toward Father Divine and his followers, most maintained a cordial relationship with their new neighbors. Always smartly attired in a three-piece business suit with a gold pocketwatch dangling across his vest and his pocket bulging with pens, Father Divine inspired confidence and respect. He was short but handsome, with a cleanly shaven head and a dignified mustache. His charming personality paved the way for acceptance in the community. In private he was soft-spoken, gracious, and self-assured. In his dealings with the white patrons of his employment agency, his sincerity and humor won their trust. The honesty and industry of the domestic servants and handymen he supplied impressed the wealthiest homeowners. The local business community also came to respect the minister who patronized their stores and purchased substantial quantities, always paying in cash. The *Suffolk County News* commented that Father Divine "met all his obligations promptly and the local tradesmen speak well of him."[19]

Affluent landholders, many from New York's high society, and businessmen were the most influential elements in Sayville. By serving their needs and gaining their acceptance, Father Divine and his followers were exempted from at least some racial hatred. No public outcry followed when the black minister, driving home late one night, hit and injured a white bicyclist. Authorities did not question his explanation that "he did not see the man on the bicycle until too late to avoid striking him." For several years, the approval of local leadership protected him and the household from the grosser manifestations of racism—and expulsion from the village.[20]

The rapport between Father Divine and Sayville's upper and business classes produced a moderately safe climate for the promotion of his ministry. In March 1922, at his request, the *Suffolk County News* willingly ran a short article, "Divine Home Has No Solicitors":

> The Rev. M. J. Divine, a colored clergyman, who has a charitable rescue home on Macon Street, this village for poor people only, asks the News to say that he does not do any soliciting for funds nor does he have any soliciting done on the streets or in the churches as his work is not financed in that way, and he wishes it understood that no one has any authority to solicit money in his behalf or for his work. He advises strongly against contributing to strangers who frequently come to town soliciting for charitable work, much of which is done by fakirs. Mr. Divine tells of a colored man who arrived in town at five o'clock one afternoon this week and who boasted that before bed-time he had succeeded in collecting $15.[21]

More than an attempt to warn Sayville not to fall prey to con men, the story was a discreet effort to stimulate interest in his sect. The article documented that Father Divine's mission was to help the poor and that his funding did not come from contributions. The tone was intentionally vague, in an effort to increase curiosity but not hostility, and the piece served as a cautious step toward spreading his theology to the surrounding community.

Father Divine yearned to preach his message openly, but the employment agency, the rescue mission, the upkeep of his property, and the fear of reprisal from the local community forced him to evangelize circumspectly in his home. But he remained restless. After over three years in Sayville, his following had not grown significantly, and he felt the lure of the itinerant circuit. He began to plan another missionary trip, waiting until the household's' savings were sufficient for followers to quit their jobs. Then in the winter of 1923, Father and Mother Divine and their nine followers each packed one suitcase, piled into a Hudson automobile, and left Sayville to spread his teachings around the country.[22]

Father Divine and his band began their journey in New York City and traveled south to Florida before turning back. As before, he preached on street corners and in churches, and served banquets in many homes. In towns where the missionaries received a warm reception, the party stayed and held three-day revivals. During the trip several congregations cheerfully hosted him and participated enthusiastically in his devotional services. But in many ways the trip proved disappointing, for despite sincere interest in his teachings, most of those who worshiped with the tiny band refused to abandon their families and possessions to follow him. In the spring, when he and his flock returned to Sayville, they brought home only one additional follower, an African-American woman converted in the Deep South. The disciples returned to their jobs, and Father Divine found that obligations in Sayville allowed few if any excursions beyond Long Island.[23]

Although Sayville isolated him from many potential converts, he remained confident that his following would grow, and in 1924 he initiated a curious project. Even though the Macon Street home comfortably housed all twelve residents, he embarked on a massive expansion of the dwelling, adding a large dining area and several more rooms, almost doubling the size of his home. His property assumed an even grander appearance, and the local residents watched their eccentric neighbor with wonder.[24]

While Father Divine quietly carried on his ministry, patiently waiting for his flock to grow, he continued to study religious literature. He frequently patronized the public library and checked out books on theology and religion. Advertising executive Bruce Barton's *The Man Nobody Knows* became one of his favorite works. Barton's book explored the life of Christ and the applicability of his teachings to the business world, rejecting the passive and fragile characterization of Christ and portraying him as a rugged and aggressive spiritual leader. Jesus Christ, according to the author, sold his teachings to the public by efficiently meeting humankind's needs. Christ's example, which encouraged honesty and effective service, furnished a successful model for businesspeople. Barton's entrepreneurial Christ and his formula for prosperity appealed to Father Divine, who had just begun to realize the profits of his spiritually piloted employment agency.[25]

Yet he almost exclusively preferred New Thought literature, which had gained increasing popularity throughout the twenties. This era of prosperity drove Americans to ideologies like New Thought that outlined formulas for the acquisition and retention of wealth. At least some of the preoccupation with mind-power and God's inner presence stemmed from the contradictions that surfaced during the Roaring Twenties. While the poor puzzled over the route to riches, affluent Christians tried to reconcile their desire for wealth with their abhorrence of greed. The New Thought formula rationalized moneymaking and prosperity within a Christian context.

Father Divine immersed himself in this literature. He closely studied Robert Collier's *The Secret of Gold,* a Christian guide to channeling God's spirit for the achievement of prosperity. Another New Thought devotional, *Christ in You,* reaffirmed Father Divine's hypothesis that heaven was on earth, God existed in everyone, and health and wealth derived from positive states of mind. But *Christ in You* was more than a regurgitation of standard New Thought ideas. Indirectly and unintentionally, the work offered remedies for social ills. "It is wonderful, to realize that we are one great and unlimited whole," the author wrote. "We are working all over the world to establish pure unity and brotherhood." The ideology that Father Divine discovered in *Christ in You* promised to heal social, economic, and even racial divisions.[26]

He also carefully researched works directly influenced by Eastern thought and mysticism. *The Kingdom of Happiness* by Jeddu Krishnamurti concentrated on spirituality and ignored material affairs, but was compatible with New Thought. Krishnamurti urged his disciples to follow "the voice of intuition," an internal spiritual beacon that steered humankind toward truth and happiness.[27] Although he opposed conformity, Krishnamurti insisted that his followers surrender their individuality and strive to achieve a group consciousness. In Krishnamurti's view, men and women continued to be reincarnated until they actualized a "oneness" with spiritual truth that could be found through any religious tradition.[28]

Father Divine was also impressed with Baird T. Spalding's *Life and Teaching of the Masters of the Far East*. Despite the questionable reliability of Spalding's account of his travels in India and his interviews with "the Great Masters of the Himalayas," his work became popular among New Thought devotees.[29] Spalding's party had conveniently encountered groups of Indians completely cut off from Western civilization who spoke fluent English and subscribed to an amalgamation of Buddhism, Hinduism, and New Thought Christianity. His book promoted New Thought and asserted that "the second and last coming of the Christ" had occurred within humankind's consciousness. Spalding's discovery of the existence of New Thought among these isolated Indians seemed to validate mind-power ideology.[30]

Father Divine also continued to follow the progress of Charles Fillmore's Unity School. By the 1920s, the Unity School had organized its own publishing house, which issued numerous periodicals and books. Membership had increased, and Unity centers extended across the country. "Silent Unity" had evolved into a busy telephone hotline for those in need of prayer. Unity's expansion increased the organization's financial stability, and in 1920 Fillmore organized a collective farm just outside Kansas City, Missouri. At the farm, which housed Unity's businesses, Unity School members escaped the harmful effects of city life and found a communal environment that furthered their study of Fillmore's theology. Father Divine continued to monitor Fillmore's model ministry closely through Unity publications.[31]

Father Divine admired the religious literature of the twenties and believed that his favorite authors displayed an acute understanding of spiritual truth. Some studies argue that his later sermons exhibited extensive and incoherent borrowings from New Thought works of the 1920s, but Father Divine, influenced primarily by Charles Fillmore, had embraced New Thought ideology and terminology long before 1920. Although his sermons were spontaneous, sometimes rambling, and filled with original vocabulary like *tangeblated* and *physicalating,* they had a consistent and comprehensible core. Indeed, he was as intelligible as any New Thought advocate. He did not pilfer the ideals of his fellow New Thought proponents but frequently praised and cited respected New Thought authors in his messages.[32]

He continued to take home armloads of library books, and before long he noticed that his disciples, faithfully following his example, had begun to study the tracts. Soon the household buzzed with discussions and debates on the perspectives of various New Thought authors. Excitedly, Father Divine realized: "After the different ones read them, I saw they were bearing witness to the truth. I said, 'It is immaterial whether people know ME, just so they get the message.' "

Quite by accident, he had stumbled onto a new evangelizing technique. He began purchasing and passing out his favorite New Thought works, excluding Unity books (because they were imprinted with a price, he feared that people would want to pay for them). Anyone who visited his home left with a printed reminder of his teachings. This literature not only legitimized his message but also allowed him to avoid the limelight, so that "the glory and honor might be given to the SPIRIT and not the PERSON or PERSONALITY." He anticipated that the distribution of New Thought works, combined with word of mouth, would disseminate his theology and attract more worshipers to his Sayville home.[33]

Slowly his new approach began to work. The few who visited his home and participated in the banquets returned to their homes with New Thought literature and tales of the remarkable minister. But New Thought books were tedious reading and irrelevant to the lives of many lower-income blacks, these works serving only as a stale reminder of his dynamic message, astonishing healing abilities, and incredible affluence. Stories of the mysterious Long Island clergyman began to circulate, and increasing numbers ventured out to Sayville to inspect the reported miracle maker. By late 1927, guests were streaming to the Macon Street commune. Father Divine later remembered: "You see, you come to your limit. You were willing to give and give and give and give and then you will get so big, you will want to GIVE the whole world, absolutely free, and take nothing for yourself apparently. When you do that, you are lost completely. That was the mystery, and that is the way it was out in Sayville. The whole world came to ME." Even when he stopped dispensing books, the numbers of followers and sympathizers continued to increase. His expanding congregation included people from all walks of life—young and old, rich and poor, healthy and infirm, black and white—who worshiped together under his roof.[34]

The vast majority of new converts to Father Divine's fold were black domestics and unskilled laborers. Several, like the West Indian couple Thomas and Verinda Brown, introduced to Father Divine by a domestic named Priscilla Paul, worked in homes of wealthy Long Island families. Naturally, those African Americans who lived on Long Island were the first to take advantage of the generous meals and vibrant worship services, but later, blacks from outlying areas became increasingly involved in his mission. Regardless of location, most black domestics worked long hours for modest pay. Father Divine provided anyone who lived on a marginal income, even Long Island domestics, with much needed social assistance.[35]

Economic hardship heightened Father Divine's appeal to the black working class. Most of his biographers link his rise in popularity to the 1929 stock market crash, but the diminutive evangelist's following blossomed two full years before the onset of the Great Depression. Nevertheless, even in 1927, as the country basked in prosperity, financial instability pressured many African Americans to join his flock. Historically, economic depression was a constant reality for the African-American community, and the affluence of the twenties skipped over most blacks. Father Divine furnished food, clothing, and shelter to destitute blacks, but he also provided a theology that promised a better life and a brighter future to anyone, regardless of economic status. Father Divine personified the Horatio Alger myth, and his success proved that even for blacks, America was a land of opportunity.[36]

Social relief and symbolic materialism were only two of the elements that attracted members of the black community to Father Divine. For many African Americans, his appeal was primarily religious. He skillfully placed himself at the center of the most powerful component of black life—the church. The dissemination of his philosophy through an institution fundamental to the African-

American community contributed to his growing popularity. With the exception of Holy Communion banquets, his worship services structurally resembled those found in many black denominations. The healings, audience participation, and music were rooted in the black church. His fusion of the sacred and profane worlds shared many theological tenets of black religion. Additionally, New Thought ideology had become increasingly popular among blacks, and the Unity School had opened churches in several African-American communities around the nation. Many new members of his spiritual family found a satisfying blend of their past religious experiences in his theology.[37]

Father Divine's theology also borrowed from self-help ideology, the dominant educational philosophy in black schools, familiar to many African Americans in the version espoused by Booker T. Washington. Marcus Garvey was also an advocate of self-help. But Father Divine's self-help was even more appealing, for he presented the philosophy in a religious context, an avenue previously unexplored by self-help advocates.[38]

Economic necessity and philosophical attraction do not explain the sudden surge of interest in Father Divine in late 1927. He had provided relief and taught his philosophy for many years. Probably he benefited from a void in the leadership of the African-American community in 1927 when the U.S. government deported Marcus Garvey to Jamaica after the courts had convicted him of mail fraud. Garvey's absence was especially noticeable in New York City and the surrounding area where the UNIA had its strongest support. After Garvey's departure, many African Americans sought new channels for expression and protest. For some swept up by the spirit of the Harlem Renaissance, Father Divine provided another outlet for the celebration of black potential.[39]

But not all those drawn into his fold were black, and a smattering of whites appeared in his congregation. Like African-American disciples, new white converts came from a variety of backgrounds. At the time, interracial groups were rare outside the NAACP and certain Renaissance circles. Some whites from affluent backgrounds probably learned of Father Divine through their contacts in the Renaissance. In addition, Euramerican Renaissance intellectuals and patrons were joined by working-class whites. One of the earliest white followers was Barbara Jones, a minister's widow who worked as a Long Island domestic. A deeply religious woman, Jones had learned of Father Divine from black domestics and came to ask him to heal a sick friend. Impressed by his curative abilities, she became a dedicated disciple and in September 1928 moved into 72 Macon Street. Like their black brothers and sisters, white disciples joined the fold for a variety of reasons—economic assistance, spiritual guidance, intellectual gratification. In his Macon Street home Father Divine had begun to establish his vision of an integrated America.[40]

For years, white Macon Street residents had tolerated their eccentric black neighbors. But as the congregation grew, so did the impatience of Sayville residents. The racial mixing and increasing numbers of African-American visitors alarmed his white neighbors. Many began to fear that his activities and the presence of more blacks in Sayville would drive down property values. His evasiveness and mysteriousness contributed to residents' resentment. Suspicious of his inexhaustible affluence, one white neighbor attended several banquets and finally confronted him about his finances. He steadfastly insisted that his wealth came directly from God. Rumors that he sent followers into New York City and other parts of Long Island to collect money began to circulate around Sayville. As neighbors' anxiety increased, the gossip about Sayville's black preacher grew more extreme. Some residents alleged that he maintained a large harem of women and engaged in wild sex behind closed doors at 72 Macon Street.[41]

Initially the Macon Street neighbors responded with petty harassment. Several got together and protested that his Hudson made too much noise. He desired a good relationship with the community but remained determined not to give in to intimidation. To keep the peace, he sold his Hudson and purchased a quiet Cadillac. The appearance of a Cadillac in his garage intensified the animosity of Macon Street residents, who were solidly middle class and lived modestly. They resented him for flaunting his wealth and further exasperated, began to flood the district attorney's office with allegations about his immoral behavior and complaints about the noise that drifted from his house each night.[42]

On Thursday, April 10, 1930, the evening's Holy Communion banquet began as usual. At 6:30, Father Divine entered the dining room, and twenty-six adults and four children rose reverently from their seats. The minister took a dinner bell from a silver tray and rang it, and the household burst into applause. Several members of the household emerged from the kitchen carrying platters of food, which he blessed and passed around. That night Father Divine served tea, milk, postum, rice, macaroni, potatoes, peas, baked beans, mashed turnips, corn, baked tomatoes, turkey, pork chops, corn bread, biscuits, graham bread, cake, pie, peaches, and salad. He demanded that the serving dishes never touch the table until emptied. His spiritual children piled their plates full and exploded into song. Occasionally the singing stopped for testimony by followers and guests. Before long, the worshipers were on their feet, shouting, dancing, and speaking in tongues.[43]

In the middle of the pandemonium, the doorbell rang. Joseph Gabriel left his seat and returned with an attractive black woman in a tattered dress. Gabriel introduced the young woman, Susan Hadley, to Father and Mother Divine, who warmly invited her to join them for dinner. Surprised by the generosity of her hosts, she tentatively filled her plate, surveyed the devotionals, and listened carefully to Father Divine's sermon. No one suspected that the pretty young waif had been recruited by Suffolk County's district attorney to infiltrate Father Divine's sect.[44]

At 10:30, the worship service ended, the household retired, and Hadley, claiming to be unemployed and homeless, approached Father Divine to ask for help. He hesitated. Explaining frankly that young people lacked commitment and left the fold once they secured jobs, he warned Hadley that if he took her in, she had to break with her family and follow his strict moral requirements. Further, he demanded that Hadley study his teachings carefully and learn to accept his divinity. Hadley insisted that she was willing to comply with his rigid standards, and impressed by her sincerity and sympathetic to her destitution, he allowed her to stay.[45]

Hadley joined a household of thirty people: eight men, twelve women, and ten children. Father Divine gave Hadley a spotlessly clean room, outfitted her in almost-new dresses, and assigned her tasks in his home. She discovered that the minister encouraged hard work. Most disciples had outside jobs, but six followers, whom Father Divine designated coworkers, labored exclusively in his home, cooking, cleaning, and tending children. Disciples had private rooms, which they shared on weekends with other followers and visitors who came to Sayville to worship. The clergyman supplied his household with the finest material benefits and had purchased a Packard and two Willys-Knights for his disciples to use. His elegantly appointed home and fleet of automobiles testified to his shrewd business sense and symbolized his union with the Godhead.[46]

Father Divine and his spiritual children patiently tutored Hadley on the principles of his theology. According to followers, the Macon Street house was not simply a home; it was heaven, where "God" and his "angels" lived "above sin." Followers addressed each other as "brother" and "sister," and insisted that if Hadley accepted Father Divine's divinity, she would live forever. Repeatedly Hadley heard that all desires could be fulfilled and mortal weaknesses overcome by channeling God's power and concentrating on the positive.[47]

Hadley also discovered that the household adhered to unique speech patterns and that Father Divine believed language subtly influenced consciousness. He forbade the use of *hell* or *devil*, for they represented negative concepts. He demanded that followers replace *hello* (which he believed referred to hell) with *peace*. In his opinion, the vocalization of the term would eventually make peace a reality and transform the world into a more positive place. Positivism was also stressed through the followers' popular mantra "It is wonderful." Even when expressing anger or disgust, his children countermanded negative statements by interjecting "It is wonderful" throughout conversations.[48]

The angels encouraged Susan Hadley to adopt their vernacular to facilitate an understanding of Father Divine's teachings. The repetition of phrases and concepts mesmerized the most resistant subject and prepared the way for acceptance of his philosophy. Furthermore, this distinct language set his angels apart from the general public and strengthened spiritual family bonds, homogenized the flock, and obscured educational and cultural differences.

When Hadley quizzed followers on their backgrounds, they refused to discuss details of their lives before they joined Father Divine's family. Disciples insisted that once Hadley recognized that he was God, she too would lose all ties to the past and be reborn. The angels speculated that perhaps his spirit would inspire her to select a new name as he had guided many disciples like Lillian

Lovelace, Queen Esther, and Prophet Ciscio to choose different names representing their new identities.[49]

Hadley discovered that the followers led an almost monastic existence, constantly strove for spiritual purity, and strictly abstained from sexual activity. All disciples subscribed to Father Divine's teaching that sex was a sin that drained the body of "spiritual energy," making the individual vulnerable to disease and death. Even followers who lived outside 72 Macon Street practiced celibacy. Husbands and wives slept in separate rooms and considered themselves spiritual siblings. Hadley came to believe that Father Divine's rumored harem was a product of malicious gossip and that he adhered faithfully to his own celibacy requirement.[50]

Even though Father Divine condemned sexual intercourse and ordered disciples to disclaim all kinship, he welcomed followers with children into his home, insisting that parents take responsibility for properly raising their children. In his view, children required nurturing until they were able to care for themselves:

> I have often said that the animal kingdom came nearer to expressing GOD's Love in this respect, than mankind. . . . In the animal kingdom the mother is a mother to her little ones, only until they are able to go out for themselves and after that time the relationship ceases. . . . But in the human kingdom, the mother-love tries to hang onto the children and call them "my" children after they are grown up. . . . GOD loaned you that love for you to protect those little ones until they were able to protect themselves and then HE intended for you to return that love back to GOD.

He provided impoverished and broken families the support and stability they lacked. Not only did the minister offer basic necessities, but he also furnished a spiritually rigid environment that prevented children from getting into trouble. His collective colony appealed especially to single working mothers. His coworkers supplied daycare, and he enrolled the older children in school. His philosophy placed limitations on women's childrearing responsibilities and allowed women to pursue activities outside the family circle.[51]

But Hadley found that not all families were completely content at 72 Macon Street. Many of the older children resented the austere lifestyle of the colony and rejected Father Divine's teachings. Lillian Lovelace, who had moved into the home with her six children, discovered one morning that her two oldest sons had run away.

Separation from her sons was painful for Lovelace, whose only consolation was the reminder that devotion to Father Divine's teachings required many sacrifices and promised great rewards. She did not try to convince her boys to return, for Father Divine insisted that involvement in his sect be strictly voluntary. He instructed disciples to pity those who rejected his teachings, for such malcontents would never enjoy immortality.[52]

Hadley found that Father Divine's promise of eternal life and the reports of his phenomenal healing powers attracted many into his fold, offering hope to those who suffered from incurable illness and had been abandoned by medical science. Hadley befriended Bessie, who had a persistent cough and was slowly dying. Hearing of Father Divine in Philadelphia, Bessie had left home and moved into the Sayville colony. At night Hadley lay in bed listening to Bessie cough. "She looks as if she will drop out any time," Hadley commented. "She seems to have lots of faith in Father Divine's spirit."[53]

While staying at 72 Macon Street, Hadley contracted a minor cold and decided to test his skills. She asked the minister to heal her, but to her surprise he refused to lay on hands, advising her to heal herself by channeling his spirit. He recommended that she "take a cold bath every morning." To her protests that frigid water would kill her he responded, "If you believe in me, the water won't be cold on you. My spirit will make it warm."[54]

Although he taught that negative thoughts produced sickness, he urged followers to respect their bodies and maintain good health. He often opened his sermons, "Peace everyone! Good health, good will, a good appetite, with good manners, good behavior, all success and all prosperity, peace and pleasure." He linked health to appetite and encouraged his followers to eat large well-balanced meals. Every Sunday and Thursday he weighed he entire household and reprimanded those who had lost weight. "He tells them to eat more so they can gain," Hadley observed, "for he wants them to be very large."

Such an attitude appears contradictory for the son of a fatally obese woman, but his practice of weighing his followers was an attempt to monitor his family's health. Since poverty had denied many of his spiritual children proper nourishment, he endeavored to revise their eating habits and improve their health. On the symbolic level, the robust appearance of the disciples, like his extravagant Holy Communion banquets, demonstrated his prosperity, infinite resources, and power.[55]

Hadley observed that about thirty followers and guests attended weeknight Holy Communion banquets. Frequently ministers and others interested in theology dropped by and spent hours discussing religion with Sayville's mystical clergyman. Many stayed for the banquet and participated in the worship service. On weekends visitors increased as the devout who lived outside the home returned for his "blessings" and the curious traveled to investigate the Long Island preacher. On Saturdays and Sundays the crowd doubled, and in the dining room, blacks and whites worshiped together into the late hours.[56]

On Wednesday evening, April 24, 1930, while Father Divine served dessert, Hadley rose to speak.

> I told them I met them when they were eating and I would like to leave them the same as I found them. As I left the dining room, Father Divine followed me out and wanted to take me to the station, but I told him I came unexpected and alone and I wanted to leave the same as I came. . . . He said his spirit would guide me to New York City.[57]

That night Hadley rushed to the district attorney's office and made her report. She insisted that Father Divine did not participate in sexual debauchery or any illegalities: "The welcome was genuine and there is nothing but a deeply religious air about the whole place—no immorality whatsoever." She had determined that he did not solicit funds for the home and speculated that his money came from an extraordinarily large inheritance.[58] The district attorney carefully examined the young woman's report and after several days issued a public statement: "We can find no reason to attack him on moral grounds. Neither can we find any tangible evidence that he has in any way violated the law."[59]

Hadley's investigation provided a sensational opportunity for the Long Island press to sell papers. The area's leading paper, the *Suffolk County News*, splashed its front page with a headline, "Sayville's Colored Messiah Investigated by Dist. Atty."[60] Another Long Island tabloid declared, "Benefactor Sets Up Utopia in L.I.: Impoverished Find Haven There Probe Reveals." The newspaper accounts increased the indignation of Macon Street residents. The stories contended that Father Divine lived lavishly and provided charity to the poor, but his source of wealth baffled investigators. Even more shocking to the citizens of Sayville were reports that he claimed to be Christ in the Second Coming. His neighbors fumed, for not only were his financial dealings shady, but his teachings appeared blatantly blasphemous.[61]

Yet local newspapers aided Father Divine and his missionary work. Reports of Macon Street's heaven provided him much needed publicity and succeeded in exciting more interest in his teachings. Promotion by the local press combined with the deepening depression lured even more people to his home. Pilgrims of all ages and races traveled to Sayville by car, bus, and train, and by spring of 1931, his weekend banquets attracted well over a hundred worshipers.[62]

Between 1930 and 1931, a growing number of whites joined the congregation. Most were well educated, from the middle and upper classes, and previously affiliated with New Thought sects. Newspaper articles drew a few white converts, but most heard of his activities at New Thought meetings or in churches. Heavenly Rest, a graduate of Boston College, first learned of Father Divine in a Boston Unity church. In 1931, she journeyed to Sayville with her sister and mother. They joined the household, and Rest became one of the minister's first secretaries. Rest recollected that during this period Father Divine attracted many New Thought and metaphysical instructors and students to his banquets.[63]

Among the new white converts was Walter Lanyon, a noted metaphysical author and lecturer. While on a New Thought lecture tour late in 1930, Lanyon attended one of the Holy Communion banquets. Father Divine's message, his unlimited wealth, and his curative abilities captivated Lanyon. He became convinced that Father Divine possessed divine powers and was God. Determined to spread his teachings, Lanyon returned to the lecture circuit and carried Father Divine's words throughout Europe. While on tour, Lanyon dashed off a book, *The Eyes of the Blind*, in which he discussed his conversion:

He is the first and only person I have ever met who speaks my language. He speaks in the present tense, first person, which is the

LIFE-giving word given in the precise manner Jesus Christ gave it.
When he said to me, "If you see me as a man do not call me Father,"
I knew this was the voice, and all personality and personal teaching
was nil. Here was the magnificent sample word that produced results far beyond the so-called demonstration—it brings about revelation and is summed up in these words, "It is Wonderful."[64]

Lanyon reflected the sentiments of many who had studied New
Thought for years. For some who struggled to capitalize on God's
internal spirit, mind-power had been a great disappointment and
produced neither health nor riches. But Lanyon and others believed that Father Divine had discovered the route to spiritual purity and offered hope to those who had failed to channel God effectively.

Lanyon was a highly respected figure in metaphysical circles,
and his conversion excited curiosity among disciples of New
Thought. With his book and lectures, Lanyon netted a few more
followers, including John Maynard Matthews, a wealthy white
Boston businessman who heard Lanyon speak in London. After
returning to the United States in early 1931, Matthews visited 72
Macon Street: "I was made welcome at the Banquet table with many
others. I saw the numbers of destitute persons [Father Divine] was
feeding, clothing and housing. . . . [He] supported them for months
and years without the cost of a penny. I saw hundreds of people
instantly healed of so-called incurable diseases." Matthews experienced a spiritual rebirth, adopted the name John Lamb, bought a
home on Macon Street, and became one of Father Divine's secretaries.[65]

The development of a highly visible white following outraged
the neighbors. White disciples not only invaded the town but also
bought property and organized multiracial households. Whites who
worshiped a black god and lived in integrated clusters threatened
the segregationist foundation of American society. Many citizens
of Sayville, becoming aware of Father Divine's menacing noncon-
formity, began to sympathize with his neighbors. Before long, even
the wealthy and the business class withdrew their support. Those
who hired his followers began to question the reliability of employ-
ees who subscribed to his unusual religious doctrines. Store-
keepers still welcomed the minister, whose purchases were larger
than ever, but businesspeople fretted that the increasing numbers

of blacks would bring crime to Sayville and make their property and businesses worthless. As more powerful sectors of Sayville rallied behind the residents of Macon Street, authorities became more responsive to complaints lodged against Reverend Divine.[66]

In the spring of 1931, Sayville authorities decided to take action against Father Divine and his flock. Late one April evening, Officer Richard Tucker interrupted a raucous Holy Communion banquet and warned Father Divine that if the noise continued, he would arrest the household for disturbing the peace. Shortly afterward, Tucker attempted to take into custody a twenty-seven-year-old black woman named Belle Grant, whose family claimed she had been missing from her South Carolina home for two weeks. She refused to leave and insisted that she had no relatives "down South no more" and had become one of Father Divine's children. A week later, the authorities again returned to the home to investigate the death of Clarence Clemons, a resident. Although the coroner determined that Clemons had died of an acute heart attack, the death contributed to Father Divine's sinister public image.[67]

Between 1927 and 1931, Father Divine's relations with his neighbors deteriorated while his following expanded and diversified. By May of 1931, the citizens of Sayville could no longer tolerate the massive, emotional Holy Communion banquets. At noon, May 8, 1931, a knock came at heaven's door. It was the deputy sheriff, and he had come to arrest God.[68]

Father Divine, c. 1932.

Father Divine conducting a Holy Communion banquet in the 1930s. At left is his first wife, Peninniah. The Schomburg Center for Research in Black Culture, the New York Public Library, Astor, Lenox and Tilden Foundations.

Peace Mission grocery, Harlem, 1936. The Schomburg Center for Research in Black Culture, the New York Public Library, Astor, Lenox and Tilden Foundations.

First Peace Mission in Los Angeles, Compton Avenue. *Los Angeles Daily News* Photograph Collection, UCLA Department of Special Collections.

Property purchased by followers in 1937 for expansion of the Los Angeles Peace Mission. *Los Angeles Daily News* Photograph Collection, UCLA Department of Special Collections.

A private home opened as a Peace Mission, Los Angeles, 1937. *Los Angeles Daily News* Photograph Collection, UCLA Department of Special Collections.

A group of followers, including the niece of Herbert Hoover, boarding a plane in Los Angeles to visit Father Divine's East Coast headquarters. *Los Angeles Daily News* Photograph Collection, UCLA Department of Special Collections.

Hugh MacBeth, former Garveyite, member of the Utopian Society, and Peace Mission leader. Hearst Collection, Department of Special Collections, University of Southern California Library.

Millionaire and Peace Mission member John Wuest Hunt (John the Revelator) during 1937 trial, "getting a message." Hearst Collection, Department of Special Collections, University of Southern California Library.

Delight Jewett on the witness stand, 1937. Hearst Collection, Department of Special Collections, University of Southern California Library.

From left to right: John Wuest Hunt, Hugh MacBeth, (unidentified), Agnes Gardner (Mary Bird), and Betty Peters (Martha Tree). Hearst Collection, Department of Special Collections, University of Southern California Library.

Father Divine, Peninniah, and followers tour the grounds of his estate across the Hudson from the Roosevelts' Hyde Park home. The Schomburg Center for Research in Black Culture, the New York Public Library, Astor, Lenox and Tilden Foundations.

Banquet table, Seattle extension in the late 1940s.

The Woodmont Estate, located in Gladwyne, Pennsylvania, Father Divine's home and headquarters after 1953. Pictured is Father Divine and his second wife, Mother Divine (Sweet Angel), whom he married in 1946.

Father and Mother Divine at one of his last public appearances in
the early 1960s.

Father Divine and children at a banquet, early 1960s.

"Shrine to Life," final resting place of Father Divine, at Woodmont Estate.

5

I AM DIVINE

Now trying to stop ME, as I tell them, would
not prohibit MY Work; it spreads it that much
faster. I AM here with you all Personally for
your own personal good and to appease your
human mortal concept concerning ME, and
your fears, but, with or without the Personal
Presence, I will rule millions of homes and
houses, for I AM DIVINE, and that is not merely
a word, it is a Power.

First spoken November 1931

In early May 1931, Suffolk County court officials had succumbed to pressure from Father Divine's neighbors and initiated another investigation of the minister and his establishment. Over twenty-five Sayville residents testified before the Suffolk County Grand Jury and finally convinced authorities to indict Father Divine for maintaining a public nuisance. The arresting officer, Glover, found Father Divine a cooperative prisoner, but as he led the clergyman away, Michael St. John, a follower, begged to go to jail in Father Divine's place. Bemused, Deputy Sheriff Glover waved St. John away, citing the illegality of "such an act of self-sacrifice."[1]

Trailed by a caravan of angels, Glover transported the minister to Riverhead to face the grand jury. Father Divine was represented by a black Harlem attorney and recent convert, Ellee J. Lovelace. The minister pleaded innocent, and the judge set his bail at $1,000. The court looked on with surprise as Peninniah reached into her purse, produced $1,000 in cash, and promptly paid her husband's bail.[2]

On May 11, Father Divine, joined by his lawyer, his wife, and his faithful followers, confronted a mob of angry neighbors in court. During the hearing Sayville citizens reported that bizarre rites transpired at 72 Macon Street, alleging that the singing, shouting, and screaming of Father Divine's children reverberated throughout the neighborhood every night after dinner and continued into the late hours. Neighbors' inquiries had revealed that the object of this aberrant worship was Father Divine. The residents of Sayville, mindful of the approaching vacation season, were anxious for action, but the court provided no immediate satisfaction. The judge remanded the case to the county court, which postponed the trial until the fall session. It was going to be a long summer for the citizens of Sayville and the Macon Street evangelist.[3]

The crowds congregating in Father Divine's home definitely disrupted this once sedate residential area. However, he and his children endeavored to preserve order and respect the rights of their neighbors. A sign posted at his driveway warned guests: *NOTICE—Smoking—Intoxicating Liquors—Profane Language—Strictly Prohibited.* Contrary to the charges of Sayville residents, angels claimed that Father Divine prohibited singing after eight o'clock and by ten o'clock had closed all windows and blinds.[4]

Actually the noise and crowds were a minor irritation that provided an excuse to harass Father Divine and his angels. Conspicuous racist indignation fueled the attacks on Father Divine and his household; the citizens of Sayville were alarmed by the increasing number of blacks in their community. Not just temporary visitors, many African Americans had moved into his home or other houses on Macon Street. In a scathing editorial, Francis Hoag, editor of the *Suffolk County News,* frankly expressed the underlying motives of Sayville citizens. Hoag urged Father Divine to reestablish his home in an "isolated" spot, because "of course everyone knows that the flocking of colored people to any locality acts as a blight upon property values." But, he insisted, he was not a "bigoted" man:

> The writer has no prejudice against colored people so long as they do not offend against the law and established customs of the land. On the contrary he has during the past 30 years given employment to many, most of whom have been self-respecting colored servants from the south. He does deplore, however, the influx of hordes from the black-belt of Harlem, and the undesirable notoriety that the village has been receiving ever since this man with the mysterious financial backing established his home here with the strong lure of free eats.[5]

Even though Reverend Divine had lived undisturbed in Sayville for over ten years, the changes in his ministry frightened his Sayville neighbors. As long as he and his followers seemed to accept their inferior status, Sayville tolerated their presence. However, his emergence as a leader with a significant following of blacks and whites threatened the social order. Thus the whites of Sayville, terrified by his symbolic rebelliousness and his rise to power, became determined to rid their village of his unsettling presence.

Vacationers returning to the once peaceful seaside hamlet in the summer of 1931 found Sayville sizzling with tension. White villagers stewed while Father Divine, undeterred by the pending trial, continued to gather more disciples. The grand jury's indictment successfully excited more interest in his teachings, and the white residents' belligerence transformed his plight into a cause célèbre in the African-American community. Even more blacks attended Holy Communion banquets, lured by the desire to exhibit racial solidarity, Father Divine's captivating theology, and his social-welfare programs.[6]

His white following also continued to grow. Newspapers ran updates on the minister's arrest, advancing his teachings in the white community. Walter Lanyon and John Lamb also contributed more white followers to the congregation. Lanyon continued to transverse the globe lecturing on Father Divine and exciting international interest in Macon Street's metaphysician. In June and July, John Lamb addressed several meetings of the exclusively white International New Thought Alliance in London. Alliance members responded enthusiastically, and several later joined Father Divine's flock.[7]

Back in the United States, pilgrims came from all over the eastern seaboard to visit Father Divine's heaven. The relative seclusion of Sayville made finding transportation to his home a real challenge. Some followers came by train; others rode uncomfortably for hours squeezed into private cars; several groups chartered buses for the long trip to Long Island. A few enterprising Harlem residents who owned cars shuttled worshipers to Sayville for a fee. On weekends, traffic jams were common, cars and buses lining the streets around his home. By the end of the summer, an average of six hundred people attended Sunday Banquets, and on special occasions he drew as many as three thousand worshipers.[8]

Encouraged by the increase in followers, John Lamb began transcribing the minister's messages and recording activities of the congregation in his journal. In an early entry Lamb wrote:

> The fervor of the past two days in the Kingdom and the grandeur of FATHER's Teaching and the high vibrations HE conveyed have been beyond words. It seems as though we have been lifted each day a step higher until we are left speechless before the wonder of it all. It has been impossible to get down much of what was said because of the constant shouting and because of the feelings aroused in me.[9]

Emotion played a critical role in the spiritual transformation of followers. Banquets were passionate celebrations. Father Divine encouraged public confession, and disciples struggled to cleanse themselves of their pasts by relating—sometimes tearfully, sometimes joyfully—their previous sins. Openness drew the followers closer together and, they believed, nearer to God. The devotionals, lasting for hours, could be physically and emotionally draining. Father Divine encouraged this, for he believed that exhausted disciples were more receptive to his guidance. These intoxicating spiritual encounters heightened followers' commitment to Father Divine, and many, like John Lamb, actively sought to testify and bring others into the fold.[10]

The expansion of the congregation induced changes in the structure of the ministry. Father Divine continued his free employment agency and still cared for the destitute, but ministerial duties increasingly dominated his time. From early morning until midnight, he served Holy Communion banquets. Throughout the day, he counseled disciples in private appointments and over the phone. His secretarial staff assisted him in correspondence, but the mail was so voluminous that he often worked until 5:00 A.M. answering letters. After a couple of hours of rest, he rose and took a walk before resuming his ministerial obligations.[11]

Despite additional responsibilities, hosting the banquet table remained his central duty. By late September, the number of Sunday worshipers averaged over one thousand. Since the banquet table seated only fifty-three people, he began serving continuous "sittings" throughout Saturday and Sunday. Household members ushered in a set of visitors who would dine, offer testimony, and listen to Father Divine's message. Once the diners finished, they vacated their seats, which were immediately filled by the next set of congregants. When the telephone or a personal interview called Father Divine away from the table, Mother Divine carried out his duties. After a sitting, disciples and guests milled about the house and adjoining gardens, visiting with friends, debating Father Divine's teachings, and relating stories of his healings. Between sittings and appointments, he circulated among the guests, chatting, joking, and elaborating on the principles of his theology. Many followers stayed overnight, turning the weekend into a true spiritual retreat.[12]

The neighbors did not bear the burden of his booming popularity gracefully. Forced by the court's sluggishness to endure another summer of frenzied worship by Father Divine's children, the citizens of Sayville continued to vent their animosity. Neighbors circulated petitions calling for his expulsion. By early August, Sayville police, contending that he provided a refuge for felons, began regularly patrolling the area around his home. The authorities checked the licenses and registrations of all black motorists. The constant surveillance of the home netted few criminals, and the harassment of African Americans did little to deter people from attending worship services.[13]

By the end of the summer, tempers had worn thin, and suddenly the flock became the target of a violent outburst. Late one night, a car pulled up in front of 72 Macon Street and showered the house with bottles and trash. The attack did not damage the home, but it startled residents and upset the usually unflappable Reverend Divine. "HE went through the house from front to back," John Lamb noted in his journal, "and looked very searchingly into everyone's eyes as if he were seeking someone or something." Despite his years of jostling with racism, such cruelty continued to bewilder and torment him.[14]

This display of hatred reflected the growing impatience of white Sayville residents with Father Divine and his flock. On September 23, they aired their grievances before a meeting of the town board. One resident claimed to have counted over 125 cars and 3 buses parked along and around Macon Street on the preceding Sunday. Another neighbor complained that his property wasn't "worth two cents," and Peter Guthy, of 71 Macon Street, told the board: "There is a continual unloading of passengers, slamming of doors and talking and shouting from morning till night. . . . We can't stand it any more. My wife is a wreck. We'll have to get out of there."

The board sympathized and limited parking on the streets surrounding Father Divine's home to thirty minutes. But the parking restrictions were a minor annoyance to the minister and his flock. Several profit-minded residents sold food and drinks to hungry pilgrims and rented their driveways to his guests.[15]

Despite his determination, the white community continued to malign the pastor and his congregation. The *Suffolk County News* regaled readers with stories of mysterious deaths at the home, women who abandoned husbands and children for the minister, and arrests of criminals attracted to the free feasts. Merchants who had welcomed Father Divine's business now shunned his patronage. Attendants at Sayville's garage refused to service a bus filled with members of Harlem's Colored Unity Center who had come to worship. The mechanic curtly informed them that the station did not serve blacks.[16]

By November, Father Divine and his neighbors had grown restless awaiting their day in court. Interestingly, it was Father Divine who brought the conflict to a breaking point. He calculated when and where the dispute would climax and in mid-November purposefully precipitated an incident that became a milestone in his ministry.

Throughout Sunday, November 15, 1931, the Macon Street devotionals grew increasingly lively. Father Divine's continuous messages electrified the throng, and the worshipers danced, spoke in tongues, and sang with extra exuberance. The services continued into the evening, and as the hour grew late, the mob became delirious. John Lamb noted in his journal: "This demonstration at such a late hour was contrary to the usual custom. . . . Thus it was apparently FATHER's Will, as HE was present at the table continually." By midnight, frenzy gripped the worshipers. The entire congregation was on its feet, waving hands, shouting, screaming, and crying.[17]

At 12:15, on the other side of town, a phone call from an irate Macon Street resident bolted Officer Richard Tucker out of bed. Within a few minutes, Tucker arrived at Father Divine's door but found Michael St. John unusually obstinate. Tucker pushed past

St. John into the crowded dining room where the worshipers stood with eyes tightly shut, "trembling with the vibrations of the spirit." Suddenly several spied the patrolman and shrieked. Tucker quickly fled.[18]

Tucker alerted Assistant District Attorney Joseph S. Arata. Within an hour, other members of the district attorney's staff, state troopers, five deputy sheriffs, and the fire department had arrived at the scene. Outside, enraged neighbors filled the streets. Several in the crowd carried clubs and other makeshift weapons, and authorities feared that a riot would break out. Arata, deciding that the only way to terminate the services was to arrest the entire flock, called for two buses to transport Father Divine and his followers to jail and ordered officers to surround the home with fire hoses in case the congregation resisted. Arata cautiously entered the home and informed Father Divine that they had fifteen minutes to surrender peacefully. The minister ordered the celebrants to stand in silence for ten minutes. Then he calmly reminded the throng, "I will keep him in perfect peace whose mind is stayed on me," and quietly led them to the waiting buses.[19]

By two in the morning, hundreds of Sayville citizens swarmed the streets surrounding the court house. Inside the judge processed seventy-eight prisoners—fifteen white and sixty-three black disciples. Those arrested came from all parts of the country and included followers from the West Indies, Canada, and Europe. Tension ran high during the proceedings, and at one point Peninniah fainted and fell to the floor. Ignoring Father Divine's protests, Arata held a match before Peninniah's face. According to a follower, Father Divine clutched his hand to his breast, and lightning flashed from his body. The *Suffolk County News* reported that Arata "jumped about four feet," Mother Divine sat up, and cries of "It is wonderful" filled the courtroom. The proceedings were again interrupted by followers who refused to give their legal names. Frustrated and angry, authorities locked stubborn disciples in cells and beat them until they cooperated.[20]

The hearing continued throughout the night, and slowly the crowd outside the courthouse dispersed. Forty-six followers pleaded guilty to disturbing the peace and paid $5.00 fines. The thirty-two remaining defendants, including Father Divine, entered not-guilty pleas. Father Divine was charged again with maintaining a public nuisance and immediately paid his $1,500 bail in cash. By 7:30 Monday morning, the judge had finished arraigning all of the prisoners, and the weary flock walked home through empty streets.[21]

On Friday night the community returned to the courthouse for the trial of Father and Mother Divine and thirty of their children, defended by Ellee J. Lovelace and another black Harlem attorney, Arthur A. Madison; they were tried en masse. Eighteen witnesses testified against them. One Macon Street resident said that he "heard a lot of hollering and shouting from 10:30 on"; another confessed that he peered through the window and saw "a lot of people shouting and jumping all around, making different noises." After a short deliberation, the court found twenty-eight of the thirty-two defendants guilty of disturbing the peace and fined each defendant $5. Father Divine paid his children's fines, which totaled $140, with a $500 bill. Unable to make change, the chagrined court promised to send the amount due to Father Divine the next day.[22]

Father Divine's public-nuisance charge remained unresolved, and the townspeople, weary of the protracted dispute, decided to take matters into their own hands. Throughout the week following the raid on the minister's home, fliers appeared around the village announcing a meeting "to devise some means of removing these individuals from our midst."[23] On Saturday night, November 21, seven hundred people, including forty of Father Divine's followers, gathered in Sayville's high school auditorium. The chairman called the meeting to order, stating: "To my mind this is a very serious situation. Unless this man, this Messiah, is driven from this village, we might as well shut up shop."[24]

At the meeting residents of Macon Street and local businesspeople complained about the noise and the devaluation of their property. Father Divine's home, they asserted, would destroy their vacation hamlet and turn Sayville into a "Harlem Colony." Many of the speakers suggested that if legal methods did not succeed, they would find other means. Excitedly, Francis Hoag suggested that a southern town would instinctively know how to solve the problem. The audience cheered.[25]

Throughout most of the meeting the chair ignored Father Divine's followers but finally allowed John Lamb to speak. Lamb stated that he had been a resident of Sayville for three months. Someone in the audience yelled that it was three months too long, and chaos broke out. After the chair restored order, Lamb calmly announced that if the residents of Sayville wanted Father Divine to move, the minister would comply. As Lamb recounted Father Divine's good works, boos and hisses rifled through the audience, compelling him to take his seat. Despite Father Divine's offer, confusion reigned throughout the remainder of the meeting. Although the residents aired their grievances and proposed different solutions, the community made little headway toward resolving the situation. By the end of the evening, the town selected a committee of seventy-five Sayville property owners to develop an expulsion plan.[26]

Following the mass meeting, Father Divine's household lived in fear of violent retaliation. Rumors that the Klan was plotting to burn down the home circulated around town. A steady stream of traffic passed in front of the house as the curious and hostile strained for a look at Father Divine's heaven. Reporters harassed followers, and neighbors made menacing overtures. He constantly reassured his children that "minds stayed on him" received protection from all harm.[27]

During the following week, the committee, working with three of Father Divine's representatives, hammered out a resolution. Speaking on the minister's behalf were Arthur Madison; a white lawyer and noted metaphysical author and lecturer, Eugene Del Mar; and a former Harlem journalist, Millard J. Bloomer.[28] The three reported that Father Divine was willing to leave Sayville if the district attorney dropped the case. The committee agreed to withdraw the charge if he promised to terminate worship services by nine o'clock and leave Sayville by the first of January. On Tuesday night, November 24, Madison, Del Mar, and Bloomer reported to the children that they had reached a compromise with the citizens of Sayville. But the three did not elaborate on the details and cautioned the children not to believe anything they read in the papers. They claimed Father Divine had a few surprises in store for his opponents.[29]

Neither Father Divine nor his representatives ever specified the strategy behind their deal with the committee. Most likely his advisors knew that the committee did not have the power to drop the public-nuisance charge. They anticipated further legal battles, and at the end of November, Father Divine accepted the free legal services of James C. Thomas, a former assistant U.S. attorney and reportedly one of the richest black men in Harlem. Thomas felt that the committee had produced an unfair compromise and pledged to defend the clergyman from "the un-American and prejudiced treatment accorded to you and your followers in deprivation of constitutional rights of property and freedom of religious worship." As the supporters of Father Divine anticipated, the district attorney failed to withdraw the charge, but the compromise suppressed the hostility of the residents and eased the tension in the village. While neighbors still remained unfriendly, the threats against the household subsided.[30]

The compromise attracted even more attention from the press. Prominent New York papers picked up the story of Father Divine's brawls with his Sayville neighbors and effectively publicized his teachings to an even larger audience. Predominantly inaccurate, the sensationalized coverage contributed to the mystique surrounding his ministry. Schooled in advertising by the works of Bruce Barton, he understood the importance of publicity and knew that the newspapers provided a free and powerful forum for self-promotion.

His increasing notoriety was part of a relatively new trend in American culture, the American celebrity. Beginning in the twenties, the media provided Americans with a new array of idols. Individuals with special talents from ordinary backgrounds replaced the soldier and statesman heroes of the past. People like baseball player Babe Ruth, actress Mary Pickford, aviator Charles Lindbergh, and preacher Billy Sunday won the admiration of Americans during the twenties.[31] Father Divine recognized that these figures had tremendous power, and he endeavored to climb into their ranks. Although he created publicity stunts to catapult himself into the public eye, his battle for attention did not develop solely from a desire for self-promotion. Racism denied blacks entry into American society, but the news media offered him an opportunity to express his views publicly. He understood that celebrity status and the efficient manipulation of the media allowed him to influence society and further his efforts to remodel America according to his theological vision.

The expansion of his congregation, his growing notoriety, and the restrictions of his compromise with Sayville residents altered

his crusade. Increasing demands forced him to delegate more responsibility to his disciples, and followers began to have more control over the movement. By early December, proselytes organized
nightly meetings in rented churches, halls, and auditoriums around
New York City. Often followers arranged several engagements in
different locations on the same night, and he darted between meetings. Although disciples limited by time and money omitted banquets from the services, their meetings drew crowds averaging over
one thousand worshipers.[32]

The rented churches and halls were too small to accommodate
the hordes of people who sought Father Divine's spiritual enlightenment, and followers, envisioning even larger meetings, searched
desperately for a suitable location. Finally, at the end of December,
several disciples booked Harlem's Rockland Palace, formerly a swank
casino, which seated over five thousand people. One enthusiastic
disciple distributed hundreds of fliers around New York and Long
Island that read: "Something on 'U.' The truth brought to mankind
again by FATHER DIVINE at Rockland Palace, 155th Street and Eighth
Avenue Manhattan, Sunday December 20, 1931 at 3 P.M. All are
welcome. Admission free! free! free! No collection. no! no! no! Not
by Might, Man or Power, But by My Spirit Saith the Lord."[33]

By ten o'clock Sunday morning, December 20, hundreds had
gathered in the streets in front of Rockland Palace. Most of the
crowd was black, but a few whites also turned out. At three o'clock
in the afternoon the doors opened, and ten thousand worshipers
flowed into the auditorium. On stage sat twenty black and white
angels, who promptly began the proceedings. After two hours of
testimony and song, Father Divine triumphantly entered the hall,
followed by Mother Divine and thirty Sayville children. At the sight
of Father Divine, the audience jumped up and filled the old casino
with thunderous cheers and applause. "Peace Everybody," he cried
out from the stage. "Peace Father," the crowd rang back. Then he
yielded the floor to several Sayville children, who told of his ability
to materialize money and to pour endless cups of coffee from one
small pot. Others claimed that he healed blindness, sickness, and
alcoholism. Excitement pulsed throughout the hall, and with each
speaker the crowd grew more jubilant.[34]

After the Sayville children concluded their testimony, Father Divine mounted the podium. He opened his message by condemn-

ing his Sayville neighbors, whom he characterized as a lynch mob. The crowd shrieked as he leapt high in the air and landed declaring that because God manifested his spirit through his body, nothing could harm or stop him. His mission was to bring salvation to men and women. He reminded the throng: "I am a free gift to mankind. Of the plenty and abundance which I have I give to you freely. I ask of you only faith. I take from you nothing. I take your sorrows and give you joy. I take your sickness and give you health. I take your poverty and give you peace and prosperity, for I am the spirit of success and health." The depression, he told the assembly, was simply a state of mind conquerable by a revision of attitudes. He reiterated his belief that positive thinking and faith in his powers conquered all adversities. Finishing his message, he surveyed the crowded auditorium and concluded with "I thank you."[35]

The assembly burst into rapturous applause, and as he shook hands with those on stage, the crowd lunged to the front of the hall. Although the platform was several feet high, many forced their way onto the stage, and soon "a struggling mass of people" encircled the evangelist. The police arrived and escorted him to his car, but the crowd followed. For over thirty minutes he and his entourage were surrounded by a mob touching and kissing his car, shouting his name. Finally the authorities cleared the streets, and he and his angels sped homeward.[36]

They arrived in Sayville about three in the morning, and the household sat down and unwound around the banquet table. The Rockland Palace meeting revealed that Father Divine's popularity had grown tremendously and demonstrated the public's receptiveness. Thousands had warmly accepted his notion of God's inner-dwelling spirit and his offer of eternal life. Thousands had witnessed that he preached free of charge. And even though black and white Americans rarely mixed during public gatherings, thousands of blacks had worshiped together with a significant number of whites. At the Rockland Palace meeting, he had realized all of the goals he had set in his row house in Baltimore. However, the December meeting marked only the beginning of his rise to power.[37]

Father Divine preached in Rockland Palace many times throughout 1932, drawing larger crowds and adding more people to his movement. Many of the newer disciples had been exposed to strains

of New Thought and metaphysics. One follower who was converted during a Rockland Palace meeting, Righteous Endeavor, had
attended classes conducted by a yogi in Harlem. The yogi taught a
variation of New Thought and restricted his students to a diet of
nuts. Endeavor recalled that one day a rebellious pupil brought a
bologna sandwich to class. When confronted by the yogi, the pupil
brazenly told the class that a minister named Father Divine and
considered God by his followers espoused a similar philosophy but
encouraged his disciples to eat everything. Disgusted with the limited diet, Endeavor dropped out of the yogi's classes and decided
to attend a meeting at Rockland Palace. That night the audience
spilled out of the old casino and into the surrounding streets. Unable to get into the auditorium, he pushed through the crowd and
into the basement, where he listened to Father Divine's message
on loudspeakers. As the evangelist passed through the basement
on his way to his car, Endeavor caught his first glimpse of him.
Struck by what Endeavor described as his "meekness," he followed the diminutive evangelist to Sayville and moved into the
Macon Street colony.[38]

The Rockland Palace meetings were only a part of a series of
lectures Father Divine delivered between December 1931 and May
1932. Followers set up engagements in churches and auditoriums
around New York City, Long Island, and New Jersey, and they
shuttled him at a breakneck pace between meetings and small banquets in followers' homes or church dining halls. Constantly surrounded by secretaries, he answered correspondence in his car.
Although middle-aged, he remained healthy and energetic, and
apparently enjoyed his whirlwind lecture tour.[39]

The exhaustive evangelizing paid off handsomely. His personal
appearances and the newspapers' coverage of his activities expanded the movement throughout New York, into New Jersey and
beyond. With the assistance of followers and sympathizers, word
of his activities spread nationwide. In late November, Eugene Del
Mar composed a heartfelt testimonial letter:

> All that I have seen, felt and ascertained regarding the life and teach-
> ings of Father Divine have illumined my understanding beyond
> anything I have heretofore experienced. His teachings are both ex-
> tremely simple and deeply profound. . . . His teaching is that of es-
> sential Unity and Oneness: that body, mind and soul are One; and

that when the Christ Life is lived in its fullness, the body is spiritualized so that it partakes of the Spirit of God, and is no longer subject to Death.

Del Mar's letter circulated among New Thought adherents and drew followers from as far as the Pacific Northwest into Father Divine's flock.[40]

Another white exponent of Father Divine's teachings, Reverend Albert C. Grier of New York's Church of Truth, compiled a pamphlet that described Father Divine's theology and chronicled his clash with the Sayville community: "For twelve years Father Divine has fed and clothed a hundred or more people with the use of money that he received directly from God. No, I do not mean through prayer or requests he receives money from people. His money comes from the hand of God." Grier marveled at Father Divine's success in "the field of finances" and praised the minister's fusion with "the Divine mind." To attract the attention of whites, Grier included testimony from Euramerican followers with texts of Father Divine's sermons. Grier's booklet went into several printings and enjoyed wide circulation, even in California.[41]

The most valuable figure in promoting Father Divine's teachings during this period was a former Christian Science practitioner, Henry Joerns of Seattle. Since 1929, Joerns had published the weekly *Metaphysical News*, which circulated primarily in Washington, Oregon, and California. Each issue carried messages from various New Thought leaders, stories on metaphysical organizations, and a national directory of "Truth Centers."[42]

In early December 1931, Joerns received a letter from John Lamb detailing the Sayville conflict and requesting that he publish some of Father Divine's sermons. Later in the month, Joerns ran an article on Sayville's metaphysician and the late-night raid on his home. Letters from Father Divine, Walter Lanyon, and John Lamb appeared in subsequent issues. By March 1932, Joerns began to reprint portions of Father Divine's lectures, which stimulated the curiosity of many readers of the *Metaphysical News*, and familiarized the American metaphysical community with Father Divine's philosophy.[43]

Through literary channels, Del Mar, Grier, and Joerns propagated Father Divine's teachings across the nation. These three men, all white, tapped their exclusively white religious circles to attract more Euramericans into Father Divine's spiritual family. The spread of Father Divine's theology outside the Northeast through lectures and literature attracted converts who were predominantly white, well-educated, and financially secure. Most important, like their earlier counterparts, the new children had previously experimented with New Thought and believed that Father Divine harnessed God's power and validated mind-power theology.

Even with the new white converts, the majority of Father Divine's children were black. Since neither he nor his staff kept membership rolls, the precise racial composition and exact number of followers by spring of 1932 are impossible to determine. The number is further obscured by the informal structure of the movement, for membership in Father Divine's congregation did not require baptism or an initiation ceremony. Followers had only to follow his theological and moral codes. A true angel lived a strictly celibate and communitarian life, but Father Divine often included people who maintained "harmonious" beliefs—Christians, Jews, and advocates of New Thought—in his following. Many of his followers participated in worship services but refused to modify their lives completely according to their leader's rigid standards. Willing to assist in the programs and activities sponsored by the movement, those who remained on the periphery provided the bulk of his support. By early 1932, an average of twelve thousand worshipers attended his lectures. Since he held meetings in widely separated locations, the number of followers and supporters may have ranged between twenty and thirty thousand. Father Divine, always thinking positively, estimated in the spring of 1932 that over 3.5 million people were "believing in ME and calling on ME."[44]

As the movement grew, he spent less time in Sayville. The demands of the lecture circuit forced him to discontinue his employment agency and take in only the most destitute. In an effort to appease his neighbors, he had suspended all public services at 72 Macon Street. He began to emphasize increasingly the "impersonal" aspect of his power and reminded his disciples that he was always spiritually present. "I have gone to the general public for the purpose of reaching those that cannot come out to Long Island," he explained to his Sayville children.[45]

Finding the trip to Sayville every night draining and inconvenient, Father and Mother Divine and their staff moved in March of

1932 to an elegant home in Harlem owned by a New York City follower. The new locale cut the commuting time between speaking engagements and permitted him to accept more invitations. Furthermore, most of his followers lived in Harlem, and support from the surrounding community allowed him to resume working out of his home.[46]

Relocation altered the structure of his ministry and transformed his sect into a movement. The Sayville home became the movement's first branch and served as a model for other "extensions" organized by followers. Throughout the Northeast, new disciples attempted to reconstruct Father Divine's collective colony and to recreate Holy Communion banquets in their homes. At the banquet tables followers reserved places for Father and Mother Divine, and filled the plates set before their empty chairs. Through the extensions now spread across New York and New Jersey, followers took a more active role. It was the angels who named Father Divine's crusade the Peace Mission movement.[47]

The disciples soon realized that their movement transcended religious concerns and could become a vehicle for widespread social change. Although Father Divine's teachings contained strains of social criticism, his plan for restructuring society remained vague. In his messages he focused on theological themes and individual prosperity. Reverend Grier, like other staunch supporters, recognized the limitations of Father Divine's ministry:

> The miracles and wonders that FATHER was doing were alright, but there was something of greater importance, the saving of civilization from going down to destruction. . . . Reverend Grier said he hoped we, including himself, who were so close to this great work of Father's would not be blinded by the immensity of it and stress the material benefits extended overlooking the great importance of salvation of the world.[48]

Father Divine had achieved affluence and provided impressive social relief, but his theology did not furnish a cohesive program for large-scale social reform. Followers like Grier began to urge him to broaden his activities and address American social, political, and economic problems.

Despite the pleas of disciples, he resisted plunging into secular issues and filtered his remarks on society through a theological lens. He explained that politics only minimally interested him, for he viewed governments as a human creation and therefore filled with imperfection. He considered the Constitution an admirable achievement but an expendable product of the "human plane." He declared that if the Constitution could not be enforced, the document should be "torn up" and a "limited government" instituted. Even though at this time his comments were few, they represent the most radical statements he would make on politics and government during his career.[49] He not only considered the foundation for American government dispensable but also spurned American nationalism. "I am none of your nationalities," he told one audience. "You don't have to think I AM an American. . . . I AM none of them."[50] At this point in his career, he refused to identify with America or its components and concentrated on promoting his ephemeral plan to "elect Christ King of Kings."[51]

On the other hand, the devastation of the depression nudged him toward a more concrete approach to the flaws in the American financial system. His critical attitude toward politics did not carry over to economics, and he enthusiastically praised capitalism. In his opinion, capitalism was not at fault; the individual was to blame for the depression. He contended that Americans had created the depression with their negative attitudes and alienation from God's internal presence. Only through positive thinking and channeling God's spirit could the country pull out of the downward economic spiral. Despite the suffering brought on by the depression, he actually considered the crisis beneficial, for it increased his following and spread his teachings.[52]

Father Divine's theological orientation also influenced his outlook on racism, the one secular topic he addressed frequently. In his view, racism, like all adversities, was a product of negative thinking. While he ardently attacked segregation and discrimination, his attitude toward bigotry was fundamentally conservative. In his opinion, blacks bore much of the blame for the inequalities in American society. The theme of individual responsibility dominated his outlook, and he concluded that blacks "had committed the sin in setting up color in the first place. They set it up in their consciousness and they would find it everywhere they went and *they* and no one else would be responsible."[53] From Father Divine's perspective, African Americans perpetuated their own oppression and should shoulder much of the responsibility for eradicating racism.

He accepted many of the unflattering characteristics ascribed to black Americans by whites and believed that African Americans who defined themselves as black internalized and manifested negative qualities. In front of one predominantly black congregation he insisted: "Now I am not poor because I do not belong to a poor, downtrodden race. If I was attached to a poor downtrodden race like some of you think you are, . . . then I would be like some of you."[54] He rejected identification with African-American people and during another meeting announced: "The other night someone got up and said there were lots of c[olored] people from New Orleans [present]. . . . I don't care anything about c[olored] people. I haven't them in me . . . [and] cast them out of my consciousness and do not allow them to exist there."[55]

Father Divine's position on racial pride did not go uncensured by his flock. During one banquet when whites occupied the seats nearest him, blacks in the congregation began singing, "Oh, just to sit at His Feet." Father Divine shot back: "Rather than be misunderstood and taken as an instigator of racial prejudice, I would slit this throat and let all that prejudicial blood run out. All that I have sacrificed, all that I have done has been for the purpose of stamping out that prejudicial belief and if that is not accepted, I will go away."[56]

At a time when many black Americans celebrated African ties, his sermons never mentioned Africa or its legacy. He was Victorian in taste and strove for the more elegant material objects of America and Europe. While in later years his secretarial staff was conspicuously integrated, during this early period his personal secretaries, the major positions of power in the movement, were all white, even though the movement had attracted a number of qualified blacks.[57]

To liberate his flock from what he considered damaging racial divisions, he demanded that followers cease identifying people by race. In his opinion, race did not really exist and was a damaging artificial construct of the mind. A product of negative thinking, the notion of race had produced destructive deviseness in American society. But his denial of blackness indicates that he endeavored to alleviate racial conflict by conceptually eliminating blacks from the population. Although he contended that African Americans created their own oppression, he believed that whites also played a role. Like blacks, white Americans embraced the concept of race and required a transformation of consciousness.

Before long, he had instituted integrated seating at banquets, alternating black and white worshipers. He enforced the pattern even in his private cars and encouraged followers to walk together in integrated pairs. Given the intense racial hostility and rigid segregation of the 1930s, these simple requirements were exceptionally progressive. Acutely aware of historical repression, he urged black disciples to surrender their old names, not only because they symbolized mortality but also because surnames were "your Daddy's master's name." Although his stands on racism were contradictory, Father Divine conceived of himself as a leader in the fight against oppression and often equated himself with Mahatma Gandhi.[58]

Despite Father Divine's occasional utterances on worldly concerns, the six months following his arrest were the least political phase of his ministry. Ideologically, he failed to provide a solid base for social action. On many issues he was a conservative and an advocate of rugged American individualism. His occasional criticisms of America's shortcomings were countered by philosophical inconsistencies and the cloudiness of his solutions.

Furthermore, alterations in the movement curtailed his most effective tool for change, his social-relief program. Sporadically, he served Holy Communion banquets to a restricted number of worshipers, but the banquets no longer provided effective aid; they were essentially a symbolic demonstration of his power. Even so, his appearances continued to draw larger and larger crowds. Most historians argue that Father Divine attracted the hungry and the poor primarily through his massive banquets, but the expansion of his following without the incentive of free food indicates that he maintained a strong intellectual and spiritual appeal. Many people—hungry, homeless, and malnourished—waited in line for hours and endured crushing crowds without the promise of a free dinner just to hear the message of the Reverend M. J. Divine.[59]

Although expense limited the number and size of Holy Communion banquets, they remained the sole and central ritual of the Peace Mission movement. Followers continually attempted to recreate the feasts and finally, on Easter Sunday 1932, organized services that culminated in an enormous Holy Communion banquet. The Easter celebration began with a parade of five thousand followers and supporters through the streets of Harlem. Thousands of spectators packed the sidewalks along the parade route. Interspersed among caravans of cars, followers proudly marched in loose formation carrying banners declaring PEACE WHERE MY FATHER DIVINE LEADS I WILL FOLLOW. The parade ended at the doors of the Rush Memorial Baptist Church in Harlem, which was so full that the flag-bearer spent forty-five minutes weaving through the crowd to get to the altar. In spite of the cramped conditions, the audience enjoyed an Easter celebration filled with song and testimony, and after Father Divine's message, adjourned to the church dining room for Easter dinner.[60]

The dining room, which accommodated only six hundred guests, turned into a mob scene. Those without seats stood behind the diners, hoping to hear Father Divine's remarks and eventually take communion. As the hungry congregants sang and testified, the room grew hot and stuffy. Outside, a crowd of over fifteen hundred people gathered in the streets and pushed toward the doors of the dining room. Through quick maneuvering, Father Divine seated the overflow in the church across the street and divided his time between the two sets of worshipers. As he served an elaborate banquet to those lucky enough to be seated in the dining room, he commented: "I preach Christ not only in word, but in deed and action. What I have to offer is only an outward expression of a per cent of the limitless blessings I have in the store house for you." The Easter devotionals proved a triumph for the Peace Mission movement. One newspaper compared the celebration to those held by the UNIA and praised Father Divine for awakening a community that had been dormant since Garvey's fall.[61]

Father Divine's Easter services may have been a publicity coup, but the banquet failed even to approximate the colossal feasts served in his Sayville home. On that Sunday, Father Divine served only six hundred people, a fraction of the crowd participating in the devotionals. But the Easter banquet was the first large-scale Holy Communion service organized outside his Sayville home. Symbolically, his ability to provide large quantities of food attested to the soundness of his teachings. This abundance in the depths of the depression must have amazed many of Harlem's residents, who struggled for basic necessities of life. Although it offered Harlemites no real social relief, it raised many people's hopes and excited their curiosity.[62]

Not everyone in Harlem was thrilled by the rise of Father Divine. As his following grew, so did opposition to his teachings. The most vocal criticism came from Harlem's African-American clergy, led by Bishop R. C. Lawson of the Refuge Church of Christ of the Apostolic Faith. Lawson arrived in New York City in 1919 and began as a street-corner preacher in Harlem. By 1931, he had built a network of churches in twenty cities and organized a school and an orphanage. Threatened by the growing popularity of Reverend Divine and appalled by his unusual doctrines, Lawson initiated a campaign against the Sayville minister. From his pulpit, in the press, and before several public meetings, he labeled Father Divine "the forerunner of the anti-Christ" and charged that the minister had bilked his unwitting disciples out of thousands of dollars.[63]

Father Divine skillfully exploited the affair to generate more publicity for his movement. He initiated a dialogue in the media, charging that Lawson was jealous of the Peace Mission movement's success. From Father Divine's perspective, the clash arose out of theological differences. For instance, he rejected Lawson's acceptance of an afterlife: "Now, of course Mr. Lawson is in a different world. He is in the orthodox world and he has a place to go to Heaven and hell, and we are not supposed to go to either."[64]

Philosophical differences ran even deeper. Lawson may have been orthodox on the question of life after death, but in Father Divine's opinion, the pastor of the Refuge Church was too radical on the issue of sanctification. Influenced by the Apostolic faith, Lawson insisted that after total-immersion baptism, the individual was unable to sin again. Father Divine declared that he preferred the approach of Methodists and Baptists, who "say the inner man is the one to be saved, but the old body is prone to sin." Overall, Lawson's persistent attacks did little to disrupt the momentum of the movement. Father Divine remained undisturbed and contended that "meek and lowly is the way. I don't have to defend or protect myself in any way."[65]

During the conflict with Lawson, Father Divine focused more

on their intellectual disagreements than on the debate within the African-American community over the obligations of the church to the poor. He did not advocate the implementation of full-scale welfare programs in black churches, for charity was against his convictions. He championed instead a spiritual and occupational reeducation of the poor. But the majority of black ministers dismissed him as a fanatic whose programs were unreasonable. African-American clergy became more involved in social welfare in part because the black middle class was beginning to feel the pinch of the depression, awakening them to the plight of poorer blacks and the dreaded possibilities for themselves.[66]

In addition to opposition from the religious community, legal problems plagued the movement. Shortly after the November raid, authorities whisked Rebbekah Branch from the Macon Street colony. Branch, formerly Julia Arras, was an immigrant from Spain who taught Spanish to New York socialites. At the insistence of two of her former students, the Sayville court arrested and detained Branch for psychiatric evaluation. During her sanity hearing, Branch testified that while playing roulette during a vacation in Buenos Aires, Father Divine had kicked her and warned her to stop gambling. After returning to the United States, strange visions haunted her until "spirit vibrations" drew her to the home in Sayville. She told the court that though she had never had any private conversations with Father Divine, she firmly believed he was God. Court-appointed doctors diagnosed her as a "religious paranoiac" and committed her to Central Islip State Hospital. Branch received the sentence with dignity. She rose confidently, shook hands with the officers of the court, and bade everyone "Peace."[67]

Other followers suffered similar persecution at the hands of authorities. In April 1932, citizens summoned police to one of Father Divine's Harlem extensions. In a tiny apartment police found thirteen worshipers singing, dancing, and shouting. One woman, Louisa Reed, sang and danced clothed only in a sheet. Wilfred Boxill, another follower, explained to the officers: "We're Father Divine's children. We dance. We're older than Methuselah." The police broke up the celebration and transported Boxill and Reed to Bellevue.[68]

The strongest opposition to Father Divine and the Peace Mission movement loomed in Sayville. Even though Father Divine had relocated, the district attorney did not drop the charges as promised, and Sayville residents were determined to expel the remainder of the sect from town. In the intervening months, James Thomas and Ellee Lovelace plotted their strategy and sparred with the legal system. In April, the attorneys filed for a change of venue, arguing that because of the blatant prejudice of residents, it would be impossible for Father Divine to get a fair trial in Suffolk County. The court granted a change of venue and set the trial for May 24 in Nassau County, whose residents had developed a strong dislike for Reverend Divine, fearing that he planned to move there.[69]

On Tuesday, May 24, Father Divine and his neighbors squared off in the Nassau County Supreme Court, presided over by Justice Lewis J. Smith. The prosecution presented many witnesses, most residents of Macon Street, who repeated their complaints, charging that his operations drove property prices down and caused emotional distress. The stories told by the beleaguered homeowners quickly won Smith over. According to the *Suffolk County News*, at one point during the proceedings, Smith interceded for a flustered witness:

> Mrs. Marie Connelly testified she was disturbed by the shouts from Divine's place and volunteered the statement that Divine claims to be the Messiah. "He says he is Jesus come back to earth," said the witness.
> "Did he say it to you?" Mrs. Connelly was asked. "No, but I read it in the papers," she said. "He says it to everybody. I heard some people that had been to his place say, 'That is heaven over there.' "
> "Did the noises you heard sound like heaven?" Mrs. Connelly was asked by Assistant District Attorney L. Barron Hill of Suffolk County.
> "How could she tell? She had never been there," interposed Justice Smith.

The testimony shocked Justice Smith, who was a staunch Presbyterian, and throughout the questioning, he demonstrated unabashed sympathy for the complainants.[70]

The defense attempted to prove that Father Divine was a legitimate religious leader and that Sayville authorities had violated his constitutional right to freedom of worship. In an effort to establish Father Divine's credibility, his attorneys called several respectable nonfollowers to the stand. Arthur Madison testified that he had attended over one hundred Holy Communion banquets and found the services orderly. Emphatically he insisted he had never heard Father Divine directly claim to be God or a messiah. Anne Mareine, a Christian Science practitioner, observed that while Father Divine's worship services and messages were nontraditional, they reflected spontaneity, not blasphemy. She maintained that Father Divine never professed the ability to cure illnesses but taught the sick to heal themselves.[71]

A number of defense witnesses refuted charges that Father Divine claimed divinity, but several followers testified that they believed that he was God and that he cured illnesses. "I believe that the same as everybody who has a God in them, Divine is the perfected expression of God," declared John Lamb.[72] As Smith listened to the followers, he grew increasingly agitated. His impatience climaxed when Heavenly Rest took the stand and professed her devotion to Father Divine and her belief in his divinity. Convinced that she was a minor, he grilled Rest about her age. When she claimed to be twenty-six, Smith snapped back, "I don't believe you are that old."

He recessed the court and detained Father Divine, hoping to charge him with a more serious crime. But after questioning Rest's mother and confirming the young woman's testimony, he reluctantly reconvened the court. The defense concluded the examination of its witnesses without calling Father Divine to the stand. Then Justice Smith recessed the court until the following morning.[73]

That night Father Divine returned to New York City and spoke at the Union Temple Baptist Church in Harlem. Several thousand worshipers attended the meeting, which proceeded as usual despite the anxiety of the trial. Father Divine was full of energy and delivered a lively sermon. The message, which he considered one of his best, reflected the state of his theology. For most of the sermon he concentrated on spiritual affairs and reiterated the central notion that Christ was present in all people. "Christ is in every joint, every sinew, every limb, every bone, every vein and fiber, every cell and atom of your bodily form," he proclaimed. People who forced Christ to surface became "lumps of radium" and "Glorays of God." He urged the crowd to surrender all their mortal habits and recognize that God's "light" was "expressed in . . . this body." He had come, he told the audience, to establish heaven on earth and light the way to eternal life.[74]

At the end of his sermon, he turned to the impending trial and reminded his children that his "prosecutions and persecutions" were for their sake. He assured the throng that his enemies in Sayville had not hurt the movement but had helped spread his message. "Every knock is a boost, every criticism is a praise," he insisted. He attempted to console and encourage the followers:

> So whatsoever you see and whatsoever you hear, whatsoever happens and whatsoever does not happen, know that I have borne it for righteousness' sake, and I AM not ashamed of the Gospel of Christ. That is what gives ME so much pleasure, because it is the Gospel, and it is the Power of GOD unto salvation, to every one that believeth and I thank you so much.[75]

Early the next morning Father Divine and his followers returned to court. After hearing the closing arguments, Justice Smith instructed the jury to ignore the statements made by witnesses not present on the night of the raid. Smith's order invalidated most of the testimony in Father Divine's favor and severely crippled the defense. The justice also rejected allegations that the arrest violated freedom of worship:

> There is no issue as to the form of religious worship in this case, but one cannot use religion as a cloak for the commission of crime. Jurors should bear that in mind. There may be those who believe this defendant is God. There are undoubtedly many who believe he is not God, and those who do not believe he is God are entitled to have their rights protected the same as those who believe he is God.

Even the prosecution could not have pleaded more persuasively for the residents of Macon Street, and after only fifteen minutes' deliberation, the jury returned a guilty verdict.[76]

On June 5, Father Divine appeared before Justice Smith for sentencing. In the meantime, suspicious of Father Divine's mysterious past, Smith had investigated the evangelist's background. Before the sentencing Smith announced that his research revealed that Father Divine had deceived both his followers and the public. The justice stated that Father Divine's true name was George Baker and that he was not an ordained minister. He claimed that Father Divine had been born in the Deep South, was not legally married to

Peninniah, and had a wife and children living in another state. He charged that Father Divine had broken up families, tricked his congregation out of thousands of dollars, and destroyed the mental health of his followers. Smith concluded that Father Divine was "a menace to society." He imposed the maximum sentence of one year in jail and a fine of $500. Shocked at the severity of the sentence and frustrated with the justice's demeanor, Thomas declared he would file an appeal. Outside, as the police hustled the little clergyman out of the courthouse and into a car, his followers waved and shouted, "Good-bye, Father."[77]

On Thursday evening, June 9, Justice Smith and his wife climbed into the family car and enjoyed a drive around Long Island. The justice had worked hard to clear the court calendar and looked forward to a relaxing vacation. He and his wife had planned a party the next day to celebrate their twenty-fifth wedding anniversary. They expected to attend their oldest son's graduation from Colgate College later in the month. The couple returned home from their drive and retired. At midnight, the justice woke his wife, complaining of chest pains. Mrs. Smith telephoned the family physician, but by the time the doctor arrived, Justice Lewis J. Smith, fifty-five, had died of a heart attack.[78]

6

These Outside Directions

We are going to start a general political clean-
up campaign and we are going through with it
if it costs a million dollars to the glory of GOD
and the salvation of mankind. . . . That is why
we had to carry on our work in these outside
directions much as we would have preferred
to remain exclusive in our chosen field.

New York News, August 6, 1932

On the death of Justice Lewis J. Smith, African-American journalist Ralph Matthews, in his nationally syndicated column, hailed the rise of Reverend Major J. Divine: "The fact that the judge who sentenced the good Dr. Divine to prison dropped dead a few days later may not have any definite significance. The hand of the self-styled messiah may not have been in this particular bit of deviltry, but I prefer to believe it was." Justice Smith's death occurred at a fortuitous time in the history of the Peace Mission movement. Followers and sympathizers interpreted Smith's demise as an act of retribution by Father Divine. The press ignored Smith's history of heart disease and his recent debilitating bout with influenza, intimating that his death was shockingly sudden. The media's stories contributed even more mystical and frightening power to the imprisoned minister. Some came to fear that Father Divine possessed sinister motives and destructive talents. But for others the justice's death reinforced Father Divine's claims to divinity and endowed him with positive qualities. Ralph Matthews heralded him as a black messiah who had resisted and defeated his opposition. "Call me a superstitious old fogie if you will," wrote Matthews, "but I want to make myself believe that when it comes to being god, Major Divine is all wool and a yard wide."[1]

During Father Divine's incarceration, his movement gained momentum. Under Peninniah's careful supervision, followers continued to serve Holy Communion banquets. At those celebrations she attended, she set a place for her husband, passed each dish by his seat for a blessing, and filled his plate with food. In a letter from his prison cell, Father Divine instructed her to read selected verses from the Bible, chapters from *The Eyes of the Blind,* and his messages reprinted in the *Metaphysical News.* Disciples around New York City and New Jersey followed Mother Divine's example and continued their devotionals. The flock waited patiently, taking comfort from the letter he had written to Peninniah, reporting that "being Spirit I AM as happy as can be and as free as a bird in a tree."[2]

Father Divine remained a dedicated disciple of positive thinking. Turning prison life into a productive experience, he evangelized among the inmates and won the admiration of many. An avid reader, he studied the newspapers and closely followed the case of the Scottsboro Nine, the innocent black youths sentenced to death for the gang rape of two white teenage girls. He probably immersed himself in the available religious literature, the extra time allowing him to assess his own personal relationship with God. He jotted in his journal:

> While sitting in My cell . . . I am thinking of the things of spirit that are made flesh, yet the Spirit spiritualizes both it and them. Therefore, the spirit materialized is incorruptible, undefiled and fadeth not away. . . . And stone prison walls and iron prison bars cannot hold me for I AM spirit even tho' I AM flesh materialized. Yet in my flesh I do see God. My eyes see Him for Myself and not for others.

The sentence furnished him time to reflect on his ministry. For over a year, his life had been a whirlwind of activity, and he had had little time to plot the direction of his movement. He contemplated the secular world where African Americans faced prison, and in some cases death, for crimes they did not commit. His incarceration allowed him to think more about earthly concerns and revitalized his theology.[3]

On June 25, 1932, word circulated around Peace Missions that attorney James Thomas had secured Father Divine's release on appeal, on $5,000 bail. Joyful followers immediately organized a celebration for the following day at Rockland Palace, and before dawn a crowd had gathered in front of the old casino. The daylong service began in late morning, and by the afternoon the congregation had swelled to ten thousand. The celebration continued into the night, the crowd growing more ecstatic. Suddenly the throng was silenced by a shriek from Priscilla Paul. Father Divine proudly marched into the auditorium: "As with one voice the crowd screamed, yelled, wept, waved their arms, danced, sang and groaned in exultation. . . . He stood silently and smiled. There was a moment's hesitation, then his disciples poured toward him with outstretched hands."[4] Several angels lifted him to their shoulders and carried him to the rostrum. He surveyed the cheering assembly and with a wave of his hand silenced them. Then, he began to sing "I am the Light of the World." After the first few lines, the audience joined in, singing and swaying.[5]

In his message on this hot summer night in 1932 he discussed Justice Smith's death. Since the trial, the press had hounded him for a reaction, but he had refused to comment, reserving his remarks for his disciples: "I did not desire Judge Smith to die. . . . I did desire that MY spirit would touch his heart and change his mind that he might repent and believe and be saved from the grave." In Father Divine's view, Justice Smith had killed himself with his own negative thoughts. His death illuminated the necessity of maintaining a positive outlook and was a warning to critics that a similar fate loomed if they impeded the progress of the Peace Mission movement.[6]

In many ways, Father Divine's messages after his release resembled his previous sermons. He still encouraged his disciples to think positively and seek God within themselves. But by the summer of 1932, he had begun to shift his focus. His sermons remained thematically spiritual, but references to political events and social issues crept into his remarks. Inspired by his conflicts with the court system, the inclusion of social activists like James Thomas in his fold, and his recent reading on current events, he had become more interested in worldly affairs. The evangelist left prison convinced that America's salvation required a transformation of the political and social structures.

Despite his revised outlook, Father Divine did not become a revolutionary. He attributed American injustice and inequalities to human error and emerged as an even more conservative champion of the American system. Previously ambivalent toward the organization of the American government, he defended the Constitution as a divinely inspired document. According to the evangelist, democracy and its economic counterpart, capitalism, furnished a foundation for a potentially perfect society: "I have searched this planet through and through and around and around and the United States of America is the only place I have found that has the fundamental principle wherein the Kingdom of God can be legitimately established if lived up to."[7]

Father Divine's solutions were clear-cut. Corrupt and immoral politicians hindered America from realizing its true potential. The country had strayed from its constitutional foundation, and through the Peace Mission movement he planned to return America to what he interpreted as the original intentions of the Founding Fathers. He insisted that followers who were not citizens become naturalized and urged his angels to register to vote. With voting power he hoped to "clean up" the political parties, impeach dishonest public officials, and inoculate the political world with his teachings. The experiences of the past year had not alienated him; he developed into a fervent nationalist who worshiped American democracy and sought peaceful change by working within the system.[8]

He set out to promote both his theological vision and his secular agenda. In July, Father and Mother Divine flew to Washington, D.C., with James Thomas and a few followers. The party received a warm welcome, toured the area, and held several banquets. His primary purpose was to meet with the editors of the Washington *Voice* and the Apalachicola, Florida, *Reporter*. While he recognized the benefits of media attention, he realized that newspaper reports had often damaged the movement, and he envisioned controlling a newspaper syndicate that would propagate his teachings. In exchange for assistance from the Peace Mission movement, the editors pledged to print his messages, chronicle the activities of the organization, and report "the news of the world without exaggeration and distortion."[9]

The second purpose of the Washington trip was to survey the capital as a potential new headquarters for his ministry. But several factors dissuaded him from leaving New York. First, the proximity to his childhood home and the painful memories associated with it probably discouraged him. Second, he may have encountered even stronger opposition to his teachings in Washington, both because it was too far south to tolerate an interracial movement and because a base of operation in the nation's capital could be misinterpreted as a threat to the American political system. Finally, in New York City he had developed a solid constituency; in Washington he did not yet have a strong following and was more vulnerable to attacks from community leaders and the general public.[10]

Before long, he had begun to build a network of congregations down the eastern seaboard and across the nation. As more people joined the movement, the list of extensions of "Father's Kingdom" grew. Many followers dedicated their own houses or apartments to the movement; others pooled their money and rented or purchased buildings. While some Peace Missions operated simply as meeting halls, others were run as rescue homes where angels provided assistance to the public in accord with their leader's principles of cooperative living. All Peace Mission residents lived in sexually segregated quarters and shared work and financial responsibilities. Most missions were humble establishments, simply furnished and spotlessly clean. Pictures of Father Divine and homemade posters and banners proclaiming his divinity adorned the walls. At least once a week, the children conducted Holy Communion banquets open to the public.[11]

The extensions of Father Divine's Kingdom lured many people into the Peace Mission movement. In northeastern cities, missions attracted a large number of blacks who had migrated from the South in a vain search for opportunity. One such convert was Viola Wilson of Dublin, Georgia. Wilson, who in the South worked as a domestic, migrated north and opened a little neighborhood market. Her business quickly failed, and she was forced onto the streets. Homeless and emaciated, she wandered the alleyways of Newark clothed in rags and eating from trash bins. Before long, she contracted tuberculosis and became an alcoholic. After suffering a severe blackout, she sought assistance from an acquaintance, who deposited her at a Peace Mission.[12]

The angels welcomed Wilson and offered her shelter, food, and clothes. On the day of her arrival, a disciple took her to a Holy Communion banquet served by Father Divine. Captivated by him and impressed by his followers' kindness, she made immediate public confession of her sins. At a time when few treatments ex-

isted for alcoholism, the Peace Mission offered support-group therapy that encouraged alcoholics to take control of their lives.

With the assistance of Father Divine's children, Viola Wilson regained her health and self-esteem. She dedicated herself to the Peace
Mission movement and assumed the name Faithful Mary. Her
portly, robust appearance made her one of Father Divine's most
striking success stories, and he frequently used her as an example
of his ability to transform the most desperate lives. As a gesture of
gratitude, Faithful Mary opened her own mission in Newark and
endeavored to help other unfortunate souls.[13]

As ambassadors for the Peace Mission movement, the angels
were instrumental in extending it into other cities across the United
States. In 1932, a Jamaican who had joined the Peace Mission
movement in New York, Brother Alexander, brought the movement to Los Angeles. He established a modest mission on Compton Avenue in a predominantly African-American neighborhood
and drew black Angelenos into the Peace Mission movement. One
local resident who discovered the movement through Alexander's
mission was Martha Craig, a single working woman with several
young children. A religious seeker, Craig had investigated several
Holiness sects and the Seventh Day Adventist church but left each
one dissatisfied. After attending a Holy Communion banquet at
Alexander's mission, her religious restiveness disappeared. She
became a devoted follower and raised her children in the movement. Followers with intriguing pasts like Faithful Mary's attracted
attention, but a large portion of Father Divine's children were like
Craig, responsible and hardworking people who struggled against
great odds to provide for their families.[14]

The Peace Mission movement also continued to expand into white
communities, but through different channels. In late 1932, two of
Henry Joerns's white colleagues, Thomas J. Hampton of San Francisco and Ross Humble of Seattle, made a pilgrimage to Harlem to
meet Father Divine. His dynamic preaching captivated both men,
who like Joerns were former Christian Science practitioners. In a
letter to Joerns, Hampton wrote that Father Divine "is a very unusual character, that he is living the life of Christ more nearly than
anyone else I have ever contacted." The two men hit the lecture
circuit and raced around the country speaking to various white
New Thought alliances and organizations, successfully stirring in-

terest in Father Divine's teachings. Throughout the United States groups of white followers began to sponsor lectures and discussion groups on his theology. The dissemination of his philosophy through lectures and literature attracted white converts who were avid readers and accustomed to participating in study groups. Most whites who joined the movement were financially secure and well educated.[15]

The branches of the movement differed fundamentally from their parent organization. Father Divine's personal management of missions in New York City and surrounding areas ensured complete integration. However, the movement was unintentionally segregated in extensions outside his direct control. De facto segregation and the spread of his teachings through different channels created a network of racially separate Peace Missions. While blacks celebrated Holy Communion banquets in ghetto missions, whites worshiped Father Divine in their homes and meeting halls.[16]

Though Father Divine easily attracted blacks from a variety of income levels, most white followers were middle and upper class. Poor and working-class whites were unfamiliar with New Thought and the metaphysical ideology that facilitated acceptance of Father Divine's theology. In addition to the aberrational nature of his theology, deeply ingrained racial prejudice made it impossible for many whites to accept his assertions of divinity. For most whites, integration was inconceivable, and the notion that God was black was repulsive. A *New York Times* reporter, George Corey, observed that racism was so powerful that needy whites "had to be desperate to come up [to Harlem] and eat a black man's food."[17]

Father Divine masterfully forged his coalition of followers. The affluent blacks and whites provided financial stability, while the less fortunate angels furnished dedicated collective labor Pooling their resources, his children embarked on a brave project: in the midst of the depression, they established a chain of independent businesses based on his notions of collective enterprise. Since few followers could afford to finance a business, they joined in cooperatives and divided the profits evenly among the partners who contributed money and muscle. Peace Mission businesses combined communalism with capitalism to make lucrative enterprises that drew still more followers, especially those interested in profitable commerce.[18]

The first Peace Mission enterprises were restaurants opened in 1932 around New York City and Newark. Immaculately clean, these restaurants offered hearty meals at low prices. Angels cut costs by purchasing day-old bread, overripe produce, and edible food from markets and restaurants. Father Divine demanded that Peace Mission restaurants charge only five or ten cents for a complete meal and insisted that his followers refuse all tips. Peace Mission restaurants quickly became popular and attracted the poor seeking a hot meal as well as the affluent searching for a bargain. Many who spurned Father Divine's teachings gladly patronized Peace Mission restaurants and made these enterprises successful.[19]

Before long, angels dived even deeper into the business world and opened hotels, markets, dress stores, and garages. Like the Peace Mission restaurants, these businesses undercut competition by providing high-quality goods and services at low prices. Followers sought Father Divine's advice and approval on each business, and his strict guidelines for personal finances yielded a sound foundation for Peace Mission enterprises.

He prohibited followers from borrowing money, insisted they pay back all debts, and required them to make monetary restitution for any unpunished crime committed before they joined the movement. He forbade the use of credit and ordered followers to make only cash purchases. He also demanded that followers eschew insurance since such policies indicated a lack of faith and increased financial overhead. Deeply distrustful of banks, he cautioned followers against depositing their money there, and since the American banking system remained dangerously unstable throughout 1932, his advice protected many followers from financial ruin. Thanks to his rigid requirements, Peace Mission enterprises throve in the thick of economic chaos. Because he was simultaneously a supporter of capitalism and a critic, his movement appealed to those interested in business but disillusioned with the American financial system. One follower observed, "We never suspected that we would have 'business' in the Kingdom of Heaven but *true* business is just beginning in a wonderful way. For the activity of God is practical and not mystical."[20]

While his disciples did not directly donate money to his ministry, their financial resources were critical to the movement. Since his days as an itinerant, he had refused to take cash contributions and relied on the cooperation of his followers to perpetuate his ministry, accepting support only from his most faithful disciples. The angels voluntarily provided Father and Mother Divine and their staff with food, clothes, housing, and cars.

> [My followers] live consecrated to and for the good of all, even though they own all things individually, severally and collectively. The legal claim of all things are to those whose legal claim they are, those who are the actual title owners of personal and real property. I, Myself, and My immediate staff and co-workers and followers who are consecrated to the service from a spiritual point of view of course we give our service gratis for the common good of humanity, without remuneration, without any love offerings and without any donations or without anything of that sort. And by so doing, according to the Gospel, in return for whatsoever is necessary and those things come automatically without any effort on our part, any physical act of coercion, in the way of trying to get something in return for that which we are sacrificing. So we are abundantly blessed in that way.[21]

Accepting tributes did not conflict with his theology, for he had constructed a spiritual family and contended that no private ownership existed within families. His standard of living depended on his followers, as he acknowledged: "You see you are helping ME to always be wealthy. . . . You are helping me to always be successful and prosperous. Because you declared it and you believe it and you have faith and I have received it."[22] Although the public praised Father Divine's contributions to social relief, the followers provided the real public assistance. The Holy Communion banquets in Rockland Palace were never more than symbolic and did not furnish the extensive relief required by the increasing number of impoverished Americans. The destitute could find help at the Peace Missions run by rank-and-file members who fed and sheltered them in exchange for labor. Peace Missions did not provide welfare but offered reeducation and job training. Their relief programs were strengthened after Father Divine and his staff reconstituted his free employment agency, which was immediately inundated with requests for his honest and hardworking followers.[23]

By the fall of 1932, many Peace Mission members had profited handsomely from their business ventures. Several angels decided to combine their earnings and sponsor a series of excursions on the Hudson River. For fifty cents followers enjoyed a day-long outing on a cruise ship. Music was provided by a brass band, but the angels had to bring their own lunches. From the upper deck Father and Mother Divine observed the flock, who sang and worshiped throughout the trip. He addressed the throng several times during the cruise, and the day ended on shore with an enormous Holy Communion banquet. The trips were popular, sold out quickly, and became a yearly tradition.[24]

Peace Mission cruises furnished African Americans with a recreational opportunity normally restricted to upper- and middle-class whites. In the twenties, Garvey and the UNIA had organized similar outings on the Black Star Line, but mismanagement of the line's business affairs abruptly curtailed the cruises. In contrast, Father Divine's inexpensive excursions demonstrated that he could triumph where other capable leaders had fallen short. He and his followers seemed to be untouched by the deteriorating economy. While millions of Americans languished in economic despair, his children delighted in their outings on the Hudson.[25]

As the Peace Mission movement continued to expand and prosper, opposition also increased. In New Jersey, a Peace Mission stronghold, the Ku Klux Klan burned a large cross inscribed *Father Divine* and threatened to attack local extensions.[26] Hostility to his teachings also smoldered in the black community. The *Baltimore Afro-American* ran a letter that expressed the sentiments of many African Americans: "If Father Divine or whatever his real name is has only mystic power with which he sways the gullible to the absurd belief that he is god you can rest assured that it is of devilish origin."[27] Previously friendly toward the Peace Mission movement, the *New York Amsterdam News* turned against Father Divine and ran a front-page interview with the Reverend Bishop Saint John the Vine, who charged that Father Divine was nothing more than a simple "hedge-cutter" from Baltimore named George Baker. In the article, the Bishop claimed to have originated the teachings that provided the foundation for Father Divine's philosophy, and he insisted that Father Divine had stolen and perverted his theology. Allegedly, Father Divine's version broke up families and undermined the morality of the African-American community. "It ain't as if I was trying to knock Father Divine," said the Bishop. "I merely want to see that my people are not led astray."[28]

Despite the escalating animosity, his popularity continued to grow. The rapid expansion of his movement, combined with his increasing focus on secular issues, attracted the attention of politicians. During the 1932 presidential race between Herbert Hoover and Franklin Delano Roosevelt, the Democrats courted his support, hoping to win the black vote. The party sent New York City mayor and Democratic party leader John O'Brien to address a Peace Mission banquet and urge the angels to vote for Roosevelt. But the Democrats' assertions that Father Divine influenced only African-American voters offended the clergyman. Angered by the party's failure to acknowledge that he controlled votes of an integrated following, he rejected their overtures. He directed the angels to compare the records of Hoover and Roosevelt, and announced that it was "essential for every man to accept, therefore, Mr. Hoover who promised to support and protect equal rights." Before 1932, African Americans consistently voted Republican, and Father Divine made no attempt to break with tradition. He supported a party that offered blacks opportunities for marginal participation, maintained sympathy for big business, and rejected federal welfare.[29]

Father Divine was not alone in clinging to the Republican party. Roosevelt's pandering to southern Democrats and his refusal to support civil rights insulted African Americans. In spite of the escalation of black unemployment under Hoover, two-thirds of the African-American vote went to the Republican ticket. Nevertheless, Roosevelt triumphed without black votes, promising economic recovery through his New Deal programs.

Once the course of Roosevelt's policies became clear, Father Divine became openly critical of the New Deal. He interpreted FDR's relief projects as a dole system that forced the unemployed into a state of dependency. He believed that instead of ending the depression, New Deal policies perpetuated poverty. His earliest attacks on the New Deal centered on Roosevelt's bank holiday: "Now we do not care anything about the banks closing. Those of you that have summed your salvation up in finances will find them failing you. . . . The banks must fail! . . . They may open soon again apparently, but they still must eventually fail." In addition, Roosevelt's repeal of Prohibition alarmed Father Divine. But his impatience with Roosevelt peaked when it became obvious that the New Deal would bypass most of the African-American community.[30]

Several promising signs in early 1933 encouraged Father Divine's outspoken opposition to the more powerful sectors of American society. On January 9, 1933, a higher court overturned Justice Smith's ruling: "We think prejudice was excited in the minds of the jurors by comments, rulings and questions by the Court throughout the trial. The Court went beyond reasonable and proper limits in the cross examination of defense witnesses."[31] Freed of legal entanglements, Father Divine and his followers poured their energy into advancing the Peace Mission movement. The *New York News* joined his news syndicate and ran his messages with his picture on the front page of each issue. The *Metaphysical News* became even more dedicated to the dissemination of his teachings. In late 1932, at the urging of Hampton and Humble, Joerns visited Father Divine's Harlem headquarters. At a large banquet, Father Divine introduced the Seattle metaphysician and announced that the *Metaphysical News* editor had promised "to give away not merely thousands, as he has been getting subscriptions for thousands without a fee, but he means to give away millions. . . . [Joerns] has declared that he will send out these periodicals absolutely free as a gift to man gratis to the world. It is wonderful!"[32] After returning home, Joerns exclaimed in his paper, "The highest concept that anyone has ever formed of God and Heaven . . . is now in actuality a reality in New York City."[33] Initially, Joerns continued to cover a potpourri of national spiritual events in the *Metaphysical News* and reported on Father Divine's activities in a companion paper, the *Light*. But by May of 1933, Joerns had abandoned his first paper and concentrated on publishing only the *Light*.[34]

The efforts of Joerns and his associates assisted in the propagation of Reverend Divine's teachings. Hampton and Humble distributed copies of the *Light* nationally, and Peace Missions began to sprout in the cities on their lecture circuit. Between lecture tours, Ross Humble organized a unique Peace Mission on Vendovi, an island just off the coast of Washington State. Staffed by an integrated group of twelve angels, the community operated according to Father Divine's teachings. It was self-sufficient, growing most of its food. The angels followed Father Divine's outline for collective labor and shared the responsibility for maintenance. Every night, island residents celebrated Holy Communion at a communal dinner table. The angels welcomed anyone interested in Father Divine's teachings to their island retreat and frequently entertained other members of the Peace Mission movement who went to Vendovi for relaxation and spiritual renewal.[35]

During 1933, the Seattle area reigned as the movement's major outpost. But before long, the rapidly expanding Los Angeles following surpassed the Seattle extensions. Since the late nineteenth century, Southern California had hosted a variety of nontraditional religious sects, and Los Angeles furnished a fertile ground for the growth of the movement. During the depression, the movement joined the Theosophists, Rosicrucian Brotherhoods, the Vedanta Society, the Church of Religious Science, Zoroastrianists, and the many other New Thought orders that thrived in Los Angeles.[36]

This abundance of religious alternatives fascinated the journalist and activist Carey McWilliams, who suggested that the presence of large numbers of migrants stimulated the formation of these new faiths. Like the urban centers of the East Coast, Los Angeles attracted newcomers from all parts of the country and the world, the development of new religious doctrines in Los Angeles paralleling the rise of black storefront churches. As migrants reestablished religious practices and asserted new identities, their experiences and exposure to other belief systems altered their religious traditions. Many blended their past faith with elements of popular New Thought ideology. Furthermore, as McWilliams observed, Los Angeles, popular for its mild climate and warm weather, attracted the elderly and infirm. Because religious sects influenced by New Thought promised to restore health, they lured many who suffered from untreatable illnesses.[37]

Until early 1933, the Peace Mission movement in Los Angeles remained confined to the African-American community. But early that year, a Beverly Hills matron identified only as Sister Betty began holding the first white Peace Mission meetings in her home. Shortly afterward, Ross Humble delivered a series of lectures that "filled one of the largest auditoriums" in the city to capacity. Inspired by Humble, another local resident organized public meetings. Soon Peace Mission gatherings drew over one hundred worshipers every night. Many affluent white followers financed missions, dormitories, businesses, and auditoriums that served as extensions of the movement. Working to unite with their black brothers and sisters, the white angels selected sites in integrated neighborhoods. As the movement expanded and followers moved into racially mixed hostels, white and black followers drew closer together.[38]

Humble tapped the growing enthusiasm for Father Divine's teachings and organized bus trips to shuttle West Coast disciples to headquarters in New York. The excursions cost fifty dollars; included food, lodging, and transportation; and attracted followers from Los Angeles to Seattle. Singing and worshiping, the pilgrims crossed the country in buses trimmed in banners declaring *Father Divine is God*. Whenever possible, the caravan stopped at Peace Missions along the route. In regions without extensions, the angels sought affordable restaurants and hotels. Frequently the integrated group faced racial discrimination and hostility. But when hotels or restaurants insulted or refused to accommodate black followers, the entire group marched out. The bus trips symbolized a challenge to the racism that infected American society.[39]

In New York City, the angels received a warm welcome from their brothers and sisters. The children entertained West Coast followers with special deference, furnishing their guests with their best food and accommodations. The East Coast disciples treated the visitors to elaborate Holy Communion banquets and a tour of Peace Mission properties. The trip climaxed in a private interview with Father Divine and a massive Holy Communion feast in his headquarters.[40]

Throughout 1933, disciples across the nation joined together, opened missions and businesses, and spread the teachings of Father Divine. The spirit of voluntarism governed the movement. Although Father Divine closely supervised his angels, he also allowed them freedom. "I stress the great significance of individuals being governed by their highest intuition and moving according to their own volunteer-volition," he explained during one sermon.[41]

Extensions of his movement appeared around the country, but he continually refused to form an official church. As a result, the movement developed into a network of independent groups united under his teachings. Father Divine insisted that extensions work together and reminded his angels that their activities were "controlled by the Spirit of My Presence."[42]

During the first months of 1933, the movement expanded unfettered by legal conflicts, but by the summer, the New Jersey branch had become embroiled in court battles. In June, the police arrested the leader of the Newark extensions, Bishop John F. Selkridge. The court convicted Selkridge of disorderly conduct and sentenced him to ninety days in jail. An escalation of complaints that Father Divine lured wives and mothers away from their families compounded the controversy surrounding the movement in New Jersey, and a Newark grand jury initiated an investigation of his activities. After several months of inquiry and the questioning of numerous witnesses, including Sayville authorities, the panel issued a mixed review. The court concluded that Father Divine tricked followers into believing he was God and was guilty of "blasphemy," a misdemeanor in New Jersey, but found that he was partially a beneficial influence and that "practice of this religious belief has a restraining effect upon persons of former criminal or morally loose character."[43]

According to the *New York Times* in November 1933, Father Divine's influence had spread nationwide, and his movement had attracted over two million followers. Father Divine himself estimated ten million disciples. The actual size of his following is impossible to determine because the Peace Mission did not keep membership rolls. Newspapers reported that ten thousand to forty thousand people attended his Easter services in 1933. If, as these figures suggest, there were as many as forty thousand disciples and sympathizers in New York City and surrounding areas, the number nationwide could have approached fifty thousand. Admirers, as opposed to disciples, probably composed the bulk of Peace Mission participants, for Father Divine's theological restrictions required a drastic alteration of lifestyle and tremendous sacrifices.[44]

In some ways, the exact size of the movement was insignificant, for much of the American public believed that Father Divine had a vast following. An increasing number of politicians became convinced that he controlled a large number of votes, especially in the African-American community. During the 1933 mayoral race in New York City, both parties courted his support. Incumbent John O'Brien attended a banquet and appealed to the angels for their votes. O'Brien's opponent, Fiorello La Guardia, appeared before the same banquet a couple of hours later, pledging to fight crime and soliciting Father Divine's assistance. Despite Father Divine's increasing concentration on politics, the angels remained uninterested in the candidates and their remarks. One follower asked a reporter, "La Guardia—who's that?" Nevertheless, the appearance of two major politicians at a banquet advanced the credibility of Father Divine's leadership.[45]

Politicians' attempts to flatter him did not impress the Harlem clergyman. He refused to endorse either candidate because neither shared his spiritual commitment. As he told the *Times*, "I'm not advocating a person, but a principle." Although he had become more interested in political affairs, his theological vision remained disengaged from the secular realm: to revitalize the city government, he simply directed citizens to subscribe to "the identical life of the Christ as it was in a person called Jesus." At the same time, he knew he could not afford to alienate the next mayor, nor could he risk supporting a losing candidate, for a defeat threatened to undermine his power in both the political and spiritual worlds. Despite his reluctance to become fully involved, the attention of major political officials ultimately drew him more into politics.[46]

While significant pressure to engage in political affairs came from external sources, by late 1933, most of the impetus originated within the Peace Mission movement. The spread of his teachings brought many individuals formerly involved in activist organizations into the movement. The flexibility of the Peace Mission allowed these new members to propel the movement into a new and more political direction.

Former leaders of the UNIA were one of the most significant additions to the movement. While some Garveyites probably transferred allegiance to Father Divine in the late twenties, their numbers increased at the onset of the depression. By the mid-thirties, the movement included several of the UNIA's most important officers, notably Maymie Leon Turpeau De Mena, previously the UNIA's assistant international organizer and editor of the Garveyite publication *Negro World*.[47]

In January 1934, De Mena issued the first edition of the *World Echo*, printed on the presses of the defunct *Negro World*. Dedicated to propagating Father Divine's theology, the *World Echo* published his messages (translated into five languages), reported Peace Mission events, and announced activities. De Mena had two objectives in mind, to maintain her old readership and to harness a new audience. In the first edition, she welcomed her readers: "Greetings to thousands of our old *friends* and to tens of thousands of our new *friends* who are eagerly waiting to welcome *World Echo*."[48]

De Mena appeared to embrace Father Divine's teachings in her paper, declaring that she believed he was "the personification of God in the fathership degree."[49] While De Mena dedicated most of the paper to Peace Mission news, she also ran articles and editorials on external affairs. The *World Echo* assumed an aggressive political tone absent in other publications promoting Father Divine's teachings; it championed civil rights, called for federal anti-lynching laws, and covered the African-American struggle for liberation. "*World Echo* emerges at this critical moment in world history with a definite program of spiritual economic, political and industrial emancipation and of securing an enduring peace," she announced. Through her publication, De Mena educated Father Divine's following and highlighted his fight against racism. Her work pleased him, and the paper won his endorsement.[50]

Although Father Divine's picture and words replaced those of Marcus Garvey in De Mena's paper, Garvey's influence was still visible. De Mena resisted particular aspects of Father Divine's philosophy, continuing to use racial labels. In one story, "Negro Has Scored Greatest Success in Insurance Field," De Mena extolled the opportunities offered by selling insurance. Despite Father Divine's denunciation of Roosevelt's New Deal, De Mena supported the program and in another article, "How NRA May Benefit Negro," praised its potential for black America. She also continued to publicize African colonization programs, central to Garveyism but incompatible with Peace Mission philosophy.[51]

The divided tone of the *World Echo* developed from several factors. Throughout the early thirties, the *Negro World* had suffered from underfunding and appeared only intermittently. Seeking finances for her journal, De Mena may have muted some of her beliefs in exchange for Peace Mission backing. Still, she had shifted from one organization to a vastly different one, a change that seemed to require an alteration in self-conception.

The core ideology of the Peace Mission movement ran counter to the philosophy of UNIA. Black pride and racial separatism were at the center of Garvey's philosophy, while Father Divine labeled blacks "insignificant" and "lowly," and campaigned for complete integration. Black Americans who joined the Peace Mission movement had to reconcile their desire for affirmation through racial pride with his denunciation of black awareness.

But for former Garveyites, the transformation must have caused much internal conflict. Perhaps some became frustrated with Garvey's ineffectiveness and were willing to experiment with Father Divine's integrationist approach. For others, his ideology may have confirmed the negative self-image caused by racism. By tapping these feelings, Father Divine attempted to construct a new route to dignity completely opposite from that offered by Marcus Garvey. He tore down the racial identification of his followers and refashioned their self-perceptions.

Father Divine offered African Americans a new identity, self-confidence, and dignity. He taught that through mind-power, his African-American followers could assume command over their destiny within a society that attempted to rob blacks of the right to control their lives. Clearly this feature attracted Garveyites, for in 1932 the *Negro World* observed that Father Divine's "confidence in himself has been the keynote of his entire teaching and it is this belief that he has succeeded in imparting to his many followers."[52]

But some African Americans may have ignored Father Divine's pronouncements against blackness and heralded the clergyman as a black god who inspired self-respect. After reading Garvey's criticism of Father Divine, one convert formerly active in the UNIA wrote Garvey: "I have discovered that you had forgotten what you had told us on more than one occasion; that GOD is supposed to be looking like us." Therefore, while the disjointed tone of the *World Echo* reflected De Mena's own ideological struggle, that struggle may have been shared by both UNIA crossovers and other black disciples.[53]

Despite their differences, UNIA and Peace Mission philosophies shared some ground which eased the transition between the movements. During the Sayville affair, the *Negro World* ran several articles sympathetic to Father Divine and his crusade. Both Marcus Garvey and Father Divine embraced capitalism and economic nationalism, and encouraged African Americans to open businesses. More important, New Thought also strongly influenced Garvey's plans for racial uplift. According to Garvey, positive thinking and "self-mastery" were powerful weapons against white oppression, especially when combined with economic advancement. Members of the UNIA developed an interest in New Thought organizations and ideologies, as evidenced by the *Negro World*'s frequent advertisements and articles on Unity, Rosicrucianism, spiritualism, and the power of positive thinking. In Father Divine, former Garveyites discovered a leader who seemed to manifest the success promised by New Thought ideology.[54]

The exodus from the UNIA into Father Divine's fold was not limited to New York City. Many members of Newark's UNIA, another Garvey stronghold, defected to the Peace Mission movement, led in New Jersey by Bishop Selkridge, who had previously served as a UNIA commander. Several prominent UNIA officials in Los Angeles, including the newspaper publisher Carlotta Bass, became active supporters of the local branch of Father Divine's organization. In Oakland, former Garveyites transformed a UNIA headquarters into a Peace Mission. The eager new converts wrote and visited their exiled leader and implored Garvey to accept Father Divine as God.[55]

In addition to defectors from the elite of the Garvey movement were many like Sister Mary Bee, a former rank-and-file Garveyite who became a dedicated disciple of Father Divine. Following Father Divine's directive that disciples make restitution for past debts, in 1936 Sister Bee sent Marcus Garvey two dollars that she owed the UNIA's African Redemption Fund. Although the UNIA had suspended the project, Garvey accepted Sister Bee's money, noting that he would apply it to the UNIA's general account. Undoubtedly, ordinary UNIA members like Sister Bee composed the bulk of the Peace Mission converts.[56]

Marcus Garvey had little patience with America's black messiah and denounced Father Divine in articles appearing in the *Black Man:*

> There is no god but One Almighty Being of Heaven, wherever Heaven is. He is the Creator of the universe. Man is but a small part of his creation, and Father Divine is but man. He is physical flesh and blood and of spirit just like another human being and if it is true that he assumes the role of God, then he must be mad or a wicked contriver of deception.[57]

To stop the flow of converts to the Peace Mission movement, the UNIA attacked Father Divine's ministry at a regional conference in Canada in August 1936. UNIA delegates led by Garvey passed several resolutions condemning the Peace Mission movement and charging that Father Divine's theology was blasphemous and morally corrupting. Garvey alleged that the movement was a "colossal racket" contrived by Father Divine and an inner circle of self-serving whites seeking to bilk people of African heritage out of their earnings.

Ironically, Garvey, who in the 1920s had accepted support from white-supremacist groups, attempted to discredit Father Divine with allegations that the minister "was being subsidized by organizations on the order of the Ku Klux Klan."[58] In addition, Garvey zeroed in on Father Divine's teachings on race and celibacy, which, he argued, "constitute a gross attempt at race suicide, leading to the complete extermination of the Negro race in the United States in one generation."[59] But the campaign against Father Divine came too late, for by 1936, the UNIA's founder was no match for Harlem's world-famous evangelist.

Further desertions to the Peace Mission movement included several well-known African Americans, notably the handsome, flamboyant Colonel Hubert Julian, one of Harlem's most romanticized figures, who joined the flock in 1934. A pioneering black aviator, Julian was famous for his safety invention, the "parachuttagraveprerisista," and his many daring aerial stunts in the skies over Harlem. He was known as the Black Eagle, and word of his achievements in a field that discriminated against African Americans spread worldwide. Julian became a favorite of the Ethiopian president Haile Selassie and, as a tribute to the African ruler, named his plane *Abyssinia*. His relationship with the Peace Mission movement began in 1933 when Father Divine contracted Julian's services. Julian claimed that during a perilous flight, Father Divine had appeared in his cockpit and piloted him safely home. Julian renamed his plane *Angelica* and pledged to further Father Divine's mission.[60]

Julian refused to surrender his sex life and racial pride, and remained on the ideological outskirts of the movement. Nevertheless, he was a valuable addition to the organization. Like other former members of the UNIA, he infused a degree of militancy into the movement and promoted Father Divine's appeal among more racially conscious blacks. His skills benefited the movement; he gave the angels flying lessons and provided Father Divine with free transportation. Julian's services contributed to Father Divine's public image of wealth and refinement, and by 1934, the newspapers ran stories on Father Divine's aerial tours in his private plane.[61]

The former Garveyites had a significant impact on the movement. With their experience in direct political action, they pushed Father Divine and his followers to campaign more actively for equal rights, the movement for the first time supporting black activist organizations. It was probably former Garveyites who brought the movement into the boycott of Blumstein's department store because of its discriminatory hiring practices. Organized by a former member of the UNIA, Sufi Abdul Hamid, the protest allowed Father Divine's angels to experiment with political crusades. Father Divine's pronouncements on politics and racism increased, and the movement developed programs to fight against discrimination in employment. Although Father Divine's theology remained fixed, the highly politicized Garveyites and De Mena's journalistic militancy refined his spiritual approach to social change and propelled the Peace Mission into direct action. His lasting reputation as a forebear of the civil-rights movement probably derives in part from the influence former Garveyites had over the direction of the Peace Mission movement.[62]

In 1934 the Peace Mission's annual Easter parade drew a larger crowd than in the previous two years. Supporters, angels, and curious onlookers crowded the sidewalks and filled the windows of buildings on the parade route. Droves of followers, singing and chanting, marched past with signs declaring Father Divine's divinity. Cars full of angels rolled slowly down the street; marching bands played uplifting tunes. Suddenly, in the midst of the celebration, a small plane appeared overhead. A hush fell over the crowd, the procession halted, and all faces turned skyward. It was the *Angelica*, carrying Father and Mother Divine and trailing a banner that read *Peace to the World—Father Divine's Mission*. The spectators burst into cheers and hurried to meet Father Divine at a mammoth Holy Communion banquet.[63]

Each media stunt brought more followers into the fold, expanding the movement's contacts and inching Father Divine toward increased political involvement. Beginning in spring 1934, the movement became fully engaged in a series of alliances with other organizations pushing for social change. Father Divine began to pledge tempered support to several groups that combated segregation and discrimination. Although these partnerships did not alter Peace Mission ideology, they continued to refine his spiritual approach to social change.[64]

One of the first and most prominent groups to ally with the Peace Mission movement was the Communist party. The only major American party openly committed to fighting for racial equality, the Communists hoped to incorporate oppressed black Americans into their struggle. By 1934, the Communists' United Front, a program aimed at affiliating the party with non-Communist groups on issues of common interest, spread into Harlem. The Communists courted many of Harlem's religious leaders and focused on Father Divine. Their commitment to equal rights and defense of the Scottsboro Nine impressed Father Divine, and he willingly supported many party activities.[65]

The Communists and the Peace Mission movement shared an uneasy and uncomfortable alliance, for they were united only by a common interest in civil rights; therefore, almost no interaction occurred between rank-and-file members of the two groups. Many American Communists balked at cooperation with a group they believed to be deceived by an oppressive religious doctrine. The advances made to Father Divine especially displeased black party members. While attending a Peace Mission banquet with a white colleague, the author and party member Richard Wright commented, "Oh whitey, deep down in your heart you think we're dirt—this confirms your opinion of us."[66]

According to FBI files, the Communist party expelled members vocally opposed to cooperation with Father Divine. Several ousted African Americans issued a publication, *Negro Voice*, that called Father Divine "the most dangerous faker that thus far has appeared in Black America." The group warned that Communists "will reap a whirlwind of destruction for playing with DIVINE. The Divine movement is nourished by the enemies of Communism. Its primary purpose is to annihilate the Communist influence in Harlem. It is not accidental that the Divine movement arose and became powerful precisely when the Communists were beginning to make marked headway in Harlem." Party leaders countered all criticism by assuring members that Father Divine and his followers would surrender their bizarre religious beliefs, convert to the party line, and join with the masses to overthrow their oppressors.[67]

But the Communists, deceiving themselves, had not come to terms with the dedication of Father Divine and his followers to Peace Mission theology. He was profoundly aware of the differences between his philosophy and communism, and sought to exploit the party to further his fight against racism and increase membership in his movement. He believed that a little proselytizing would draw Communists into his fold. In an interview with the Harlem Renaissance author Claude McKay, he explained his relationship with the party:

> Father Divine said that he was always willing to cooperate in his own way with the Communists or any group that was fighting for international Peace and emancipation of people throughout the world and against any form of segregation and racial discrimination. But what the Communists were trying to do he was actually doing by bringing people of different races and nations to live together and work in peace under his will. . . . He did not need the Communists or any other organization, but they needed him.[68]

Father Divine clearly saw the Communists as subordinates and in no way compromised his views to accommodate them. During a May Day parade in 1934, he and his followers composed the largest division in the procession and provided a striking contrast to the marching contingents of workers and party members. Surrounded by his disciples, he rode along the parade route in a "luxurious automobile with a chauffeur and a footman," an image that reinforced his passion for capitalism and bourgeois values.[69] In speeches and sermons Father Divine frequently attacked issues of central importance to the Communists with complete indifference to their reaction.

Opposing unions since his days in Baltimore, he lashed out against the labor movement and demanded that his followers surrender their union membership. "Practically all the different unions, they think they have dominion over people and force them to work or force them not to work, and yet give them nothing. I have RISEN TO PUT IT DOWN. . . . I will strike on them." Nevertheless, the Communists, desperate for black support, attributed Father Divine's utterances to ignorance and strove to maintain friendly relations with the Peace Mission. The strained alliance rested for several years on this unsteady foundation.[70]

Between June 1932 and the fall of 1934, the Peace Mission movement had undergone intense evolutionary change through its association with political groups. Yet Father Divine remained a reluctant political leader who retreated to vague spiritual solutions for complicated social and economic problems. "Now I am not a politician," he warned one banquet. "I don't want you to make me that."[71]

However, the inclusion of politics in his perspective made his theology more appealing to a larger sector of society, and the addition of new members added new dimensions to the Peace Mission movement. But each time the membership multiplied, the ministry changed. Responsibilities for his national following ultimately limited his activities. He was present for only a few Holy Communion banquets, which by this point were almost always restricted to followers and their guests. To compensate for his absence, angels played wire recordings of his sermons at banquets and in their restaurants.

No longer did the mild-mannered clergyman putter around his Sayville garden, tending his chickens and ducks. Now he dashed from mission to mission, serving banquets, dedicating extensions, and delivering sermons. In his Harlem home he spent most of his time in his third-floor office receiving visitors, giving interviews, and advising his disciples. Followers found it difficult to obtain appointments with him, and he relied more and more on his assistants.

Those lucky enough to meet with him discovered an impressive elegance that reinforced positivism. Several cages of canaries lined the stairway to his richly appointed office, and two stuffed doves on pedestals, inscribed *Peace* and *Love*, flanked his desk. A battery of secretaries surrounded him and recorded his every word. In the corner of his office stood a microphone connected to speakers placed throughout his headquarters, and when moved, he rose from his desk, flipped a switch, greeted angels with "Peace everybody," and delivered a few inspirational remarks.

The followers' dedication seemed unaffected by the increasing impersonality of his ministry. While a journalist was visiting the Peace Mission headquarters, Father Divine broadcast one of his impromptu messages, and an angel observed, "Isn't it wonderful? Lord God Almighty is up there sitting at his desk. Father Divine is God."[72]

7

As a Sample and as an Example

Then consider this Peace Mission Movement
from this angle of expression, in the name of
the INTERNATIONAL RIGHTEOUS GOVERNMENT
CONVENTION, as a Sample and as an Example,
to be the leaven to leaven the whole world
with RIGHTEOUSNESS, TRUTH, and JUSTICE. If I
can bring the millions into subjection, and
cause them to cease to commit sin, vice and
crime of every kind, do you not think this is
worth considering for you to use as an inter-
jection into your political parties.
Spoken Word, January 14, 1936

One afternoon in the fall of 1934, over one hundred of Father Divine's angels descended on the Santa Fe railroad station in downtown Los Angeles. As a train carrying passengers from the East
Coast pulled in, the songs and chants of the Peace Mission members echoed throughout the depot. Suddenly, a cheer went up from
the followers as a matronly woman stepped from one of the cars.
The fuss over the unassuming traveler must have perplexed onlookers, but to Father Divine's children she was no ordinary guest.
The woman at the center of attention was his most trusted emis-
sary, Faithful Mary, sent to inspect Peace Mission extensions in the
West.[1]

By 1934, Faithful Mary had become a celebrity in the movement.
Frequently appearing at Father Divine's side during banquets, her
spellbinding testimony impressed even dispassionate observers.
Claude McKay remarked, "When she spoke her face was full of a
warm illumination, like a beam of truth making credible the strange
atmosphere." In two years she had made miraculous progress and
lived an exemplary life. To reward her devotion, Father Divine
summoned her to New York and placed her in charge of a large
mission. Within a short time, Faithful Mary transformed a dilapi-

dated Turkish bath into a refuge for homeless women and single mothers. With her sharp entrepreneurial sense, Faithful Mary quickly expanded her undertakings and opened a restaurant, a market, a dress store, and a coal business. For the angels, her amazing conversion and subsequent success validated their leader's ties to divinity. Father Divine hoped the California children would benefit from her example and her keen organizational abilities.[2]

Faithful Mary's tour of Los Angeles extensions revealed that the California children had progressed quite well alone. While in most Peace Mission outposts black and white disciples continued to worship separately, by 1934 the Los Angeles membership had surmounted racial lines and class barriers. The most striking attempt to cement the relationship between black and white angels came with the purchase of the Dunbar Hotel. Built by a black dentist in 1928, the Dunbar was the only hotel in Los Angeles that accommodated African Americans. The Dunbar offered first-class service and lodging, and many African-American entertainers, leaders, and celebrities stayed there. In the summer of 1934, angels transformed this showplace into another multiracial colony in Father Divine's kingdom. The hundred-room hotel became a hostel for black and white Peace Mission members, and the children used its large dining room for Holy Communion banquets and extensive office space for Peace Mission activities.[3]

The large number of wealthy and progressive followers in the Los Angeles area promoted racial unification and the expansion of the movement. A significant number of wealthy Beverly Hills matrons, attracted by Father Divine's business-oriented spiritualism, had followed Sister Betty into the fold. One of the most important additions to the Los Angeles branch was Florence Wuest Hunt, a former Christian Scientist and heiress to a dairy fortune. She and several other prosperous Angelenos financed many of the local chapter's projects. Their vast monetary resources brought black and white angels together in numerous business endeavors and forced disciples to overcome segregation. Affluent angels contributed their talents as well as their money to the organization. Hunt's two sons, John and Warner, who ran an advertising agency, also joined the movement and used their promotional skills to publicize it. A frenzy of activity ensued, making the Los Angeles branch the most active extension of the movement.[4]

In October 1934, disciples working out of the Dunbar Hotel published the first edition of the *Spoken Word: The Positive Magazine,* which was printed by the local African-American newspaper, the *California Eagle.* The editorial staff distributed the first issues free and charged five cents a copy for subsequent editions.[5] Although the *Spoken Word* stated it was not Father Divine's official organ, the magazine promoted his teachings. A.D.F.D. followed the date on each copy—"Anno Domini Father Divine." The front page carried a picture of the Peace Mission's founder with the caption "AND GOD SAID: LET THERE BE LIGHT AND THERE WAS LIGHT—AND GOD SAW THE LIGHT THAT IT WAS GOOD—AND THE WORD WAS WITH GOD AND THE WORD WAS GOOD—AND THE WORD WAS MADE FLESH." Along with Father Divine's messages, the publication included Peace Mission news and songs dedicated to Father Divine set to the tunes of popular or sacred music. The *Spoken Word* also contained articles on scientific curiosities, positive thinking, and religious affairs. Advertisements were scattered throughout, many emblazoned with *I Thank You Father* in bold letters.[6]

The *Spoken Word* was an important contribution to the Peace Mission movement, for previous journalistic endeavors had proved disappointing. Suffering from financial insecurity, the *Reporter* and the *Voice* had folded, and the *Light* appeared only sporadically. Plagued by insufficient funding and unresolvable ideological differences with Peace Mission theology, De Mena discontinued her support of Father Divine's movement and transformed the *World Echo* into the *Ethiopian World.* The *New York News* had a stable circulation but was available only in New York. In contrast, the *Spoken Word* came out regularly and reached a national audience, its success deriving from the soundness of its financial backing and the freshness of the operation. In the first six months of publication, the *Spoken Word* expanded its circulation from five thousand to ten thousand.[7]

The magazine differed significantly from the other periodicals showcasing the movement. In addition to chronicling Peace Mission activities, it covered local, state, and national politics. The editors conceived of the *Spoken Word* as a religious and political paper dedicated to "liberal truth and thought."[8] Most articles included a critical assessment of the social, economic, and political climate of the depression-ridden United States. The staff ran features on race relations and in support of antilynching legislation. Frequently the paper attacked the Roosevelt administration and New Deal policies: "If man can imagine a dole system and give it being, why can't men envision a cooperative state where wealth is created for use and not for hording. . . . A revamped mental attitude is needed. Visualize the good and the positive that you visualize must come into expression." During local and state electoral campaigns, the *Spoken Word* served as a forum for political debate, and many candidates advertised in its pages.[9]

Despite its radical ring, the *Spoken Word* represented little ideological deviation from Father Divine's social, political, and economic polemics. The editors envisioned a state based on collective enterprise where workers labored in cooperatives and divided the profits evenly.[10] In one issue, a commentator called for a "share [of the] opportunity" over a "share of the wealth."[11] The editors did not reject capitalism but called for a renovation of the American economic system: "'Rugged individualism' of the super greed type, (the present brand of capitalism), is dying; the reward of every man according to his several abilities and the function of hiring a man may conceivably find a place in the new state. Capitalism, in its inherent sense, should not be confused with stifling special privilege."[12] They believed that if the government repealed legislation that favored the elite and promoted racism, the standard of living for all Americans would rise through unfettered competition and hard work.

Basically, the only difference between Father Divine and his West Coast followers was focus. Between 1932 and 1934, he had become more directly involved in worldly affairs, especially in campaigns against discrimination. Although he had evolved into an effective social critic, his blueprint for secular change remained vague and spiritually restricted. The *Spoken Word* articulated his theology through an organized program for the revitalization of American society.

It is not surprising that the California angels displayed a preoccupation with politics. During the depression, California emerged as a hotbed of political activism, with several leaders proposing alternatives to the New Deal. Dr. Francis Townsend of Long Beach advocated a pension plan that would increase taxes on businesses and, from the revenue, pay $200 a month to senior citizens. Designed to redistribute the wealth and prime the economy, the Townsend Plan required pensioners to spend their allotments within thirty days. Socialist author and California resident Upton Sinclair offered another remedy. His End Poverty in California movement, known as EPIC, denounced social welfare and called for job programs that encouraged self-sufficiency among the unemployed. Sinclair agitated for the governmental purchase of closed factories and fallow farms, to be transformed into collective enterprises by jobless Americans.[13]

Caught up in the political fervor that swept the state, many members of the Peace Mission movement maintained ties with the numerous activist groups in California. The *Spoken Word* ran articles sympathetic to Townsend and Sinclair, and reported on the progress in both camps. EPIC received particularly supportive coverage, and the first edition of the *Spoken Word* featured an article by Sinclair. But the magazine most favored a movement that embraced both the Townsend Plan and EPIC—the Utopian Society of America.

Founded in Los Angeles in 1933, the Utopian Society was an interracial and "semi-secret" political alliance that endeavored to return America to "true" democracy. Members of the group enacted "cycle rituals" based on Masonic practices and designed to dramatize solutions to the depression. The Utopians rejected New Deal relief and devised a plan to pay American citizens a monthly allowance composed of their normal salary and an equal portion of aggregate national profits. Utopians envisioned an increase of employment "opportunities" that they believed would disseminate wealth equally among Americans. Although the works of the socialist utopian Edward Bellamy inspired the society's leaders, they denied radical leanings and considered the movement "liberal." The Utopians were patriots, proud that the organization's initials spelled USA. They wanted to redistribute capital by implementing "needed reforms in our economic structure through peaceful, legal and constitutional means." Several influential leaders of Father Divine's Los Angeles flock had been active Utopians and incorporated the language and philosophy of the society into the Peace Mission movement.[14]

In 1933, one of the founding members of the Utopians, Roy Owens, led the migration from the society to Father Divine's movement. Owens, who was white, became a frequent speaker at Los Angeles banquets and a contributor to the *Spoken Word*. According to Owens, the depression resulted from weaknesses in the banking system, which he insisted could be eradicated by complete governmental control of financial institutions.

Other Utopians followed Owens into the Peace Mission movement, each bringing a special expertise. A former priest in the Liberal Catholic Church, John Roine, who had written several articles on Utopianism for papers around the country, "threw away his robe" and joined Father Divine's flock. Born in Finland, Roine had connections in continental Europe and a strong interest in international affairs. Other defectors included Hugh MacBeth, an ex-Garveyite and former Los Angeles assistant district attorney. MacBeth, who had represented the Utopian Society in a voting-rights case before the state supreme court, offered his legal services to the movement and became an active leader in the Los Angeles branch.[15]

Former Utopians found the passage between the society and the Peace Mission fairly smooth, since the ideologies of the two organizations were compatible on several levels. Both groups shared a distaste for the New Deal and welfare programs without compromising their patriotism and trust in the Constitution. Furthermore, the society strove for integration and fought for antilynching and antidiscrimination legislation.

But the parallels extended beyond political matters. A cultish atmosphere surrounded the Utopian Society of America. After initiation, members assumed new names and participated in elaborate secret ceremonies. Many Utopians also exhibited interest in religious affairs, and the organization maintained a metaphysical auxiliary. The society's newspaper, the *Utopian News*, carried a column that explored Theosophy, Christian Science, and other variations of New Thought. An editor observed, "Many Theosophists are Utopians and the Utopian Movement obviously objectifies theosophical predications and expectations." Father Divine's organization furnished religiously inclined Utopians a familiar theology that contained political concepts resonant with their past affiliations.[16]

Father Divine also provided an appealing economic philosophy to the business-oriented members of the Utopian Society. The society originated from the classic fear of displacement by uncontrollable economic forces. Its official history identified the founders as "men who had prospered in prosperous times, but suffered reverse of fortune when the depression came." Several Utopians had solid ties to the business community. Hugh MacBeth invested in mining ventures and served on the board of directors for the Lower California Mexican Land and Development Company. In the 1910s, MacBeth and his business partners purchased over eight thousand acres in Baja California and attempted to sell plots to African Americans to build a black settlement. They had hoped to reap a sizable profit, but the onset of the depression halted the project. Utopians like MacBeth must have found validation in Father Divine's support of capitalism, for the clergyman's programs operated more effectively within the existing economic structure than the Utopians Society's proposals. Father Divine's revised capitalism assured individuals complete command of their lives through positive thinking and helped those threatened by the depression to combat feelings of helplessness.[17]

Despite Los Angeles's congenial atmosphere, Father Divine's followers encountered some opposition. In the midthirties a flyer appeared around the city:

> We want you to know that all various followers of Negro worshippers, including white women who give their physical bodies over to niggers, put themselves lower than the lowest criminals and traitors. Intelligent people of this day and age need not resort to Negro religious degradation and become religiously enslaved to any black sweet-smelling Negro, who perfectly symbolizes ignorance, darkness, corruption and the curse of God.

Such animosity reflected a national trend of increasing belligerence toward Father Divine and his ministry that was appearing even within the African-American community. Ralph Matthew's sympathy had turned to hostility, and in his column he charged that Father Divine was a freeloading charlatan. Concerned citizens and relatives of Peace Mission followers shared his sentiments and pleaded with local, state, and national agencies to take action against Father Divine.[18]

In New York City, where Father Divine's influence was strongest, the courts began vigorously to pursue complaints against the

Peace Mission movement. Police arrested angels and remanded them to Bellevue Hospital, where psychiatrists treated the followers for "depressive psychosis."[19] Authorities indicted Father Divine in an effort to curtail his activities and determine the extent of his personal wealth. The court charged him and Faithful Mary with the unlawful operation of a boardinghouse for children because neither had obtained the required permits. At the trial, Arthur Madison proved that none of the deeds to Peace Mission property bore Father Divine's name and contended that he was not responsible for activities carried out in followers' missions. Madison also argued that Faithful Mary's mission housed both mothers and their children, and therefore was exempt from city approval. The court ultimately acquitted the two defendants.

Despite the inconvenience of constant litigation, Father Divine's legal battles kept him in the public eye. Whenever he appeared in court, followers and sympathizers filled the streets, hoping for a glimpse of him. Articles on the mysterious clergyman and his movement appeared frequently in the papers, bringing more publicity. Emerging from tedious court sessions, he was engulfed by cheering crowds, and as he departed they ran behind his limousine shouting, "He's God, He's God."[20]

The increasingly complex legal entanglements and opposition failed to hinder expansion of the Peace Mission movement. The *Spoken Word*'s partial directory of extensions, which included followers' homes, businesses, missions, dormitories, and auditoriums, indicated that the movement continued to grow in size and wealth. In 1934, the Peace Mission movement claimed 72 extensions; the following year the number had risen to 134. According to the *Spoken Word*'s listings, many U.S. cities boasted at least one Peace Mission.[21]

By 1935, followers had opened extensions in Europe, Australia, Canada, and the West Indies. As in the United States, foreign outposts attracted former students and disciples of New Thought and mind-power. A former Christian Science practitioner, converted to Father Divine's teachings by Walter Lanyon's works, organized Peace Mission meetings in France. A hypnotist, Joseph Jacob Greutmann, founded the first Swiss extension.

Foreign branches, however, differed from their parent organization. With the exception of Canadian and West Indian followers, a majority of international disciples were white, and most angels in foreign countries did not organize businesses or missions. These disciples worshiped in private homes or rented halls, and focused more on Father Divine's theology than on secular activities. However, his international children proved as dedicated as their American brothers and sisters. Greutmann, in an interview with *Time* magazine, stated: "We worship Father Divine because he is the second incarnation of God. . . . We are all white but we think there should be no differences between human races. . . . It is just a symbol to mankind that God chose the body of a Negro when He came to earth this time."[22]

The expanding size and diversity of Father Divine's following induced further changes in his ministry. New converts asserted increasing influence over the direction of the Peace Mission and channeled the movement into new avenues. In Los Angeles, followers initiated political forums that attracted local activists, office seekers, and elected officials. To promote political awareness and participation, the Los Angeles meetings often included lectures on American history and government.

In the summer of 1935, at Father Divine's request, the *Spoken Word* relocated in New York City "where first hand news of Father Divine and his movement was more available." The move brought the Californians closer to their leader and incorporated these highly politicized disciples into the hierarchy of the movement. The assimilation of the *Spoken Word*'s staff into the movement's leadership altered the focus of the Peace Mission. These Los Angeles followers drew Father Divine further from the tactics of moral suasion and forced him into a new style of political evangelism.[23]

The *Spoken Word*'s staff arrived in Harlem to find that their coreligionists had launched a voter-registration drive. Over the previous year followers on the East Coast had broadened their activities and slowly become more political. But a single event shattered any remaining spiritual complacency in the movement. On the evening of March 19, 1935, a rumor circulated around Harlem that police had killed a black teenager they were holding in custody. Harlem residents took to the streets in protest, and later that night a riot broke out. The next morning, 4 people lay dead, over 100 had sustained injuries, and 121 Harlem residents were in jail. The community lay in ruins, and the authorities estimated property damage at over one million dollars. The Harlem riot of 1935 shocked followers of the Peace Mission movement and increased their desire for more direct political involvement.[24]

The editors of the *Spoken Word* harnessed the Peace Mission's growing political energy, encouraged further development, and funneled the angels' zeal into more structured campaigns. In July the movement held a massive voter-registration rally at Rockland Palace where Father Divine announced his intention "to make the laws through aldermen and Congressmen and Senators, just the same as I make laws through these Peace Missions of mine." Immediately, angels organized the Fighters for Righteous Government on Earth among Men, dedicated to registering disciples to vote. But the angels' enthusiasm quickly turned to frustration, for the election board rejected almost all applications from Peace Mission members. State law required that new voters pass a literacy test, and many of Father Divine's followers could barely read or write. The board also refused to register those who used spiritual names because the names were not legally verifiable.[25]

The leadership of the Peace Mission decided to fight and began maneuvering to place their brothers and sisters on election rolls. To overcome the literacy barrier, Father Divine urged followers to get an education. In response, adult angels packed New York City's night schools to capacity. In an effort to accommodate all of them, extensions opened private "Kingdom Schools" that taught courses in basic skills and American government. Father Divine's legal staff initiated suits against the election board and demanded that officials register followers under spiritual names. Between 1935 and 1936, the court several times granted, revoked, and again granted the right to vote under spiritual names. The movement had just begun its fight and, with the assistance of the West Coast disciples, pressed further into the political realm.[26]

The politicizing influence of the Los Angeles faction was seen most clearly in the 1936 International Divine Righteous Government Convention. A committee headed by Arthur Madison and composed of John Roine, the staff of the *Spoken Word*, and several other disciples organized the convention. The three-day affair in early January drew five thousand delegates from Peace Missions around the world. Although President Roosevelt, several governors, and Mayor La Guardia declined Father Divine's personal invitations, several representatives of the major parties, candidates for local office, and community leaders attended and addressed followers. The warm reception extended to speakers contrasted dramatically with the angels' indifference to O'Brien and La Guardia less than four years earlier.[27]

The Righteous Government Convention's major purpose was to draft a platform that incorporated Father Divine's teachings into a coherent political program. Records of the sessions and the agenda itself indicate that although Father Divine guided the delegates, followers wrote most of the platform. In the resulting International Righteous Government Platform, Peace Mission representatives framed their vision of the future within his teachings. "We are advocating RIGHTEOUSNESS, JUSTICE and TRUTH in every walk of life," the authors declared. "Therefore we request the cooperation of all governments in LEGALIZING these QUALITIES and the participation of all right-thinking people in Universalizing a RIGHTEOUS GOVERN-MENT."[28]

The convention climaxed at the last session as John Lamb read the final version of the platform to the delegates. The document contained four sections and a series of accompanying planks interspersed with quotations from Father Divine. The first section, "Principles," delineated convictions of Peace Mission members and presented Father Divine's teachings to the secular world. It called for strict guidelines on the union movement, an end to capital punishment, and the repeal of laws requiring the purchase of insurance. Several planks focused on the eradication of racism, demanding equal job opportunities and the elimination of racial terms. The authors called for "legislation to abolish lynching and outlaw members of lynch mobs in all states and countries." Under the influence of John Roine and the foreign delegates, the principles assumed an international tone. Alarmed by the events in Europe and Ethiopia, conventioneers called for the destruction of all weapons, commanded aggressive nations to evacuate occupied territories, and declared that followers would refuse to bear arms against another human being.[29]

The economics section recommended specific changes and exhibited the direct influence of Los Angeles disciples, echoing Father Divine's criticisms of the New Deal and, like the Utopians, championing "EQUAL DISTRIBUTION OF OPPORTUNITY; a chance for every man; plenty of work with good wages; prices reduced to a minimum, and all the advantages for the masses, we are now enjoying these things and we know they can be enjoyed by all."[30] The platform denounced FDR's crop-destruction policy and public assistance, and advocated an increase in work programs.

Some of Roy Owens's ideas appeared in the document, which endorsed the nationalization of the banking system and imposition of limitations on personal profits. Although Father Divine taught that affluence reflected a state of grace, he opposed excessive wealth gained through selfishness. With some encouragement by the California contingent, he had come to blame greed for the uneven distribution of capital in America, but he continued to preach that negative attitudes created dependency and poverty, and occasionally threatened to "cut out so much feeding of the unemployed." The Californians also introduced some of Sinclair's ideas into the platform, and one plan, recommending the collective operation of "idle plants," resembled EPIC in spirit and language. But the delegates espoused these radical proposals without abandoning capitalism or the work ethic.[31] For example, those workers involved in reopening factories would retain the profits and would "be paid a living wage until income exceeds expenses, then the wage scale [is] to be increased and maintained at as high a rate as conditions permit."[32]

Interestingly, the political and educational sections of the platform were relatively short. The political section contained only two planks—the direct election of all public officials and an end to political patronage in the Civil Service. The educational section called for the use of "peace" in place of "hello" and for immediate school desegregation.[33]

Hoping to gain a head start, Father Divine and his staff timed the convention to take place at the beginning of a presidential election year. The delegates aspired to more participation in the electoral process and expected to incorporate American political parties under Father Divine's direction. Peace Mission representatives repeatedly denied that the convention was an attempt to organize a third-party movement, and Father Divine pledged to support any presidential candidate who endorsed the entire Righteous Government Platform.[34]

While Peace Mission leaders welcomed the endorsement of any

party, the convention blatantly courted the Communists and anticipated absorbing the party into the movement. The Communists
had a similar ambition and sent two major party figures, Robert
Miner and James Ford, to the convention.[35] Despite obvious differences, shared interests continued to provide common ground for
the two groups. The delegates flattered the Communists by sprinkling Father Divine's praise of the party throughout the platform:
"The communist ideas must be endorsed—I mean to say some of
them. At the day of Pentecost, they had many things in common
did they not? . . . This is an abstract expression of the communistic
ideas, making all things in common, claiming nothing for yourself
as an individual."[36]

But Father Divine sought to incorporate the Communists on his
own terms. Although he defended them from attacks by conservative delegates, he was unafraid to challenge them. When Robert
Miner proclaimed the Communist party the "emancipator" of the
American people, Father Divine responded bluntly: "RIGHTEOUS-
NESS, JUSTICE and TRUTH—these Qualities I have brought into action for you. . . . I will lift the whole nation out of depression,
lacks, wants and limitations. Speaking of your freedom, you will
have your Emancipation for the Spirit of My Presence will give it
so freely according to the Scripture." Father Divine saw himself as
the sole liberator of the masses and declared to the delegates, "Now
you may shout the victory for I have it for you."[37]

He closed the convention with the prediction that American political parties would accept his platform. But despite the new secular dimension to his ministry, he held fast to his spiritual core,
seeing himself as primarily a religious figure, a perception shared
by his followers. Millennialism dominated his message in which
he declared that he fulfilled the prophecies of the Book of Revelation: "Therefore I can declare, 'You are in another Day.' "[38] As the
newsreels rolled, massive demonstrations broke out, and delegates
paraded around the floor chanting, "GOD—GOD—GOD."

Father Divine closed his remarks by assuring delegates that the
movement would triumph: "Even though all may not be legalized
we will take a stand for them, for I will spiritually and mentally
legalize them and command the Cosmic force of Nature to endorse
them. I thank you." Cheers and applause filled the hall, and Peninniah led the crowd in a song:

> Sing and Praise Him, Sing and Praise Him,
> Sing and Praise Him for the Glorious Work
>   He's done.
> Sing and Praise Him, Sing and Praise Him,
> Glory Hallelujah for the Work He has done.

Across the auditorium, the throng waved white handkerchiefs in unison, and Father Divine announced, "White handkerchiefs represent the Spirit of Peace, the Spirit of the Movement."[39]

As a final act, the convention established a Righteous Government department within the Peace Mission movement and recommended that each extension organize a branch. Following the example of the Los Angeles angels, followers around the country began to hold weekly forums exploring political matters. Most chapters launched voter-registration drives, offered public lectures on civics and government, and compiled studies on local elections, forwarding noteworthy information to Father Divine's headquarters. The New York City Peace Mission assumed responsibility for national affairs and dispensed reports to the extensions. Through the implementation of Righteous Government departments, the convention catapulted the entire movement into the political arena.[40]

Religion dominated even the movement's political undertakings. The *Spoken Word* described Righteous Government forums as a cross between "a praise meeting" and "an impromptu political meeting." In addition to committee reports and speeches from political figures and community representatives, the angels sang, testified, and sometimes banqueted during forums. The Righteous Government departments were educational and evangelical instruments, giving Peace Mission disciples an awareness of political issues and a taste for activism. However, Father Divine's followers saw the forums as primarily attempts to proselytize among the politicians and secure their support for the Righteous Government Platform.[41]

Although the Righteous Government departments converted few politicians to Father Divine's crusade, the forums increased the local communities' interest in and understanding of politics. Whereas the rigid structure and well-entrenched hierarchies of political parties shut out many Americans, the loose communalism of the Righteous Government forums invited participation from everyone in the neighborhood, regardless of race, class, or gender. The Righteous Government departments opened doors to African Americans and women, who assumed active roles and leadership positions. Furthermore, the platform was not a static document, and forum participants often discussed and recommended revisions. Several amendments and resolutions approved by Father Divine and the Righteous Government Committee in New York were added to the platform throughout 1936.[42]

Peace Mission members focused on new political horizons but did not neglect old projects. During 1936, the movement matured both politically and economically. The success of Peace Mission enterprises and the increasing number of wealthy converts provided a sound financial foundation. This security allowed angels to tackle even more elaborate investments.

In 1935, several of Father Divine's children pooled their money and purchased lots in Ulster County, New York. Followers continued to buy property in the region, and by the summer of 1936, the holdings, known as the Promised Land, were so extensive that Father Divine spent three full days touring the area. The Promised Land headquarters, located in a large mansion in Kingston, was reserved for the use of Father and Mother Divine. The followers owned property in Kingston and bought farms, houses, and small businesses in Krumville, Samsonville, Cherry Hill, Stone Ridge, and New Paltz. In High Falls, a former resort, the angels created an industrial village complete with hotel, gas station, grocery store, clothing factory, bakery, dormitories, and candy mill. The disciples in Saugerties founded an agricultural settlement named Hope Farm, which specialized in raising poultry.[43]

Peace Mission farms constituted the majority of the followers' undertakings in the Promised Land. The settlements were organized like the cooperative farms Father Divine had known as a child in Maryland. Often the entire Peace Mission community worked together, sharing labor and equipment. Nevertheless, individual collectives owned separate farms and retained the profits from their products. These rural cooperatives supplied New York City Peace Missions with inexpensive high-quality food and ultimately benefited the entire movement. The Promised Land also provided a refuge for city dwellers. An editor of the *Spoken Word* commented: "One wonders why the people in crowded cities don't spread out more and occupy the spaces on the plains, mountains and islands. One wonders why the rest of the world doesn't adopt the same leisurely way of doing things and have the same disregard for time. One should remember that in these areas of The Promised Land time practically ceases to exist." Weisbrot compared the Promised Land to the New Deal resettlement programs that attempted to relocate unemployed agricultural laborers on collective farms, using their expertise and skills.[44]

Father Divine delighted in the farms, for he believed that the land was highly spiritual. "This country," he said, "has been inspired and Graced with the honor of the Spirit, by Spiritual Revelations for years back." He frequently mentioned that upstate New York had fostered many American religious movements and was especially proud that the founder of the Shakers, Mother Ann Lee, had launched her American ministry from a neighboring region. His teachings and Shaker doctrine had much in common, and like other New Thought devotees, he considered Ann Lee a pioneer in the theology, in several messages hailing her as a courageous advocate of religious truth who gave the Promised Land a noble spiritual legacy.[45]

The amazing affluence of the Peace Mission movement, combined with Father Divine's move into the political realm, stimulated more hostility and a lot of curiosity. Capitalizing on the public's fascination with Father Divine, the advertising executive John Hoshor published a sensationalized biography, *God in a Rolls-Royce*, a racist and inaccurate exposé that fed the public's growing fear of the Peace Mission movement. Hoshor asserted that "around Savannah's darky town there are still negroes who remember" him when he was called George Baker.[46] According to Hoshor, Father Divine duped foolish and superstitious African Americans into supporting his lavish lifestyle, thanks to his charismatic personality and genius for self-promotion. Hoshor characterized the minister as a laughable con artist who double-talked his way out of tight situations. He contended that Father Divine maintained an extensive, mindless black following who remained dedicated regardless of the questionable activities carried out by their leader. Furthermore, Hoshor dangled an unsettling observation before the public: exploring the relationship between the movement and the Communists, he quoted an African-American editor who labeled

Father Divine's political theology "unsound and un-American." According to Hoshor, Father Divine's large and loyal following adhered to a subversive political ideology that threatened the American way of life.[47]

Hoshor's biography outraged members and friends of the movement. Optimistically, the staff of the *Spoken Word* insisted, "Glib lies about Father Divine and His altogether Christlike work can only enhance His mission and cheapen the lie-maker." Positive attitudes aside, the editors urged followers not to read Hoshor's book because it attempted to undermine Father Divine's influence.[48] Several members of the black press supported the *Spoken Word*'s allegations and charged that the biography was part of a conspiracy by government officials to destroy Father Divine's political power. Sympathetic African-American newspapers insinuated that powerful national politicians had backed Hoshor's work and encouraged the constant harassment of Peace Mission members by the courts. The *California Eagle* commented, "Now his enemies, fearing his power, are seeking his destruction and dethroning among his followers."[49]

By the summer of 1936, none of the major parties, including the Communists, had adopted the Righteous Government Platform. The movement's hopes for absorbing the Communist party had dimmed considerably. The party had finally realized that it could not dominate the maverick clergyman and retreated from the alliance. The disillusionment was mutual, and the movement willingly terminated relations with the Communists, its dissatisfaction linked to a general disenchantment with the party among Harlem blacks. Communist support for the New Deal during the 1936 presidential campaign induced several African-American coalitions, including the Peace Mission, to abandon the Popular Front. But Father Divine had grown impatient with the Communists' refusal to endorse the Righteous Government Platform and no longer pandered to the party's interests. After the fall of 1936, he occasionally hailed the progressivism of select components of Communist ideology but never again praised the party.[50]

The Righteous Government Platform received support from a few candidates for local and state office, but individual endorsements were insufficient, and Father Divine refused to back office seekers until their parties had officially embraced his program for political reform. By July, he had advised his flock to prepare to boycott the polls and ordered followers to "stay your hand until you get the command." In the meantime, politicians hesitated to commit to the Peace Mission's distinctive principles. Candidates remained unsure of the extent of Father Divine's influence and continued to frequent Righteous Government forums, appealing for angels' votes. Father Divine urged disciples to be ready in case at the last minute one of the parties accepted the platform.[51]

Flustered by the political world's reluctance to endorse the platform, Los Angeles followers decided to stage their own Righteous Government Convention to garner support in California. With Father Divine's approval, a committee of sixteen Angelenos, headed by John Roine and Hugh MacBeth, scheduled the convention for July 31 through August 2.[52]

Despite California's reputation as a "bright spot of progressive social advance," the convention's steering committee faced resistance from some sectors of the Los Angeles community. City officials, for example, purposely neglected to process the movement's application for a parade permit. But the white clergy presented by far the greatest threat; shortly before the convention, a local minister, P. E. Gardner, organized a drive to prohibit the followers from meeting at the Hollywood Bowl. Gardner alleged that the Peace Mission movement was a Soviet puppet and as evidence presented a 1936 edition of the *Spoken Word* that had reprinted the Communist party platform. John Roine responded that the journal had also published Democratic and Republican party platforms during that election year.[53]

California's Righteous Government Convention proved a success, with over five thousand followers and sympathizers attending. The closing event was a mass meeting at the Hollywood Bowl, where Hugh MacBeth, serving as master of ceremonies, warned those who opposed the movement: "If you think that the thing you are fighting is ordinary maudlin religious frenzy founded on ignorance, you are due for an awakening. Father Divine insists upon that highest intelligence, upon the highest of science, and upon the finest and best of everything for all people." Following his remarks, MacBeth called various dignitaries and political activists to the podium, eliciting from each speaker full support for the Righteous Government Platform and its principles. However, regardless of the endorsements made by several influential California politicians, the national parties remained reluctant to recognize the unconventional platform.[54]

In mid-September, in a final attempt to attract support for his platform, Father Divine organized a parade through the streets of Harlem to Madison Square, planning the procession as an exhibition of the movement's political strength. The parade began with thirty mounted disciples wearing green sashes declaring *Father Divine Is God*. Behind were three thousand angels marching or riding in cars. In his elegant limousine, Father Divine rode along the parade route "perched on the back seat in the Lindbergh welcome manner." At Madison Square, politicians addressed a large crowd, though they evaded Arthur Madison's request for a public endorsement of the movement's platform. Despite the *Spoken Word*'s warning that Father Divine controlled the votes of his following and many sympathetic African Americans, the politicians would not risk alienating the rest of their constituencies by approving the Peace Mission's radical proposals. In turn, Father Divine refused to rescind his order, and his angels in all parts of the nation stayed home on election day.[55]

Roosevelt's forces again triumphed without Father Divine's assistance. Initially, the *New York Times* reported that Harlem's polls, guarded by a battery of his most trusted angels, were deserted on election day. After examining election results, *Times* analysts determined that Harlem's turnout was not unusually low and that most black voters had ignored Father Divine's orders. Father Divine's following was small, the paper concluded, numbering only two thousand, and the diminutive minister wielded little power.[56]

Father Divine was unable to influence the 1936 election for many reasons. Contrary to the *Times*'s estimate, his core following in Harlem and the vicinity averaged between three and four thousand, but because a sizable portion of this group were children, aliens, and adults registered outside the city, his political strength in Harlem may have been meager. Still, he commanded respect and admiration among many Harlemites, and his appearances often drew from ten thousand to fifteen thousand. Mainstream political parties and candidates offered little to the African-American community, and those alienated by political neglect would seemingly have supported his boycott of the polls. But many of his supporters and disciples were uneducated, disfranchised by New York's literacy requirement. Since he appealed to many excluded from political participation anyway, gauging the size of his movement by his influence over votes gave an inaccurate impression that his following was small.[57]

Furthermore, dissemination of the movement nationally made determination of his influence and popularity difficult. The circulation of the *Spoken Word* suggested that the Peace Mission maintained at least thirty thousand followers and allies. But dispersion over a wide area weakened his political clout in any single region. Discriminatory voting requirements, especially in the South, prevented many African-American followers from voting and further reduced his political power.[58]

The disappointment of the election did not significantly erode the membership of the movement, the angels' confidence in Father Divine's leadership, or their interest in politics. To a degree, the Peace Mission's first excursion into political waters proved disillusioning. But the politically oriented Los Angeles followers made a permanent mark on the movement, and his disciples did not abandon their activism. Disciples continued to stump for the Peace Mission platform and hold regular Righteous Government meetings. Candidates and community leaders attended banquets and sought Father Divine's endorsement.

But between 1934 and 1936 the Peace Mission movement had reached its political zenith. A note of dissatisfaction prevailed in postelection activities, and at a Holy Communion banquet in late 1936 Father Divine gave a message that sounded more like earlier sermons:

> I have brought RIGHTEOUSNESS, TRUTH and JUSTICE as a platform among you, that the government of our present civilization, yea the governments of all governments, might recognize the Actual Presence of God through Righteousness. Nevertheless, such governments that are founded by the conscious-thinking, mortal-minded men, it is a matter of impossibility for them to establish a Righteous Government in reality.

Father Divine returned to preaching that Americans' problems resulted more from sinfulness than from internal political weaknesses. While he did not stop trying to persuade government officials to reconstruct society according to his guidelines, his remarks reflected little faith in politicians. But he remained confident and assured his flock that change would come—if not through the politicians then eventually through God's will.[59]

8

A Kingdom without a Spot or a Wrinkle

> We shall have a glorious Church—a Kingdom
> without a spot or a wrinkle. Now we do not
> wish to hear anyone getting up testifying if
> they are continually out of employment and
> will not earn a living and meet their daily obli-
> gations. You are not representatives of ME.
> You are not acceptable, testifying, sowing the
> seeds of poverty, the seed idea of poverty and
> discord among this people.
>
> *New Day*, June 2, 1938

Of all the California disciples, none appeared more zealous than Florence Hunt's son John Wuest Hunt. His immediate family had become immersed in Peace Mission doctrine and chosen new names symbolizing their commitment to Father Divine's teachings. Florence Hunt selected Mary Bird Tree; her younger son, Warner, John the Baptist. John Wuest Hunt adopted John the Revelator and plunged fanatically into Peace Mission activities.

During the summer of 1936, John the Revelator personally delivered the Righteous Government Platform to delegates at the Democratic Convention in New York City. With the help of his younger brother, he coordinated the publicity for California's Righteous Government Convention. He also assisted in the publication of the *Spoken Word* and Peace Mission literature. He designed an official seal for the movement bearing a picture of Father Divine in a pyramid surrounded by the slogan *Justice, Truth and Righteousness*. In January 1936, he filmed the International Righteous Government Convention and produced a color movie on Father Divine's ministry. In the fall, John the Revelator and another disciple, H. B. Smith, began touring the nation and screening the film for Peace Mission audiences.[1]

Before his conversion John the Revelator's life had been filled with hedonism and self-indulgence. In an open letter of confession, he described battling alcoholism, an insatiable sex drive, and venereal disease. He told in detail of drunken parties and infidelities that resulted in three failed marriages. But acute appendicitis and a brush with death drew John the Revelator to Father Divine's teachings and "quickened the Christ in my body." He testified, "I am now living the exact life that Jesus taught and lived." Hoping to bring others into the movement, he mailed seven hundred copies of his confession to friends, acquaintances, and public officials. One landed in the hands of the postmaster general, resulting in John the Revelator's conviction for distributing obscene literature through the mail and nine-day stay in Bellevue Hospital.[2]

The incident did not deter the fervent disciple. He proselytized eagerly among friends and associates, succeeded in converting a former girlfriend to the movement, and organized caravans of his expensive automobiles to carry Los Angeles followers east to meet Father Divine. In addition to financing Peace Mission activities, his family opened the doors of their impressive Beverly Hills home to disciples and frequently hosted Holy Communion banquets. John the Revelator's generous contributions and active involvement earned respect and admiration from his brothers and sisters in the movement. This six-foot, two-hundred-pound millionaire who seemed to lead the model life of a follower offered striking testimony to Father Divine's spiritual talents. Gregarious and flamboyant, he was an engaging speaker, and his story spellbound Peace Mission congregations. Soon many angels began to consider the fiercely devoted John the Revelator one of Father Divine's official spokesmen.[3]

The flexibility of Father Divine's leadership gave disciples a large degree of control and allowed John the Revelator to gain increasing power in the organization. But the loose structure of the Peace Mission and Father Divine's theology produced a situation in the West that seriously threatened the movement nationwide. Father Divine's teachings on God's inner presence enhanced every disciple's self-confidence, especially that of John the Revelator. Before long, the Beverly Hills resident began to believe that his spiritual development had outdistanced that of his fellow angels, that he was different from the rest of the children. And he was not alone in that conclusion.

On November 13, 1936, sixty members of the Los Angeles movement congregated in John the Revelator's home for a routine Holy Communion banquet. Well into the celebration, "vibrations" seized John the Revelator: "My arms went up first. I had hot and cold contractions of my muscles. I soared around and cried and then laughed. . . . I found myself laying on the floor. Then about twenty people around me got the vibrations and pretty soon they were all laying around, yelling 'The Lord! Shiloh! It's the Second Coming.' " John the Revelator retreated to an upstairs bedroom, and when he emerged a half hour later, the throng began to worship him. From the staircase, the millionaire flung over $10,000 in cash and watched happily as his guests scrambled for it.[4]

Word of the spectacular devotionals spread, and on subsequent evenings over two hundred people appeared at John the Revelator's home. He obliged and led the mob in noisy rituals. Finally his incensed neighbors, who included actor Lionel Barrymore, alerted the Beverly Hills police, who arrested John the Baptist, H. B. Smith (who had assumed the name Joseph), and Hunt, who now claimed to be "Jesus the Christ." At the ensuing trial, Hugh MacBeth's impassioned argument that the arrest violated freedom of worship failed, and the jury found the trio guilty of disturbing the peace.[5]

Confused over John the Revelator's status and suffering from what one follower termed "mental indigestion," angels appealed to Father Divine for comment. He avoided criticizing his wealthy supporter and explained to disciples that God could be found through many channels, but he cautioned followers against worshiping a single individual and reminded "those in the west" that he was the highest expression of God's spirit. Father Divine's diplomatic warning did not inhibit John the Revelator. Although he remained devoted to Father Divine's teachings, he still thought he held a special rank. Surrounded by a cadre of angels who hailed him as Jesus the Christ, he set out on a tour of Peace Missions in late 1936.[6]

On December 16, John the Revelator arrived at a Denver Peace Mission in his shiny new Packard, the Golden Chariot. Driven by his chauffeur, Ben Hur, the Golden Chariot carried his personal secretary, Agnes Gardner (Mary Bird), and his companions H. B. Smith and Betty Peters (Martha Tree). During a Holy Communion banquet, John the Revelator preached passionately before an audience that included Lee Jewett and his family. A former agricultural agent, Jewett had turned to Father Divine's teachings hoping to cure a painful and untreatable dental condition. John the Revelator's convincing testimony and his apparent possession of "divine grace" through Father Divine's theology impressed Jewett and his wife, Elizabeth. Regular participants in Denver Holy Communion banquets, the Jewetts were flattered when the West Coast disciple invited their seventeen-year-old daughter Delight for a ride in his luxurious automobile.[7]

The jaunt in John the Revelator's Packard turned into a spiritually charged outing. As the Golden Chariot rolled along the streets of Denver, the Revelator and his entourage sang and celebrated. Delight joined in and began to speak in tongues. Captivated by the pretty teenager, he renamed her Mary Dove and treated her to an $800 shopping spree at a local dress store. On returning to the Peace Mission, he informed the Jewetts of their daughter's outstanding religiosity and hinted that Delight would make a valuable addition to his personal staff. Whether John the Revelator obtained her parents' permission is unclear, but late that night he and his companions sped away from Denver with Delight.[8]

On the trip to California, John the Revelator renamed Delight Virgin Mary. According to Delight, the Californian and his associates constantly marveled at her pure spirituality and convinced her that she possessed holy powers. Arriving in Beverly Hills in a heady state, she willingly accepted John the Revelator's claims to divinity and his prophesy that as Virgin Mary she would by "immaculate conception" give birth to a "New Redeemer" in Hawaii.[9] He initiated sexual relations with the seventeen-year-old and cabled Father Divine a triumphant message: "What God has put together, let no man put asunder."[10]

Father Divine refused to tolerate this direct violation of his celibacy requirement and immediately telegraphed stern disapproval. He admonished the two for "indulging in the appearance of human affection" and insisted: "One cannot be My Disciple unless he is willing to deny all self-indulgence and direct his energy and ambition in a different direction, according to this great conversion, that the Mind and Devotion, Love and Attention might be directed and concentrated on the Fundamental." He chastised John

for calling himself Jesus and asserted, "I do not even call Myself
FATHER DIVINE; I call Myself only Rev. M. J. Divine."[11]

Despite appeals from his mother and the Jewetts to return Delight to Denver, John the Revelator packed the Virgin Mary into
his car and traveled to the Harlem headquarters, where Father Divine reprimanded and separated the couple, assigning Delight to a
collective farm in Kingston. John the Revelator later claimed that
before leaving for the Promised Land, Delight cornered him in his
car and attempted to seduce him. He maintained that he rejected
her advances and stated his intention to obey Father Divine's com-
mands.[12]

Lee and Elizabeth Jewett were frantic. The couple left their children with friends and journeyed to New York City hoping to locate
Delight. Father Divine graciously received the Jewetts, assured the
couple of their daughter's safety, and took them to Kingston. In
the Promised Land, Peace Mission members extended generous
hospitality to the Jewetts and provided the two with food and impressive accommodations. The angels insisted on treating the couple to an extensive tour of Promised Land properties. Concerned
primarily with her daughter and impatient with the overwhelming
attentiveness of the disciples, Elizabeth Jewett constantly implored
her hosts to take her to Delight.

Finally, late one night in a female dormitory, Elizabeth found
her daughter, and the reunion was a nightmare. Delight resisted
her mother's embrace, saying, "You mustn't touch me, Mother.
You're still in mortality. I'm in immortality. Remember I'm the Virgin Mary." She recounted her escapades with John the Revelator
and attempted to comfort her horrified mother: "I'm going to have
a child by Jesus. . . . He will be the Redeemer of the World."[13]

Elizabeth could not find Lee until the following evening at a
Holy Communion banquet. Outside the dining room she recounted Delight's story to her husband. Much to her amazement,
Lee showed no interest. The orderliness of the movement and the
success of the Promised Land farms had impressed Lee Jewett.
Aware of his agricultural expertise, Father Divine had offered Lee
a position as a manager of several farms. After a meeting with Father Divine and an apology from John the Revelator, Lee forgave
the wealthy Californian and began toying with the possibility of a
permanent commitment to the Peace Mission movement.[14]

Distressed by the influence Father Divine had asserted over her husband and her daughter, Elizabeth pressured Lee to leave the Peace Mission. Her pleas probably became more persuasive after Lee requested that Father Divine furnish a monetary settlement for the damage inflicted on Delight. Father Divine's attorney, Nathan Kranzler, conducted an in-house investigation of the incident and ultimately refused to pay the Jewetts. The lawyer suggested that the family return to Denver and keep the affair quiet, stating, "The last thing we want in this matter is publicity."[15]

But publicity was exactly what the Peace Mission movement got. The Jewetts interpreted Father Divine's unwillingness to furnish financial restitution as a betrayal, gathered up Delight, and fled to New York City. In March 1937, the Jewetts offered Delight's story to the highest bidder among the New York papers. William Randolph Hearst's *New York Evening Journal*, long a foe of the Peace Mission movement, jumped at the chance. The paper provided Delight with an attorney, William Lesselbaum, and promised to pay Lee Jewett $100 a week until the case was resolved.[16]

The *New York Evening Journal* exploited the Delight Jewett affair to its fullest. Recognizing that the potential damage extended beyond a simple scandal, Hearst reporter J. D. Kerkhoff initially withheld the story from the public and alerted the FBI. After investigating the case, the bureau issued an arrest warrant for John Wuest Hunt, H. B. Smith, Agnes Gardner, and Betty Peters, charging them with violation of the Mann Act, which prohibits the transportation of minors across state lines for immoral purposes.[17]

The nationwide manhunt for John the Revelator, his dramatic surrender, and the subsequent trial resulted in a barrage of bad press for the Peace Mission movement. The national media tantalized the public with the horrifying story of the millionaire-cultist playboy who believed he was Christ and his seduction of the innocent young Delight Jewett. Major papers and magazines pictured the cheery Denver teenager embracing her sister, riding a bicycle, and practicing the piano. The portrayal of Delight directly contrasted with the characterization of John the Revelator as an obese, demented aide of the notorious Father Divine. Rumors circulated that Father Divine gave his male assistants their choice of female angels for sexual purposes, and shortly after the Jewett story broke, two former female disciples charged that Father Divine had forced them to provide sex to his closest advisers.[18]

Despite the fearsome behavior ascribed to the Peace Mission

movement, the Los Angeles trial of John the Revelator had periods of levity. The courtroom observers tittered as the case unfolded and the cast of unusually named characters testified. Delight's testimony brought guffaws from the audience and bemused responses from the judge.

> "Mr. Hunt was Jesus the Christ. I was the Virgin Mary and I was to have my New Redeemer in Honolulu, but they didn't tell me when," the girl testified.
> "Who was to be the Holy Ghost?" interrupted Judge Yankwich.[19]

Even Hugh MacBeth, serving as John the Revelator's attorney, unwittingly provided comic relief when he interrupted the proceedings, asking, "Is the Immaculate Conception, as interpreted in theology, a violation of the Mann Act, your Honor?" However, the courtroom grew quiet as Delight tearfully described being raped by the Revelator. Resolutely, Delight stated her desire to expose Father Divine's cult to prevent others from suffering a similar fate under the black messiah and his disciples.[20]

Once on the witness stand, the Revelator frankly admitted his guilt. In front of the judge and jury, he confessed the most intimate details of his exploits with the Denver teenager. Hugh MacBeth explained to the shocked courtroom that Father Divine demanded truthfulness from his followers and had instructed his disciple to confess. The attorney declared that John the Revelator would willingly accept punishment for his crimes. The jury found him guilty and acquitted his codefendants.[21]

Judge Yankwich sentenced John the Revelator to three years in prison. He assumed a new name, the Prodigal Son, and remained a devoted follower, vowing to spread the news of Father Divine among his fellow inmates and announcing plans to issue a "prison paper." Although some speculated that Father Divine would inflict misfortune on the judge, he publicly approved of Yankwich's sentence. In a letter to John the Revelator, he stated that it was "a consolation to know the court's sentence was not as severe as it might have been and that it was lenient by My Spirit with Mercy and compassion under the violation of the law of both God and man."[22]

While the movement had long withstood accusations of sexual impropriety, the Delight Jewett case brought the issue to the fore.

The trial and accompanying publicity reinforced the public's perception of the movement as a fanatical cult that brainwashed gullible victims. Elizabeth Jewett's account of Father Divine's hypnotic control of her husband and daughter appeared to prove that the diminutive clergyman practiced brutal mesmerism. Father Divine's powers had always been suspicious, but as the facts surrounding Delight Jewett's seduction emerged, his influence appeared even more sinister, the Prodigal Son's crimes revealing that Father Divine controlled a visible sector of the white community. Reverend Divine's harmful influence no longer terrorized only the black community but fundamentally threatened white America.[23]

After the Delight Jewett affair, authorities stepped up their surveillance of Peace Mission activities, which with media coverage spawned increased attacks on the movement. New York State audited the movement, intending to extract taxes from its enigmatic leader. An angry Marylander whose car had been hit by a Peace Mission bus pressured the movement for a monetary settlement through the attorney William Lesselbaum. Acting on a tip that Peace Mission stores sold "bootleg" coal, New York authorities initiated a probe into followers' businesses. Police raided one extension, arresting an angel for possession of narcotics. The tabloids reported the death of Little Morning Star, whose parents, followers of Father Divine, refused medical attention for the tubercular thirteen-year-old. In Kingston, arsonists set fire to Peace Mission property. Even the Harlem community, previously a safe haven for Father Divine and his angels, turned against the movement. Puerto Rican residents, resentful of Father Divine's wealth and claims of divinity, ambushed and beat followers on Harlem streets. Residents became so hostile that he assigned bodyguards to escort his disciples around the neighborhood.[24]

In the midst of this chaos, Peninniah fell ill during a visit to the Promised Land. Aides secretly whisked her to a Kingston hospital and registered her under a false name. As she lay dying of kidney and heart failure, Father Divine continued his ministerial duties without acknowledging her illness, briefly visiting her only once. The press, doggedly pursuing the movement, tracked down Mother Divine, publicized her illness, and castigated Father Divine for his negligence. In the light of his teachings on immortality, his wife's illness threatened the credibility of his theology. However, Peninniah, remained positive. According to a journalist who allegedly interviewed her in the hospital, Peninniah denied that she felt any pain or that she was dying: "Death is the last sin that we must overcome, Father says. It is a sin to be overcome and it is the last one for us to conquer. Some of us cannot always do it. Some of us don't have faith enough, but I have faith in my heart." Faced with death, Peninniah was Father Divine's most loyal disciple, fighting death alone in the hospital.[25]

Despite Father Divine's emphasis on patience, peacefulness, and positive thinking, the constant crises that rocked the movement angered and frustrated many of the angels. Tension finally peaked on April 20, 1937, in a violent outburst. That evening, as Father Divine finished his message, two process servers, Paul Camora and Harry Green, tried to serve the clergyman a summons. According to Camora and Green, Father Divine cried, "Go get him." The throng converged on the men, beating and kicking them. During the ensuing melee, someone in the congregation stabbed Green. The angels threw the two process servers out the front door, and as Green lay bleeding, Father Divine vanished.[26]

While he was in hiding, another disaster shook his following. With the Peace Mission at its weakest point, Faithful Mary defected. To those close to the movement, Faithful Mary's bolt was no surprise. The relationship between Father Divine and his premier angel had soured over a dispute concerning an Ohio follower, William Gottlieb. After joining the movement, Gottlieb offered Father Divine a cash contribution of almost $10,000, but the clergyman rejected Gottlieb's gift. Eventually Gottlieb met Faithful Mary, who persuaded him to donate his money to her Promised Land enterprises. She invested about $5,000 and deposited the rest in her personal bank account. The transaction, which greatly benefited Faithful Mary, angered Father Divine. He insisted that Faithful Mary immediately return Gottlieb's money. On her refusal, he demanded that she surrender her property to her coworkers and reassigned her to kitchen duty in the Promised Land.

Once Father Divine had disappeared, Faithful Mary took over High Falls, denounced her pastor as "just a damned man," and started a rival sect. Empowered by many of the factors that allowed John the Revelator to assume leadership, Faithful Mary drew several former angels into her Universal Light movement.[27]

In the meantime, police had begun an eight-state search for Father Divine. The authorities raided Peace Missions, roughed up disciples, and eventually discovered the minister hiding behind a furnace in the basement of a Connecticut extension, purportedly attempting to "invisibilize" himself.[28] A court swiftly extradited him to New York City, and as rumors of his arrest spread, a massive crowd filled the streets around police headquarters. Hearst Metrotone news captured the scene on film, and in theaters across the nation Americans watched Father Divine's disciples wave white handkerchiefs and heard them sing, "Glory, glory, hallelujah! Our God is in our land."[29]

Immediately after his release from jail, Father Divine ordered Faithful Mary out of High Falls. While the deed bore only her name, several followers had collectively purchased and renovated the property. But Faithful Mary protested that High Falls belonged to her and ignored Father Divine. Her insolence and continued occupation of the Promised Land promoted hostility between her followers and Father Divine's. One afternoon Faithful Mary's followers encountered several angels on a Harlem street. Priscilla Paul, one of Father Divine's most ardent disciples, grabbed one of Faithful Mary's followers, Humility Consolation, pulled her into a yard, and began beating her. Some of Faithful Mary's supporters came to Consolation's assistance, inducing several more angels to join the fray. When the dust cleared, four of Faithful Mary's followers had sustained injuries, Consolation suffering a dislocated shoulder, broken ribs, and numerous cuts.[30]

Faithful Mary continued her assault on Father Divine with a diatribe entitled *"God" He's Just a Natural Man* in which she revealed the "evil" operations of the Peace Mission. She claimed that he maintained a "holy Treasury" and extracted weekly payments from all extensions and businesses. The former angel portrayed him as a racketeer who preyed on his disciples to sustain his luxurious lifestyle. Although Faithful Mary's primary purpose was to alert everyone to Father Divine's detrimental effect on his disciples, much of the book directly addressed the black community. She equated followers' living and working conditions with slavery, alleging that followers toiled long hours with insufficient food and no pay.[31]

Probably nothing in Faithful Mary's exposé attracted more attention than her allegations of sexual lasciviousness in the movement. In vivid terms, she described late-night orgies involving large groups of angels. She insisted that homosexuality was common in sexually segregated quarters and was especially prevalent among female followers. According to the former disciple, Father Divine was by far the most licentious. Dubbing him the "Rasputin of America," she contended that he coaxed young female followers into sexual intercourse.[32] She claimed that he told his pretty proselytes that sex with him was a blessing from God. Faithful Mary asserted that she had been a target of his voracious sexual desire, recalling that during one banquet, "this man who was being idolized as 'God' had his legs around mine and was feeling the legs of his secretary sitting beside him."[33]

Faithful Mary's attack on Father Divine went beyond mudslinging. The former angel rejected his teachings and formulated her own theology. Since childhood, religion had been a central component of her life. Her father was a Baptist minister, and as an adult, she attended the Sanctified Church where, she claimed, she first learned of New Thought. After witnessing the abuse of power in the Peace Mission movement, she reverted to the belief that God's spirit throve equally in all persons. She declared that through her doctrine and social relief, she hoped to uplift all of humanity.[34]

In choosing to part from the Peace Mission movement, Faithful Mary had encouragement from Father Divine's most hostile critics. Later she contended that the Hearst press had backed her defection, a claim supported by her close association with the Hearst lawyer William Lesselbaum. But Hearst was not alone in his support of her desertion. A longtime Peace Mission nemesis, the *New York Amsterdam News,* also championed the Universal Light movement. Faithful Mary had no formal education, and the *News* guided the preparation of her book, sprinkling in quotes from Egyptologists, historians, and British poets. Though Father Divine's enemies exploited his malcontent former disciple, Faithful Mary herself was savvy and to an extent used Father Divine's adversaries to her advantage. She cunningly derived extensive financial support from Peace Mission opponents and ample free publicity that advanced her wealth and notoriety.[35]

Of all the catastrophes of 1937, the most damaging in the long term was initially the least spectacular. In May, Verinda Brown, the Long Island domestic invited into Father Divine's fold by Priscilla Paul, filed a lawsuit against the movement, demanding $4,476 from Father Divine. Verinda had been an active and dedicated member of the Peace Mission movement, and her husband, Thomas, was one of the angels arrested in Sayville in November 1931. Throughout the couple's association with the movement, they supplied Father Divine with linens, furniture, and expensive suits. Verinda claimed that fearing the collapse of commercial banks, the couple had deposited their life savings with Father Divine. Wishing to live together again as man and wife, the Browns left the movement in 1935, but when they tried to withdraw their savings, Father Divine flatly refused to remunerate his former angels.[36]

It was probably no coincidence that Lesselbaum represented Verinda Brown in her attempt to recover her savings. Brown was also supported by Father Divine's longtime archrival Bishop Lawson. The suit implicated Father Divine and eighty angels—including John Lamb, Arthur Madison, Nathan Kranzler, and Mary Bird Tree—in deceptive financial practices. Not surprisingly, Lesselbaum's star witness was Faithful Mary. She repeated her allegations of Father Divine's secret repository and testified that she had acted as a collection agent. Faithful Mary claimed that the minister pooled followers' money and personally dictated redistribution of funds for the purchase of businesses and property.[37]

Faithful Mary's testimony, reinforced by Lesselbaum's compelling arguments, convinced the court that Father Divine's financial affairs demanded close scrutiny. The court ruled that he had fraudulently collected money and misappropriated the organization's funds. The judge required the Peace Mission movement to pay Verinda Brown. The decision left Father Divine open to lawsuits, and several former followers, including Colonel Hubert Julian, attempted to extract money from the movement. Verinda Brown's case and the additional claims threatened the financial stability of the movement. Father Divine's legal staff immediately challenged the court's decision and began maneuvers to avoid paying Verinda Brown.[38]

Despite a history of conflict and rejection, members of the movement had never encountered the concentrated hostility they experienced in 1937. Internal factionalism left the movement vulnerable to mounting opposition. The expanding size of the movement had forced Father Divine to delegate more authority to his disciples, and his distaste for institutional religion, his reluctance to establish a church, and his optimistic nature led him to surrender too much power to underlings. The controversies created by John the Revelator and Faithful Mary induced some disciples to question their faith and weakened group solidarity. In many ways, the dissension within the movement in 1937 resembled the hazards encountered by Father Jehovia in 1912.

With the appearance of discord in the Peace Mission movement, the time was ripe for attack. In 1937 the movement's long-divided enemies united in a powerful coalition dedicated to undermining his ministry. Foremost among the black and white critics of the Peace Mission was William Randolph Hearst. With his extensive resources and powerful influence, Hearst provided the glue that bonded the enemies of the Peace Mission movement.

Several factors motivated Hearst's attack on Father Divine and the movement, above all Hearst's desire to sell newspapers. The father of yellow journalism, Hearst hunted down provocative stories to boost readership. Before 1937, his editors provided limited coverage of Peace Mission scandals, but John the Revelator's misconduct yielded a perfect target for a reporter's contemptuous and exploitative pen. Undoubtedly the *New York Evening Journal* hoped to increase circulation with the titillating tale of the deflowering of Delight Jewett.[39]

Hearst also had a political bone to pick with Los Angeles Peace Mission followers. The Utopian Society frequently attacked Hearst, and former Utopians carried their deep dislike for him into the Peace Mission movement. Hearst's deceptive actions during the 1934 gubernatorial campaign between conservative candidate Frank Merriam and Upton Sinclair especially exasperated the angels. With the help of Hearst newsreels showing thousands of hoboes drawn to California by EPIC, Merriam trounced Sinclair. The *Spoken Word* attacked Hearst and contended that the exclusion of the unemployed from California violated their constitutional rights.

Throughout the thirties, Hearst and the Peace Mission movement remained politically polarized. Hearst's links to right-wing organizations, his personal interview with Adolf Hitler, his sympathy with the Nazi regime, and his constant attacks on communism earned the publisher a reputation as a Fascist. Furthermore,

Hearst's publications exhibited candid racism. The *Spoken Word* took thinly veiled shots at Hearst, and that provocation, with the scandals surrounding the movement, drove him to take action. Often Hearst personally coordinated campaigns to defame individuals or organizations with whom he disagreed. Father Divine and his seemingly liberal political ideology furnished a perfect mark for Hearst, who pursued him in print and in court.[40]

By early 1938, the Peace Mission movement had begun to rebound from the crises of the previous year. Its enemies concentrated on the Brown case and abandoned other campaigns against Father Divine, the attacks on the movement becoming less severe and less frequent. Several positive signs reinforced the angels' faith and Father Divine's claim to divinity.

Most significant and reassuring was Mother Divine's recovery. The doctors had diagnosed her ailment as terminal, but by early 1938, Peninniah had regained her health and resumed her duties in the Peace Mission movement. The followers were relieved to see Peninniah back at the banquet table. Father Divine heralded her recovery as a great victory, a demonstration of the power of faith.

> I thought of how glorious it was for you . . . to have the privilege of observing MOTHER in perfect health—not only 100 percent healthy but ten thousand (10,000) percent healthy. . . . It is a blessing to you and to others as much as it is to her as a person. There are those who would have doubted the Majesty of My Presence, had I not brought her out of the condition under which she allowed herself to be considered. . . . I gave victory over sickness and over sorrow and over death.

While he rejoiced at his wife's return, he sternly reminded all followers, including his devoted wife, that conquering death required unquestioning acceptance of "GOD's actual presence."[41]

The movement's increasing wealth also elevated the spirits and confidence of its members. The attempts to destroy the movement's financial base had little impact on Peace Mission assets. Father Divine's children around the nation acquired more property and businesses. In the Northeast, angels bought additional property in Ulster County and expanded their colonies in the Promised Land.[42]

The Peace Mission movement scored an impressive financial coup with the purchase of Krum Elbow, an elegant country manor directly across the Hudson River from the Hyde Park mansion of President Franklin Roosevelt. The movement bought the expansive estate for almost $50,000 from Howland Spencer. According to Weisbrot, after an extensive feud over politics and property lines, Spencer sought to embarrass FDR by selling his estate to the black minister. The acquisition of Krum Elbow attracted the attention of the national media,[43] Hearst newsreels showing a beaming Father Divine, accompanied by his robust wife, strolling around the grounds of the estate. On the opening day, over 2,500 angels toured Krum Elbow and in the evening held a banquet. The newsreel commentator quipped, "Hyde Park has witnessed many strange sights in its day, but never before Heaven on the Hudson."[44]

The acquisition of Krum Elbow climaxed Father Divine's long battle against residential segregation. Since his early years in Baltimore he had tried to live in predominantly white areas. He continued to maintain his headquarters in Harlem but spent much time at the Hudson manor. For some African Americans seeking to break out of the bondage of segregation, the purchase of Krum Elbow increased respect for Father Divine and his movement. In a time when legal and social codes excluded blacks from white neighborhoods, Father Divine made his home in one of the country's finest white communities and was a neighbor of the president of the United States.[45]

Although he refused to comment openly on his new neighbor, Roosevelt exploited the situation to his advantage. The president walked a thin line between two major constituencies—African Americans and southern whites. His refusal to support antilynching legislation alienated many African Americans. By remaining silent on the affair, Roosevelt probably hoped to recoup losses among black voters. But in his off-the-record comments at a press conference, his assessment of the situation was clear. He rationalized that the distance between his house and Krum Elbow was so great that Father Divine was not really his neighbor at all, these remarks implying that he was uncomfortable with the presence of African Americans in the neighborhood.[46]

While angels celebrated the acquisition of Krum Elbow, they also rejoiced at the fall of one of Father Divine's most damaging critics. Late in 1938 a broken figure appeared at his door—Faithful Mary humbly returning to the fold. During the previous year Faithful

Mary had dabbled in a variety of projects. With the help of Father Divine's opponents, she had expanded the Universal Light movement from High Falls into Harlem. Perpetually lured to the business world, Faithful Mary tried to expand her extensive enterprises. Eventually she made her way to Hollywood, and with some assistance from Hearst's connections in the movie industry, embarked on a film career. The rotund sect leader starred in *Two-Gun Man from Harlem*, a musical produced for African-American audiences by Merit Pictures.[47]

Soon her film career stalled, and her business endeavors failed. Membership in the Universal Light movement, never large, dwindled. She claimed that with encouragement from Hearst's associates, she began drinking again and using drugs. After a near-fatal automobile accident, she began to fear that her rejection of Father Divine's teachings had brought misfortune. A vision of Father Divine haunted her everywhere: "I was running through a barbed wire fence and my dress caught and before I could snatch it from the wire, Father came through the fence with his head looking right at me. And when I went to bring my arms down, Father had come suddenly under my arm."

Father Divine's tormenting spirit drove Faithful Mary to grovel for forgiveness. Triumphantly, the minister received his wayward angel back into his spiritual family. At banquets she confessed her sins and retracted her allegations about the movement. Although Father Divine absolved Faithful Mary, he refused to give her any power in the movement and assigned her to a modest mission in Newark.[48]

By the end of 1938, he had stabilized the movement and recovered almost completely from the upheavals of 1937. But previous crises had left their mark. The struggles within the movement and battles with opponents gave a sharpness to his comments, the most hostile ones directed at Hearst:

Then I say, fret not yourselves because the workers of iniquity, FOR THEY SHALL BE CUT OFF! As I quite often say, I must say again; it has long since been declared and I declare the same, "The pen is mightier than the sword." Hearst used his pen! He thought he could slay ME and all the Works of RIGHTEOUSNESS that had been established by your SAVIOR; but it was, and it still remains, A MATTER OF IMPOSSIBILITY!

Although Hearst had not significantly reduced the number of Father Divine's core followers, the newspaper magnate's campaign sapped external support. Friends of the movement not fully committed to Father Divine's teachings slowly began to drift away. Father Divine lashed out at Hearst, aware that the dwindling support from fringe sectors left his ministry more open to attack.[49]

Verinda Brown's lawsuit, the fear of more internal dissension, and the weakening of the protective shield of public support compelled him to take decisive action. To defend his ministry, he restructured the Peace Mission movement. Before the crisis he had repeatedly refused to establish a church; he preferred to conduct his ministry in an itinerant fashion and saw his movement as a protest against the inadequacies of institutional religions. His teachings were disseminated through lectures, sermons, and the movement's publications. But the days of modified itinerancy were over. Between 1937 and 1942, he transformed the Peace Mission movement into a formal church with the legal status of a business.[50]

During the first stage of institutionalization, he attempted to centralize power and exert more control over Peace Mission members and their activities. He recognized that the most influential instruments in his movement were the newspapers. In the summer of 1937, the angels discontinued all publications except the *New Day*, a Newark publication which first appeared in 1936 and was strikingly similar to the *Spoken Word*. The editorial staff of the *Spoken Word* joined that of the *New Day* under the supervision of Warner Hunt, who had assumed the name John Devoute. Working with Devoute, Father Divine was able to supervise more directly the contents of the *New Day*.[51]

Another development contributing to the centralization of the Peace Mission movement may have occurred accidentally and had both beneficial and detrimental ramifications. Members in extensions outside the New York City area wanted to be near Father Divine. His failure to visit extensions farther than Washington, D.C., induced many angels to move east to be close to "the body." The concentration of his followers in a single area allowed him to exert more authority over his flock, but the relocation of his most stalwart followers sapped the leadership ranks in Peace Missions outside the New York area. The loss of the most dedicated members in the extensions led to an overall decline in the number of Peace Mission outposts.[52]

The next phase of institutionalization was a regimentation of the movement, and between 1938 and 1941 "orders" with specific creeds and uniforms evolved. A California woman organized the first order, the Rosebuds, initially a choral group that performed during Holy Communion banquets. By the late thirties, the choir had adopted rigid requirements for membership, and by November 1941, the Rosebuds had become officially recognized in the movement. Rosebuds were young female followers who proudly took a pledge to remain virgins. The order's creed declared that Rosebuds were always "submissive, meek and sweet; they have hearts where Christ alone is heard to speak." Their uniforms reflected Father Divine's intensifying nationalism: blue skirts, white blouses, blue berets, and red blazers with large *V*s, which stood for virgin, embroidered on the lapels. The Rosebuds became the official choir of the movement and composed and performed songs celebrating Father Divine's holiness.[53]

At about the same time, another order, the Crusaders, developed among the men. The Crusaders maintained strict celibacy and devoutly followed all of Father Divine's teachings. Their creed pledged that members would "build and maintain a Fraternal Brotherhood which is on record as an active, effective, integral member of Father Divine's Inter-National, Inter-Racial, Inter-Denominational, Universal Peace Mission Movement." The Crusaders' uniform was a white jacket, dark pants, white shirt, and bow tie. They provided music and served as waiters at Peace Mission banquets.[54]

The development of these orders, with their emphasis on virginity and celibacy, may have grown out of the sex scandals plaguing the movement. Father Divine repeatedly stressed that his Crusaders and Rosebuds embodied the "Holiness of Jesus and Virginity of Mary." He grew impatient with followers who broke his commandments and expelled longtime disciple Priscilla Paul for flirting. But the movement implemented orders not only to combat innuendo and rumors. Membership in the Rosebuds and Crusaders required Father Divine's personal approval, and through the orders he dictated the conduct of his disciples. By creating an inner circle of strictly devoted followers, he protected the Peace Mission from external threats and strengthened the internal structure of his sect.[55]

While the orders unified the movement, they also had a detrimental impact on the Peace Mission. The creeds assigned gender-specific roles to Rosebuds and Crusaders. The Rosebuds' pledge encouraged women to follow traditional norms of obedience and humility; the Crusaders' was aggressive and political. While female angels still held positions of leadership and remained active in political forums, the deferential tone of the Rosebuds' creed robbed the movement of its feminist appeal and may have discouraged female converts. Furthermore, orders imposed a hierarchy on the movement. The exclusivity of the orders and their rigid requirements further distanced the movement from friends and sympathizers. The demarcation between supporter and angel became clearer and excluded the former from complete participation, so that those peripherally associated with the Peace Mission probably felt less comfortable at banquets and gradually withdrew from the movement.[56]

The final phase of institutionalization began in the spring of 1940. That April, John Devoute and several other angels incorporated the Palace Mission Church. In 1941, followers organized the Circle Mission Church and the Unity Mission Church, all recognizing Father Divine as their official pastor and adhering to his teachings. The three churches maintained the same constitutions, disciplines, and bylaws, but each was financially independent and claimed to be free from central rule. Following Father Divine's model of collective organization, the three churches cooperated in their efforts to advance his theology. After incorporation, Peace Mission property throughout the nation came under the control of one of the three churches. The huge amount of property made incorporation of the various extensions a slow and arduous task.[57]

The unification of Peace Mission properties streamlined the movement. Following incorporation laws, each church filed public statements concerning finances and property holdings. The movement hoped to avoid further embarrassing suits from dissatisfied former followers and to regain the public's respect. Institutionalization reduced the complex network of independent cooperatives to three manageable collectives. The incorporation of Peace Mission enterprises under specific groups of angels also freed Father

Divine from legal responsibility for the vast real estate held collectively by followers. Furthermore, the channeling of official Peace Mission transactions through only three sources facilitated his supervision of the sale and purchase of properties. The organization of the Palace Mission, Circle Mission, and Unity Mission churches provided a formidable fortress of protection against internal disruption and external attacks.

The establishment of the churches also had a constraining effect on the Peace Mission. The transformation drained much of the vitality of the movement and altered the way it spread. Previously, faithful servants opened Peace Missions everywhere at any time. By the early forties, new extensions needed approval from a parent church. The formalization of the Peace Mission robbed the movement of its spontaneity and flexibility, and cost a number of converts. Additionally, followers who did not wish to surrender their property to the church may have been forced out. As Weisbrot notes, the establishment of churches created a rigid status structure in the movement. Rank-and-file disciples who were not on the board of directors of one of the churches discovered that they had less of a voice in the movement. The Peace Mission became less accessible to the average member, and institutionalization restricted the independence of each extension.[58]

The reorganization of the Peace Mission also affected the social-relief programs it sponsored. Father Divine continued his employment agency through the offices of the *New Day*, and Peace Mission businesses still offered high-quality meals, accommodations, and services at budget prices. But by the late thirties, most relief missions had disappeared, and almost all Holy Communion banquets were closed to the public. Father Divine had never been an advocate of charity, instead providing the poor with spiritual and occupational retraining. The purpose of his ministry was to instruct disciples to assume independence and responsibility. All along, he had planned to wean his flock from social relief, and by early 1938, he forbade unemployed followers and supporters from testifying at banquets. Consequently, those attracted to the Peace Mission's version of public assistance found themselves less welcome at the extensions and ultimately abandoned the movement. Furthermore, by the late thirties, the country had begun to rebound from the depression, and Father Divine's prosperity message was less timely. Thus institutionalization and financial recovery caused a decline in numbers drawn to the movement because of economic hardship. Father Divine probably did not realize the long-term cost of reorganizing his ministry because the process was slow and the decline not immediately detectable.[59]

Despite the changes, his theology remained consistent, and the movement continued many of the projects initiated before 1937. During the 1940 election, Father Divine again launched into politics, and a new focus emerged at that year's International Righteous Government Convention. He still pushed for the acceptance of the Righteous Government Platform but concentrated most of his efforts on promoting antilynching legislation and a strategy for national defense. The movement began a letter-writing campaign targeted at congress, urging the passage of an antilynching bill. The angels singled out Mississippi Senator Theodore Bilbo, the leader of the antilynching opposition, and flooded his office with letters. Even angels with limited education struggled to express their disillusionment with his attacks on the bill: "Mr. T. G. Bilbow, . . . I was just thinking how uncivilize it sounds for you to reject such a Bill as the Antilinching Bill, it only goes to show one the great crisis our Great Government now faces with such mind as your in geoing out to this people." The angels warned Bilbo that his opposition to antilynching would have dire consequences.[60]

During the election year, the followers successfully gathered 250,000 signatures on a petition bearing Father Divine's antilynching bill, but he had little influence in Congress, and he further undermined his crusade with the addition of a foreign-policy proposal to his petition. Fearing an outbreak of a "Great International Civil War," Father Divine called for the unification of North, Central, and South America under the U.S. government. He believed the plan would extend democracy to other peoples and facilitate the defense of the Western Hemisphere. In his sermons during the late thirties and early forties, he increasingly attacked Hitler and fascism, equating the two with racism. He remained a pacifist and noninterventionist, but the tone of his sermons grew more nationalistic. Although other leaders had suggested similar schemes, to those in power his proposals appeared outlandish. The mixing of issues also deterred those who supported only antilynching legislation from signing the petition. At the same time, his resolutions appealed to those who feared the spread of fascism. His fight to stop lynchings and his plans to prevent the war probably lessened the draining effect that institutionalization had on the membership of the Peace Mission movement.[61]

On December 7, 1941, the bombing of Pearl Harbor drew the United States into war and posed a difficult problem to the patriotic but pacifist Father Divine. At first he continued to order followers not to bear arms for any cause, but eventually he allowed draftees to act according to their consciences. While a few angels fought for conscientious-objector status, many marched off to fight. Father Divine supported the war effort, commanded his angels to buy war bonds, and stepped up his criticism of Hitler and fascism. But the public remained distrustful of him and showered the FBI with accusations that the minister maintained ties with the Axis powers and planned to allow Germans to land at his New Jersey shorefront property. Other informants alleged that he was a member of the "Black Dragon," a group of African Americans reportedly allied with the Japanese and plotting to overthrow the American government. Concerned that Father Divine presented a threat to national security, the FBI infiltrated the movement but concluded that the minister was not engaged in subversive activity.[62]

But the damage of 1937 left a permanent scar on the movement. The public perceived the Peace Mission not as an alliance of deeply religious citizens concerned with the nation's destiny, but as a secret aberrational cult that lured the innocent and the foolish and robbed them of their money and purity. Americans would remember the positive aspects of Father Divine's ministry—his battles against poverty and racism—only in the context of the sex and financial scandals.

Father Divine adroitly steered through most obstacles and stubbornly bounced back in the face of opposition, but Verinda Brown's claim loomed in the courts, continuously menacing the progress of the Peace Mission movement. After a series of appeals, in the summer of 1942 the New York courts ordered him to pay his disgruntled former disciple or face a prison sentence for contempt. From Father Divine's perspective, the ruling reflected the ingratitude of New York City, whose poor he had fed, clothed, and sheltered for ten years. He threatened with bitterness: "Now tell every crooked-necked and uncircumcised, unconstitutional official, if he or they cannot do something better to the general public I say . . . I HAVE LONG SINCE DECLARED I WILL SHAKE CREATION."[63]

In July 1942, as a judgment on New York City for its thanklessness and in an effort to avoid paying Verinda Brown, Father Divine fled the city, moving his wife and staff to a new headquarters in Philadelphia. Although Brown never received her settlement, Hearst and his forces gloated over Father Divine's sudden departure. But New York had not seen the last of him. His legal staff knew that New York law prohibited serving a subpoena on Sunday. For six days a week, New York was off-limits to Father Divine, but each Sabbath he presided over his flocks in Sayville, Harlem, and the Promised Land. "I need not say more," he proclaimed to one congregation, "but I stress for your consideration this little prediction, declaration and composition, 'YOU CAN'T STOP GOD. YOU CAN'T STOP GOD. *YOU CAN'T STOP GOD!* I thank you! I thank you! I THANK YOU!'"[64]

Epilogue

It is said "What if Father goes? How can I go?"
You would say in the words of the melody
composed in 1917 when I was in Brooklyn "He
lives in me, my Holy Father, He lives in me."
That would be your great battle axe when anyone tried to tell you that you and I were separated.

Metaphysical News, April 20, 1932

While Father Divine's flight to Philadelphia in 1942 marked the end of his heyday, the saga of the Peace Mission movement continued. Although during the war years, support and membership gradually declined, Peace Mission churches continued to acquire property and expand their commercial ventures.

But the movement suffered a blow with Peninniah's sudden disappearance from the banquet table. Father Divine and his staff refused to comment on her absence, but as many speculated, she had again fallen seriously ill. Sometime in 1943 at an unknown location, Peninniah passed away. Her stalwart support had been instrumental in perpetuating Father Divine's ministry, and her death left a void in the movement. At first Father Divine did not publicly acknowledge her passing, but his later remarks indicated that her loss deeply affected him.[1]

Though membership in the Peace Mission movement declined during World War II, Father Divine drew some new members into the fold. One wartime convert was a white Canadian high school student, Edna Rose Ritchings, who joined the movement in Vancouver. Ritchings became a Rosebud, chose the name Sweet Angel, and after finishing school, moved to Philadelphia. Her dedication and efficiency attracted the attention of Peace Mission leaders, and she quickly secured a position as one of Father Divine's personal secretaries. One day while working with him, Sweet Angel boldly approached the minister and announced, "I want to marry YOU because I know YOU are GOD."[2]

Surprisingly, Sweet Angel's proposal did not offend him. He had observed the young woman as she worked and was impressed with her devotion to the movement. On April 29, 1946, he whisked Sweet Angel to Washington, D.C., and married her in a secret ceremony. For months the marriage was concealed from even the closest disciples. Many states, including Pennsylvania, prohibited interracial marriages. Given racial prejudice and his celibacy requirement, the preacher probably felt that he had to prepare both the public and his followers to accept his marriage to the twenty-one-year-old white woman. In the summer of 1946, Sweet Angel's visa expired, and the immigration authorities threatened deportation, forcing Father Divine to disclose the marriage.[3]

In early August, Father Divine announced to his congregation that Peninniah had wished to leave her old body and be reborn in a "more youthful body." He claimed to have selected Sweet Angel for her virginity and spiritual purity, reincarnating both Peninniah and the Virgin Mary in the body of the young Canadian. He christened Sweet Angel the Spotless Virgin Bride who exemplified his teachings,[4] contending that his marriage was not physical and represented "the Marriage of CHRIST to HIS Church—consummated the union of GOD and man and the fusion of Heaven and earth as spoken of in the Book of Revelation."[5]

Many speculated that his marriage would snap the faith of his followers, but no mass exodus from the movement ensued. To prove that the marriage was platonic, he assigned a black female disciple to act as a constant companion to Sweet Angel. Disciples celebrated the marriage as a victory in the Peace Mission's battle for equal rights through the elimination of blackness. "It is another symbol," commented one follower, "that the black Mrs. Divine vanished and rose again, but as a young white girl."[6] Proudly the angels sent to their old racist foe Theodore Bilbo a newspaper account of the wedding with an inscription, PEACE IT IS TRULY WONDERFUL, next to a picture of Father Divine and his white bride.[7]

Father Divine's marriage to Sweet Angel both represented and induced some changes in his theology. Peninniah's death challenged his doctrine of eternal life and forced him to confront certain biological realities. Previously the notion of reincarnation had not been part of his teachings, but in his new version he offered a selective reincarnation extended only to Peninniah. He still expected rank-and-file followers to strive for immortality, and Sweet Angel, an exclusive reincarnation, assumed a special significance. After he announced their marriage, their wedding anniversary became a Peace Mission holiday. Next to the date, the *New Day* began to carry a second set of numbers recording the year of the Divines' anniversary, and on each April 29 Peace Missions across the nation organized special banquets.

In contrast to Peninniah, who had always avoided the limelight, Sweet Angel allowed her photographs and comments to appear frequently in Peace Mission publications. Articulate and outspoken, she occasionally addressed Holy Communion banquets and even granted a few interviews to the press. Disciples revered her for her virtue and worshiped their new Mother Divine. Portraits of Father Divine and his bride went up in Peace Missions all over the nation and around the world. In their wallets, followers carried "International Peace Cards" bearing a photo of Father and Mother Divine, the Liberty Bell above their heads and the White House below, as "a symbol of Infinite Protection."[8]

While internal opposition to Father Divine's new wife was not readily apparent, the marriage may have cost the movement a few important members. Not too long after the wedding, John Lamb quietly left the movement. He did not offer an explanation and refused to criticize Father Divine openly, but he now insisted that he had never believed that Father Divine was God and had joined the movement out of a desire to help the poor.

The marriage was definitely a factor in the defection of the Prodigal Son. After serving his prison sentence, the Prodigal Son had plunged back into the movement's activities with his characteristic enthusiasm. He served as Father Divine's official photographer, and his pictures often appeared in the *New Day*. He also assisted in the Peace Mission campaign to promote antilynching and desegregation legislation. In the midforties, a Philadelphia publication ran a series of his photos showing black and white male followers eating, sleeping, and bathing together. The Prodigal Son tormented Senator Bilbo with a shower of correspondence containing eight-by-ten glossy reprints of the photos, carrying the greeting *Peace Bilbo*.[9]

After Father Divine's marriage, the Prodigal Son became increasingly discontented with the movement. The former womanizer and partygoer grew restless with the strict demands of the Peace Mission movement and resented Father Divine for taking a wife. By the midforties, the Prodigal Son had become intimate with one of the leaders of the Rosebuds, Carol Sweet. Reportedly, Sweet had hopes of becoming Peninniah's successor and was infuriated when Father Divine chose Sweet Angel. In 1948, the Prodigal Son and Carol Sweet left the movement and were married.[10]

Subsequently John Wuest Hunt and his wife embarked on a campaign to undermine Father Divine and his Peace Mission. Hunt issued a diatribe against the movement, "Father Divine: Man or God?" which appeared in *Our World*, a magazine that circulated in the Northeast. The former disciple alleged that Father Divine was a con man and that Mary Bird Tree, was "now an invalid and virtual prisoner at 41st and Westminster in Philly." Hunt called the movement a "hoax" and asserted that "the mass of [Father Divine's] followers are of inferior intelligence and feel themselves rejected and unwanted by the world."[11]

Hunt did not confine himself to attacks in the media. After a series of attempts, the former angel finally convinced the FBI to investigate Father Divine for violating the Mann Act. Hunt produced several witnesses, including his wife, who testified that Father Divine had forced them to have sexual intercourse. Many of the victims were minors who claimed that the minister forced them to participate in all forms of sexual debauchery. After a long investigation, the Bureau determined that Father Divine had "engaged in numerous immoral activities with white and colored girls who are members of his religious group; however, on the basis of signed statements furnished, no evidence has been developed upon which Father Divine could be prosecuted under the White Slavery Traffic Act." But the Bureau's conclusions remained unclear, for testimony also revealed that Hunt had rehearsed all the witnesses and that Carol Sweet "readily admitted that she and her husband were out to expose or 'get' FATHER DIVINE."[12]

Despite the unceasing threats, the movement continued steadily throughout the late 1940s and into the 1950s. While national media coverage of the movement significantly declined, the press still occasionally ran a story on Father Divine, noting, for instance, that he had declared Philadelphia the capital of the world or that he claimed to have inspired the invention of the hydrogen bomb. A heightened preoccupation with international affairs increasingly dominated his postwar messages. Horrified by World War II, he promoted his own plan for world peace based on obliterating all territorial, racial, and ethnic divisions and creating a one-world government under American democracy. The *New Day*, reflecting his increased nationalism, was now printed in red and blue ink on white paper.[13]

The most significant barometer of Father Divine's patriotism was his growing hostility toward communism. He had remained fairly noncommittal on party activities until the commencement of the Cold War. Then his distaste for the Communists reflected the red-baiting atmosphere of the McCarthy era. Like many Americans during this period, the clergyman had become disillusioned with the Soviet Union's actions after World War II and considered communism a threat to American democracy. Disapproving of Communist expansionism and wanting to avoid association with the Left, the movement excised the pro-Communist portions of the Righteous Government Platform. Father Divine frequently assaulted communism in his messages and in a radical departure from his earlier strategy refused to cooperate with leftist organizations that appealed to him to support their campaigns for civil rights. In a letter to a Communist alliance that solicited his assistance in fighting segregation, he declared, "I AM NOT an N[egro] and I AM NOT representing any such thing as the N[egro] or C[olored] race; but I AM REPRESENTING THE TRUE AND THE LIVING GOD INFINITELY but as among men."[14]

During the 1950s, one of the most important events in the Peace Mission movement occurred with John Devoute's purchase of Woodmont, a seventy-two-acre estate in a wealthy suburb of Philadelphia. Woodmont, built for one million dollars in 1892 by a steel magnate, had tennis courts, a swimming pool, a coach house, stables, several other spacious outbuildings, greenhouses, a stream, walking paths, woods, and a large Gothic stone mansion high on a hill. The movement renovated the manor house, prominently displaying the American flag in front, and added neatly manicured gardens like Father Divine's in Sayville. In 1953, the imposing mansion became home to an aging and increasingly infirm Father Divine. During an open house that fall, he proclaimed the estate the "mount of the house of the LORD" and declared September 10, 11, and 12 Peace Mission holidays.[15]

Woodmont became the center of the movement, and followers made pilgrimages as often as possible in hopes of seeing and hearing their spiritual leader. Father Divine opened his doors to the public, and uniformed Rosebuds conducted tours of the mansion and grounds. To his followers the estate symbolized the material benefits derived from his teachings and was the ultimate demonstration of his vast spiritual powers. The manor house was furnished with expensive antiques, elegant works of art, and photographs of Father and Mother Divine. He worked in his sunlit Woodmont office, decorated with an oak desk, leather chairs, a long meeting table, and velvet armchairs. Each day the household staff served several Holy Communion banquets on fine china and cut crystal in Woodmont's large, ornate wood-paneled dining room. When his health permitted, he presided over the celebrations, but his appearances became increasingly rare, forcing Mother Divine to assume the duties of serving Holy Communion and delivering messages to Woodmont's guests.[16]

Woodmont provided a serene setting for Father Divine's retirement. The quiet estate in an exclusive white neighborhood represented his final challenge to residential segregation. His declining health did not slow his fight for equal rights, and in the fifties he proposed that "all nations and peoples who have suppressed and oppressed the under-privileged . . . be obliged to pay the African slaves and their descendants for all uncompensated servitude."[17] Despite the boldness of his pronouncement, he did not participate in the expanding civil rights movement, partly because of his advanced age but especially because of civil rights leaders' persistent use of racial labels. Nevertheless, he viewed the campaigns for civil rights as a fulfillment of his mandate for America and contended at one banquet, "I have said enough not only in Words, but in the actuated words of expression, for I have declared, I HAVE BROKEN THAT LINE OF DEMARCATION. . . . That's why you have the privilege and the pleasure to go up to the Mount of the House of GOD, AND YOU MAY COME IN THE FRONT DOOR."[18]

From the late fifties to the early sixties, Father Divine served fewer and fewer Holy Communion banquets. Rumors circulated in the national media that he suffered from arteriosclerosis and diabetes. Meanwhile, Mother Divine shouldered increasing responsibility in the movement. In 1963 Father Divine ceased all public appearances, a close aide commenting to the press: "Father has said everything there is to say about everything." Finally on September 10, 1965, his long ministry came to an end, and in his mountaintop home he passed away.[19]

Immediately angels organized an extravagant Holy Communion feast and announced to the press that since Father Divine was God, he could not die and had decided to "lay his body down."[20] Some followers interpreted his death as a judgment on humankind for ignoring his teachings. But Mother Divine contended that he remained spiritually present and that his passage was a "supreme sacrifice" made for the salvation of all peoples. In an interview she declared:

> Everyone should be glad that FATHER DIVINE came and exemplified Righteousness! HE presented Righteousness to the political world, to the educational world, the social world, the religious world—Righteousness! He sacrificed HIMSELF for that Righteousness and caused millions of others to sacrifice themselves for that Righteousness, and that's why that Righteousness is going to flood the earth and nothing can stop it!

She prophesied that Father Divine would eventually resurrect himself and began a patient vigil. In the meantime, Mother Divine demanded that followers continue to act as if Father Divine were physically present. Angels spoke of Father Divine in the present tense. At each banquet table, followers set a place for their leader, complete with food, and continued to worship him as they had in the past.[21]

Mother Divine firmly guided the Peace Mission movement through probably the most traumatic period of its history. She reassured the angels that those who did not achieve immortality would experience reincarnation. By the time Mother Divine assumed

complete control of the movement, Peace Mission property holdings had dwindled. But although the movement did not attract
many new members and death claimed a number of the older followers, Mother Divine's leadership efficiently perpetuated the
ministry started by her husband at the turn of the century.[22]

Like her husband, Mother Divine encountered opposition to her
ministry. At one point, she fought off cultist Jim Jones's attempt to
take over the movement. In the 1950s Jones met with Father Divine
and based some of his ministry on tenets borrowed from the Peace
Mission. In 1971, Jones brought two hundred of his followers to
the Woodmont estate. According to Mother Divine, after suffering
for several days with the "brazen and obnoxious behavior" of Jones
and his followers, she requested that the group leave. A few months
later, Jones deluged Peace Mission members with letters and fliers
encouraging them to abandon the Peace Mission and join his People's Temple. Jones sent a bus equipped with loudspeakers blaring
his messages through Peace Mission neighborhoods in Philadelphia.

Only one follower left the movement for the People's Temple,
and in December 1971 the former angel appealed to Mother Divine
to recognize Jones as Father Divine's reincarnation.[23] She bluntly
responded:

> How can you possibly think that FATHER DIVINE would reincarnate
> HIMSELF in these last days of mortality in a human likeness, much
> less in one born in sin and shaped up in iniquity, according to his
> own testimony and now married, having one child according to the
> flesh? The Sonship Degree came through a virgin birth and the FA-
> THERSHIP came with the beginning of days or the end of life.

In 1978, when the news of the mass suicide at the People's Temple
in Guyana shocked the world, the angels interpreted the tragedy
as retribution for Jones's challenge to Father and Mother Divine.[24]

The connection between the People's Temple and the Peace
Mission did not go unnoticed by the public. A 1980 made-for-
television movie on Jim Jones presented an image of Father Divine
that drew from old myths and created some new distortions. In
the film, Jones journeys to Woodmont, a sparkling palace filled
with attractive black female disciples in flowing white robes. He
confesses to Father Divine his difficulty in funding his ministry

and, even more troubling, his inability to reject the advances of women followers. A sullen Father Divine, played by James Earl Jones, offers a strategy on securing disciples' money and advises the People's Temple leader to help his female followers "bring their desires to fruition."[25]

The association of Father Divine with wealth and sex also recently resurfaced during the scandal involving television evangelist Jim Bakker. In 1987, the *National Enquirer* ran a story entitled "Jim and Tammy Bakker Are Nothing New—Preachers Have Been Raising Hell for Years," which presented Father Divine as a typical scheming preacher. The article quoted Dr. John McCollister, author of *The Christian Book of Why*, who reported that Father Divine "wore $500 suits, was chauffeured about in a Duesenburg, and flew in his own private plane with an army of beautiful women— who he was careful to refer to as his 'secretaries.' " Not surprisingly, the rumors surrounding the movement in the 1930s continued to influence the public perception of Father Divine and his Peace Mission movement fifty years later.[26]

The Peace Mission movement under the determined leadership of Mother Divine persisted throughout the 1980s and into the 1990s. As late as 1983, the Circle Mission Church in South Central Los Angeles continued to hold Holy Communion banquets. The lush green lawns, colorful flower beds, shaded terrace, and brightly painted church stood as a quiet oasis in a graffiti-scarred neighborhood. Across the street, people emaciated by addiction bought and sold drugs. Entire families suffering from poverty and unemployment crowded into hotel rooms or small dilapidated apartments. Each night the residents of the neighborhood locked themselves in their homes, fearing that they could be the next victims of the gang warfare that raged in the streets. Undaunted by the surrounding despair, Father Divine's children struggled on, distributing the *New Day*, discussing their leader's teachings, trying to spread positive thinking and offer salvation to their neighbors. A vacant but completely furnished home stood across the street from the Circle Mission Church, readied in case Mother Divine made a surprise visit to Los Angeles.[27]

Throughout the eighties the movement began to surrender various outpost properties, but not out of financial necessity; the death of many longtime disciples had eroded the membership and left fewer and fewer followers to organize Peace Mission banquets or oversee church properties. By the fall of 1986, the circulation of the *New Day* was only eight hundred nationwide. But the decrease in followers did not discourage Mother Divine and Peace Mission leaders, who compared the movement to the Shakers and contended that it was the quality, not quantity, of the disciples that was important.[28]

In 1991, a handful of Father Divine's children resided in California, Colorado, New York, and New Jersey, but Pennsylvania remained the stronghold. In Philadelphia members operated a variety of businesses, including cafeterias, dry-cleaners, and printshops. But the best known were the Peace Mission hotels, the Divine Tracy and the Divine Loraine. The Divine Tracy Hotel, across the street from the University of Pennsylvania, was patronized by visitors from all parts of the nation and the world. In keeping with Peace Mission tradition, the Divine Tracy offered immaculately clean and comfortable accommodations for extremely low rates. The hotel's staff insisted that all guests adhere to Father Divine's International Modest Code, which forbids smoking, drinking, and profanity. Furthermore, the owners enforced a dress code requiring women to wear dresses and hose and men to wear dress pants and shirts. The floors were segregated by gender, and the sexes were allowed to mix only in a public waiting room at the entrance. Since the Divine Tracy was also home to many followers, visitors gained firsthand exposure to the language, social customs, and spiritual convictions of Peace Mission members. On Sundays, Holy Communion was served in the Keyflower Cafeteria in the basement of the hotel.[29]

Woodmont remained the focal point of the Peace Mission movement. Manned by a small staff of followers, the estate continued to serve as the home of Mother Divine. Although well into her sixties, Mother Divine led an active life, taking early-morning walks, jogging, and bicycling. Most of her days were devoted to church business and spiritual affairs. She supervised Woodmont, counseled followers, gave interviews, and conducted study groups. Like her husband, she was open with the public. Woodmont still welcomed visitors during special hours in the summer and by appointment in other seasons. Mother Divine met with journalists and scholars, and discussed frankly the movement's activities and goals. While her willingness to work with those outside the Peace Mission led some journalists to write pieces that the movement perceived as inaccurate, her cooperation dispelled charges that the organization was a dangerous cult with a secret agenda.[30]

Mother Divine's tireless efforts to perpetuate her husband's ministry have left their mark on the Peace Mission movement. The *New Day* carried her messages and updates on her ministry. While she served Holy Communion in Peace Mission churches throughout Philadelphia, the most revered banquets were those she presided over at Woodmont. The fare—natural foods, poultry, vegetables, and tofu—reflected her concern with health and nutrition. Her sermons advanced Father Divine's theology, promoted American patriotism, and assailed communism. Followers hailed her as the purest example of Father Divine's teachings and looked to her for guidance. Pilgrims from the few remaining Peace Mission extensions continued to trek to Woodmont for banquets and holidays. Many angels spent time meditating within the walls of the Shrine to Life, a small hexagonal structure with large gilded doors topped with a glass pyramid. Designed by Mother Divine as a tribute to her husband, the shrine holds a red marble crypt that contains the body of Father Divine.[31]

In 1991, on the other side of the country, in South Central Los Angeles, Hezekiah Craig worked in the gardens of the last remaining Peace Mission in the West, preparing the property for its impending sale. A sign outside read *Circle Mission Church, Reverend M. J. Divine, Pastor*—the last reminder of the minister who dedicated his life to stopping the forces choking the life from this neighborhood. But despite the chaos, fear, and destitution of the community, a peacefulness prevailed in the Circle Mission Church. On a long buffet, Father Divine's portrait still overlooked the dining room. But the banquet table stood empty. Most of the chairs were gone. Plates, cups, glasses, and silverware were neatly stacked, waiting to be moved. The piano and tambourines were silent. On the counter sat a box of handmade favors celebrating the Woodmont Holiday. Printed on the favors were the words from one of Father Divine's messages, also inscribed in gold on the inner walls of the Shrine to Life in Philadelphia and chosen by Mother Divine to encapsulate the meaning of his work:

Condescendingly I came as an existing Spirit unembodied, until condescendingly inputting MYSELF in a Bodily Form in the likeness of men I came, that I might speak to them in their own language, coming to a country that is supposed to be the Country of the Free, where mankind has been privileged to serve GOD according to the dictates of his own conscience—coming sponsoring this Peace Mission and this spiritual revelation in the hearts of the children of men, and establishing the Kingdom of GOD in the midst of them; that they might become to be living epistles as individuals, seen and read of men, and verifying that which has long since been said:

"The tabernacle of God is with men, and he shall dwell with them, and God Himself shall be with them, and shall be their God, and they shall be his people."[32]

Notes

ABBREVIATIONS

LAT Los Angeles Times
MN   Metaphysical News
ND   The New Day
NYT The New York Times
SCN Suffolk County News
SW   The Spoken Word
WE   World Echo

PREFACE

1. Kenneth E. Burnham, *God Comes to America: Father Divine* (Boston: Lambeth Press, 1979). For earlier studies of Father Divine, see John Hoshor, *God in a Rolls-Royce: The Rise of Father Divine, Madman, Menace or Messiah* (New York: Hillman-Curl, 1936); Robert Allerton Parker, *Incredible Messiah: The Deification of Father Divine* (Boston: Little, Brown, 1937); Sara Harris, *Father Divine: Holy Husband* (Garden City, N.Y.: Doubleday, 1953); St. Clair McKelway and A. J. Liebling, "Who Is This King of Glory?" *New Yorker*, pt. 1, June 13, 1936, 21–28; pt. 2, June 20, 1936, 22–28; pt. 3, June 27, 1936, 22–32.

2. Mrs. M. J. Divine, *The Peace Mission Movement* (Philadelphia: Imperial Press, 1982), 178. This work provides an internal view of the history and philosophy of the Peace Mission movement. For a review, see Richard Newman, *Black Power and Black Religion* (West Cornwall, Conn.: Locust Hill Press, 1987), 176–77.

3. J. Gordon Melton, *Encyclopedic Handbook of Cults in America* (New York: Garland Publishing, 1986), 3–20. For an example of an early work on cults, see Jan Karel Van Baalen, *The Chaos of Cults*, 3d ed. (Grand Rapids, Mich.: William B. Eerdmans, 1942). For examples of the anticult school, see James A. Rudin and Marcia Rudin, *Prison or Paradise?* (Philadelphia: Fortress Press, 1980); Walter Martin, *The Kingdom of Cults* (Minneapolis, Minn.: Bethany House, 1985); Ernst Troeltsch, *The Social Teachings of Christian Churches* (New York: Macmillian, 1956); J. Milton Yinger, *The Scientific Study of Religion* (New York: Macmillan, 1970); C. Eric Lincoln and Lawrence H. Mamiya, "Daddy Jones and Father Divine: The Cult as Political Religion," *Religion in Life* 49 (Spring 1980): 6–23; David G. Bromley and

Anson D. Shupe, *Strange Gods: The Great American Cult Scare* (Boston: Beacon Press, 1981), 23 (Bromley and Shupe's definition is derived from the work of Geoffrey K. Nelson, "The Spiritualist Movement and the Need for a Redefinition of Cult," *Journal for the Scientific Study of Religion* 8 [Spring 1960]: 52–60, and "The Membership of a Cult: The Spiritualists National Union," *Review of Religious Research* 13 [Spring 1972]: 170–77); Joseph R. Washington, Jr., *Black Sects and Cults: The Power Axis in an Ethnic Ethic* (Garden City, N.Y.: Anchor Press/Doubleday, 1973), 1–18.

4. Clarence Howell, "Father Divine: Another View," *Christian Century*, October 7, 1936, 1332–33; Charles Samuel Braden, *These Also Believe: A Study of Modern American Cults and Minority Religious Movements* (New York: Macmillan, 1949), 1–76. More recently Ronald Moran White suggested that Father Divine borrowed most of his teachings from New Thought authors. Ronald Moran White, "New Thought Influences on Father Divine," M.A. thesis, Miami University, 1980.

5. Robert Weisbrot, *Father Divine and the Struggle for Racial Equality* (Urbana: University of Illinois Press, 1983). Weisbrot's work has been accepted by scholars as a significant step in advancing an unbiased view of the Peace Mission movement. See Harvard Sitkoff, "Review," *American Historical Review* 89 (1984): 542–43.

6. McKelway and Liebling, "Who Is This King?" pt. 1, 21–28.

7. Barbara Jeanne Fields, "Slavery, Race and Ideology in the United States of America," *New Left Review* 181 (May–June 1990), 95–119.

8. Divine, *Peace Mission Movement*, 117.

9. Ibid., 114.

CHAPTER ONE

1. Henry Copp, *Peerless Rockville: What It Offers to Homeseekers and Investors (How to Get Health, Wealth, and Comfort)* (Washington, D.C.: Gibson Brothers, 1890); T. H. S. Boyd, *The History of Montgomery County Maryland, from Its Earliest Settlement in 1650 to 1879* (1879; reprint, Baltimore: Regional Publishing, 1968), 139; Peerless Rockville Historic Preservation, *A Walking Guide to "Peerless Rockville"* (Rockville, Md.: Peerless Rockville Historic Preservation, 1975), 1–3; Ray Eldon Hiebert and Richard K. MacMaster, *A Grateful Remembrance: The Story of Montgomery County, Maryland* (Rockville, Md.: Montgomery County Government and Montgomery County Historical Society, 1976), 212, 217.

2. Hiebert and MacMaster, *Grateful Remembrance*, 247–49, 305, 338; Willie Mae Carey interview, October 4, 1986, Rockville, Maryland; Mary Gordon Malloy and Jane Sween interview, October 10, 1986, Rockville, Maryland.

3. *Montgomery County Sentinel*, May 28, 1897, 3; U.S. Census, *1880 Population Schedules, Rockville, Montgomery County, Maryland*, E.D. 113, vol. 15, sheet 20, line 23; St. Clair McKelway and A. J. Liebling, "Who Is This King of Glory?" *New Yorker*, pt. 1, June 13, 1936, 21. It is possible that George

Baker was born in Rockville but grew up elsewhere. However, even though there is no record of George Baker's life from 1880 to 1900, evidence indicates that he probably did not migrate to Baltimore until the late 1890s. McKelway and Liebling interviewed an early associate, Samuel Morris, who apparently did not know where Baker was born but did tell the authors that in 1899 Baker was a gardener in Baltimore. The 1900 census confirms that a twenty-one-year-old gardener named George Baker lived in Baltimore and shows that he was born in Maryland. The 1880 census lists only one George Baker living in Maryland who is of a corresponding age and birthplace, suggesting that this was the same person that Morris later knew. Since Morris probably did not arrive in Baltimore until about 1903 and could not have known George Baker before the turn of the century, it seems likely that Baker told Morris that he moved to Baltimore about 1899 and secured a job as a gardener at this time. Since he was not orphaned and his mother did not die until he was grown, it seems unlikely that he would have been separated from the rest of his family at an early age and therefore must have been raised in Rockville.

4. U.S. Census, *1870 Population Schedules, Rockville, Montgomery County, Maryland, Brighton Post Office*, 8, 9; U.S. Census, *1880 Population Schedules, Rockville, Montgomery County, Maryland*, E.D. 113, vol. 15, sheet 20, line 23; *Montgomery County* (Slave Statistics) 1867–1868 [MdHR 9876], 77. The birthdate for Nancy is uncertain. The state of Maryland slave census, compiled in 1867, was to aid loyal Maryland slaveholders who sought compensation for "property" lost as a result of the Civil War. The government never paid these masters. Nevertheless, the manuscript was eventually deposited in the Maryland State Archives in Annapolis and contains the name of the master, any past owners, and the full name and age for all slaves. Masters were instructed to record the ages of their slaves in 1864, the year the state issued a general emancipation proclamation. The 1867 census shows that Nancy was born in 1843. In 1870 Nancy gave her birthdate as 1842; in 1880 she gave it as 1845. It is likely that Nancy, like many other former slaves, did not know her birthdate.

5. Roger Brooke Farquhar, *Old Homes and History of Montgomery County, Maryland* (Baltimore: Monumental, 1952), 38; John Thomas Scharf, *History of Western Maryland*, vol. 1 (1882; reprint, Baltimore: Regional, 1968), 653–54; Hiebert and MacMaster, *Grateful Remembrance*, 116–18, 155; Barbara Jeanne Fields, *Slavery and Freedom on Middle Ground: Maryland during the Nineteenth Century* (New Haven: Yale University Press, 1985), 2–4, 11, 23–28; Frederick Douglass, *Life and Times of Frederick Douglass* (1892; reprint, New York: Collier Books, 1962), 178–89.

6. *Montgomery County* (Slave Statistics) 1867–1868, 77; U.S. Census, *1850 Slave Census, Montgomery County, Maryland, 4th Rockville Election District*, 365. In 1850, the U.S. Census compiled a listing of each slaveowner and the age and sex of all of his or her slaves. The 1850 slave census shows that Lemuel Clements owned five slaves, including a 22-year-old female and a two-year-old female. Given the uncertainties of Nancy's birthdate

and the fact that masters often paid little attention to slaves' ages, it is possible that the two female slaves were Nancy and her mother. Charles Cole recalled that when he had been a slave in Charles County, Maryland, his master "conducted regular religious services of the Catholic church on the farm in a chapel erected for that purpose and in which the slaves were taught the catechism and some learned how to read and write. . . . When a child was born, it was baptized by the priest." He also noted that priests conducted slave funerals. George W. Rawick, ed., *The American Slave: A Composite Autobiography*, vol. 16, *Maryland Narratives* (Westport, Conn.: Greenwood, 1972), 4–5, 7; Farquhar, *Old Homes*, 229; Boyd, *History of Montgomery County*, 129–30; Robert McMain, ed., *Historic Saint Mary's* (Washington, D.C.: Moore and Moore, 1963), 6; Hiebert and MacMaster, *Grateful Remembrance*, 160.

7. *Montgomery County* (Slave Statistics) 1867–1868, 77, 146. Waring claimed nine slaves; Robert Thompson, 28; Jacob Noland, 30; Nancy Smith (who later became Nancy Baker), 21; John Thompson, 20; George Smith, 11; Edward Smith, 8; Bernard Smith, 6; Mary Smith, 3; and William Cook, 1. The slaves with the Smith surname may have been relatives of Nancy Smith. Since Nancy was the only adult female enumerated, she must have been the Warings' only domestic servant. U.S. Census, *1870 Population Schedules, Rockville, Montgomery County, Maryland, Brighton Post Office*, 8, 9; *1880 Population Schedules, Rockville, Montgomery County, Maryland*, E.D. 113, vol. 15, sheet 20, line 23. McMain, ed., *Historic Saint Mary's*, 39; Hiebert and MacMaster, *Grateful Remembrance*, 61, 69, 152–54; Fields, *Slavery and Freedom*, 25. Fields's statistics show that the median slaveholding for the entire state was three slaves per master, but regionally the median slaveholding in the southern counties like Montgomery was 15. For general discussions of slavery and the slave community, see John Blassingame, *The Slave Community: Plantation Life in the Antebellum South* (New York: Oxford University Press, 1972); Eugene Genovese, *Roll Jordon Roll: The World the Slaves Made* (New York: Vintage Books, 1972); Herbert Gutman, *The Black Family in Slavery and Freedom* (New York: Pantheon, 1976); Lawrence Levine, *Black Culture and Black Consciousness* (New York: Oxford University Press, 1977); George Rawick, *From Sundown to Sunup: The Making of the Black Community* (Westport, Conn.: Greenwood, 1972); Edward Reynolds, *Stand the Storm: A History of the Atlantic Slave Trade* (New York: Allison and Busby, 1985). For a firsthand account of slavery in Maryland, see Josiah Henson, *Father Henson's Story of His Own Life* (Boston: John P. Jewett, 1858), 17, 18; Douglass, *Life and Times*, 56, 59; George W. McDaniel, *Hearth and Home: Preserving a People's Culture* (Philadelphia: Temple University Press, 1982), 51–102, 114–16, 224. McDaniel's study provides an excellent history of the material culture of black Marylanders before and after emancipation.

8. Vincent Harding, *The Other American Revolution* (Los Angeles, Atlanta: Center for Afro-American Studies, University of California, Los Angeles, Institute of the Black World, 1980), 1–70. Herbert Aptheker's *Amer-*

ican Negro Slave Revolts (1943; reprint, New York: International Publishers, 1967) provides much information on slave revolts and is a pioneering work on African-American resistance. Douglass, *Life and Times*, 35–36; Mc-Daniel, *Home and Hearth*, 126–27; Rawick, *American Slave*, 7. Albert J. Raboteau's *Slave Religion: The "Invisible Institution" in the Antebellum South* (New York: Oxford University Press, 1978) offers a comprehensive analysis of the evolution, ideology, and rituals of slave religion. For an examination of African religious retentions in the New World among slaves in South Carolina, see Margaret Washington Creel, *"A Peculiar People": Slave Religion and Community-Culture Among the Gullahs* (New York: New York University Press, 1988). See also John S. Mibiti, *African Religions and Philosophies* (New York: Praeger, 1959).

9. McMain, *Historic Saint Mary's*, 6.

10. Fields, *Slavery and Freedom*, 111–31; Noma Thompson, *Western Gateway to the National Capital, Rockville, Maryland* (Washington, D.C., 1949), 103–4; Shepard Krech III, ed., *Praise the Bridge That Carries You Over: The Life of Joseph L. Sutton* (Cambridge: Schenkman, 1981), 12; John Blassingame, "The Recruitment of Negro Troops in Maryland," *Maryland Historical Magazine* 58 (March 1963): 20–29; McMain, *Historic Saint Mary's*, 11–13; U.S. Census, *1870 Population Schedules, Rockville, Montgomery County, Maryland, Brighton Post Office*, 8, 9; *Atlas of Fifteen Miles Around Washington Including County of Montgomery, Maryland* (1879; reprint, Rockville, Md.: Montgomery County Historical Society, 1975).

11. For general overviews of Reconstruction, see Kenneth Stampp, *Era of Reconstruction: 1865–1877* (New York: Random House, 1965), and Leon Litwack, *Been in the Storm So Long: The Aftermath of Slavery* (New York: Random House, 1979). Fields, *Slavery and Freedom*, 131–66; W. A. Lowe, "The Freedmen's Bureau in the Border States," in *Radicalism, Racism, and Party Realignment: The Border States During Reconstruction*, ed. Richard Curry (Baltimore: Johns Hopkins Press, 1969), 245–64; U.S. Census, *1870 Population Schedules, Rockville, Montgomery County, Maryland, Brighton Post Office*, 8, 9; *1880 Population Schedules, Rockville, Montgomery County, Maryland*, E.D. 113, vol. 15, sheet 20, line 23; *1870 Population Schedules, Prince George's County, Maryland; 1900 Population Schedules, Rockville, Montgomery County, Maryland*, E.D. 54, vol. 36, sheet 5, line 56. *Montgomery County* (Slave Statistics) 1867–1868, 146. The 1870 census shows that Annie was attending school and lists both Margaret and Delia as literate, which indicates that they must have attended school at some point. Baltimore Association, *First Annual Report: Baltimore Association for the Moral and Educational Improvement of Colored People* (Baltimore, 1865), 5, 28–29; Nina Clarke and Lillian Brown, *History of the Black Public Schools of Montgomery County, Maryland: 1872–1961* (New York: Vantage Press, 1978), 1–10; Richard Butchard, *Northern Schools, Southern Blacks and Reconstruction: Freedmen's Education 1862–1875* (Westport, Conn.: Greenwood Press, 1980), 111, 126, 186–90; Robert C. Morris, *Reading, 'Riting, and Reconstruction: The Education of Freedmen in the South 1861–1870* (Chicago: University of Chicago Press, 1981), 1–53, 149–73; Eva

Slezak interview, October 9, 1986, Baltimore, Maryland. Luther Snowden
was the son of James Snowden, who in 1860 was free and resided in Prince
George's County. Although James Snowden was free, his wife and children may have been slaves, for marriages between slaves and free blacks
were common in Maryland. By 1870, James Snowden had reunited with
his family, including his son Luther, and relocated in Sandy Spring. *Atlas
of Fifteen Miles*, 10–11; U.S. Census, *1880 Population Schedules, Rockville,
Montgomery County, Maryland*, E.D. 113, vol. 15, sheet 20, line 23; *1900
Population Schedules, Rockville, Montgomery County, Maryland*, E.D. 54, vol.
36, sheet 5, line 56; *1860 Population Schedules, Prince George's County, Maryland, 4th Election District, Brandywine Post Office*, 116; *1870 Population Schedules, Sandy Spring, Montgomery County, Maryland, 5th District*, 47. Fields,
Slavery and Freedom, 24.

   12. Fields, *Slavery and Freedom*, 110–89.

   13. Monkey Run was not the only black enclave in the vicinity of Rockville. Northwest of Middle Lane a black settlement, which became known
as Haiti (pronounced Hay-tie), developed on land given by a wealthy planter
to her former slaves. Another black hamlet, called Texas, was situated on
a rise above Monkey Run. However, Haiti and Texas, located on the outskirts of the city, eventually drew blacks who were more affluent than
their neighbors in Monkey Run. *Atlas of Fifteen Miles*, 10–11; Thompson,
Western Gateway, 85. Mary Gordon Malloy and Jane Sween interview, October, 10, 1986, Rockville, Maryland. *Montgomery County Sentinel*, June 21,
1878. William Forrest Prettyman, "Remembrances of Rockville, Maryland"
(typewritten), n.d., Montgomery County Historical Society, Rockville,
Maryland, 9. Jeffrey R. Brackett, *Notes on the Progress of Colored People of
Maryland Since the War* (Baltimore: Johns Hopkins University, 1890), 40;
Hiebert and MacMaster, *Grateful Remembrance*, 245–46, 305, 338.

   14. U.S. Census, *1880 Population Schedules, Rockville, Montgomery County,
Maryland*, E.D. 113, vol. 15, sheet 20, line 23. The 1880 census lists the
following as members of the Snowden household: Luther Snowden, 40;
Emma Snowden, 30; Nicholas Snowden, 16; Harriet Snowden, 14; Charles
Thompson, 25; Elizabeth Thompson, 23; Thomas Bond, 25; George Baker,
40; Nancy Baker, 35; Annie Baker, 20; Maggie Baker, 16; Delia Baker, 14;
George Baker, 2; Milford Baker, 3 months. Krech, *Praise*, 4, 22, 24, 34–36,
51, 69; McDaniel, *Home and Hearth*, 47, 56, 130–86.

   15. U.S. Census, *1880 Population Schedules, Rockville, Montgomery County,
Maryland*, E.D. 113, vol. 15, sheet 20, line 23; *1900 Population Schedules,
Rockville, Montgomery County, Maryland*, E.D. 54, vol. 36, sheet 6, line 4.
Mary Gordon Malloy and Jane Sween interview, October 10, 1986, Rock-
ville, Maryland. Krech, *Praise*, 13–14, 18, 29, 30, 32, 48, 50–51, 69, 70; Hie-
bert and MacMaster, *Grateful Remembrance*, 246.

   16. For a study of black sharecropping in the South, see Roger L. Ran-
som and Richard Sutch, *One Kind of Freedom: The Economic Consequences of
Emancipation* (New York: Cambridge University Press, 1977). McDaniel,
Home and Hearth, 189–91.

17. Krech, *Praise*, 26, 16, 24. McDaniel contends that the African Americans who lived in the black farming communities fully embraced capitalism and Western economics. McDaniel argues that slavery erased African notions of collective ownership, and the oppression of blacks in American society impeded their attempts to establish collective agriculture. However, works by other historians suggest African communalism persisted during and after slavery. Since black Maryland farmers demonstrated extensive communal cooperation, it seems reasonable that a combination of African and Western traditions provided the organizational basis of their communities. McDaniel, *Home and Hearth*, 195–238; Genovese, *Roll Jordon Roll*, 311–24; Levine, *Black Culture*, 136–89, 215.

18. Krech, *Praise*, 24, 16, 26; McDaniel, *Home and Hearth*, 189; Land Records, Montgomery County: JA 3, deed: George Baker and Nancy Baker, August 30, 1886, 59, Montgomery County Court House, Rockville, Maryland.

19. Brackett, *Notes on Progress*, 13–15, 20; Fields, *Slavery and Freedom*, 132–34; Margaret Law Callcott, *The Negro in Maryland Politics: 1870–1912* (Baltimore: Johns Hopkins University Press, 1969), vii–ix. Callcott traces black voting in Maryland and argues that blacks were active participants in the electoral process. *Montgomery County Sentinel*, November 8, 1878, 3; November 7, 1879, 3; September 3, 1880, 3; October 8, 1880, 3; February 18, 1881, 3; February 17, 1882, 3; September 8, 1882, 2; February 16, 1883, 3; September 14, 1883, 2; October 26, 1884, 3; November 13, 1885, 3; April 1, 1887, 3.

20. Callcott, *Negro in Maryland*, vii–ix; Brackett, *Notes on Progress*, 60, 66.

21. *Montgomery County Sentinel*, January 16, 1880, 2; November 22, 1895, 2. Brackett, *Notes on Progress*, 80; *Montgomery County Sentinel*, January 16, 1880, 3; November 25, 1887, 3; November 22, 1895, 2.

22. *Montgomery County Sentinel*, July 17, 1885, 2.

23. *Montgomery County Sentinel*, December 2, 1877, 2; August 2, 1882, 3; August 11, 1882, 3; August 29, 1884, 3; July 17, 1885, 2; September 16, 1887, 3. Brackett, *Notes on Progress*, 80–81.

24. *Montgomery County Sentinel*, April 26, 1878, 3; December 19, 1879, 3; April 21, 1882, 3; September 14, 1883, 3. Krech, *Praise*, 52, 81–82, 88; Brackett, *Notes on Progress*, 58.

25. Hiebert and MacMaster, *Grateful Remembrance*, 196–97; Brackett, *Notes on Progress*, 22; *Montgomery County Sentinel*, June 4, 1880, 3; August 27, 1880, 2; April 22, 1881, 2; August 18, 1882, 3; August 12, 1887, 3; April 15, 1887, 3; December 2, 1904, 3.

26. *Montgomery County Sentinel*, July 9, 1880, 3; April 27, 1894, 3. The report of the board of education indicates that the absentee rate for blacks was 63 percent and the rate for whites was 67 percent. Krech, *Praise*, 48–49.

27. Butchard, *Northern Schools*, 33–75; Morris, *Reading, 'Riting*, 149–173, 248; Hugh Hawkins, ed., *Booker T. Washington and His Critics* (Lexington,

Mass.: D. C. Heath, 1974), 3–44. Booker T. Washington was the primary exponent of "self-help" philosophy. He articulated and modified a philosophy that he had acquired while a student in Freedmen schools. The educational philosophy that Washington made popular in the late nineteenth and early twentieth century had been the foundation for black education since Emancipation.

28. Willie Mae Carey interview, October 6, 1986, Rockville, Maryland. Clarke and Brown, *History*, 48–52, 176–80; Scharf, *History of Western Maryland*, 753; L. M. Hagood, *The Colored Man in the Methodist Episcopal Church* (1890; reprint, Freeport, N.Y.: Books for Libraries Press, 1971), 141–43, 168–69; Krech, *Praise*, 55.

29. Hiebert and MacMaster, *Grateful Remembrance*, 152–53; Hagood, *Colored Man*, 141–43, 159, 168–69; Lewis V. Baldwin, *"Invisible" Strands in African Methodism: A History of the African Union Methodist Protest and Union American Methodist Episcopal Churches, 1805–1980* (Metuchen, N.J.: American Theological Library Association, Scarecrow Press, 1983), 16–17; Harry V. Richardson, *Dark Salvation: The Story of Methodism As It Developed Among Blacks in America* (Garden City, N.Y.: Anchor Press/Doubleday, 1976), 50–61; Farquhar, *Old Homes*, 318; Henson, *Father Henson's*, 27, 58.

30. Sandy Springs, Luther Snowden's former residence, and Prince George's and Montgomery County, where both Snowden and George Baker, Sr., may have lived, had large Quaker settlements. Scharf, *History of Western Maryland*, 773–76; Farquhar, *Old Homes*, 195–96; Douglass, *Life and Times*, 79; Rawick, *American Slave*, 4–5, 7; Charles Samuel Braden, *These Also Believe: A Study of Modern American Cults and Minority Religious Movements* (New York: Macmillan, 1949), 76.

31. *Montgomery County Sentinel*, May 28, 1897, 3.

32. First spoken fall 1931, reprinted in *ND*, July 20, 1974, 17.

CHAPTER TWO

1. St. Clair McKelway and A. J. Liebling, "Who Is This King of Glory?" *New Yorker*, pt. 1, June 13, 1936, 21–28.

2. T. H. S. Boyd, *The History of Montgomery County Maryland, from Its Earliest Settlement in 1650 to 1879* (1879; reprint, Baltimore: Regional Publishing Company, 1968), 139; H. L. Mencken, *Newspaper Days: 1899–1906* (New York: Alfred A. Knopf, 1941), 53; Sherry H. Olson, *Baltimore: The Building of an American City* (Baltimore: Johns Hopkins University Press, 1980), 245–301; Marion E. Warren and Mame Warren, *Baltimore: When She Was What She Used to Be: 1850–1930* (Baltimore: Johns Hopkins University Press, 1983), 44–57. For an examination of African-American migration in the early twentieth century, see Florette Henri, *Black Migration: Movement North: 1900–1920* (Garden City, N.Y.: Anchor Press, 1975).

3. Shepard Krech III, ed., *Praise the Bridge That Carries You Over: The Life of Joseph L. Sutton* (Cambridge: Schenkman, 1981), 26; Olson, *Baltimore*, 275–76; Henri, *Black Migration*, 49–80.

4. Olson, *Baltimore*, 277, 273–279; Booker T. Washington, "Law and Order and the Negro," *Outlook*, November 6, 1909, 547–51; James B. Crooks, *Politics and Progress: The Rise of Urban Progressivism in Baltimore 1895–1911* (Baton Rouge: Louisiana State University Press, 1968), 211. Baltimore's black newspaper, the *Afro-American Ledger*, founded by two leading ministers, rarely noted events occurring outside black middle-class circles. Suzanne Ellery Greene, *Baltimore: An Illustrated History* (Woodland Hills, Calif.: Windsor, 1980), 166–67.

5. Eubie Blake recalled the Gans incident and many other instances of racial conflict in Baltimore. Lawrence T. Carter, *Eubie Blake: Keys of Memory* (Detroit: Balamp Publishing, 1979), 39–40; Olson, *Baltimore*, 279.

6. "Negro Segregation in Cities," *Chautauquan*, March 1911, 11–13; Olson, *Baltimore*, 275–76; Greene, *Baltimore*, 164, 168. "Pigtown" extended from the southwestern boundary of Baltimore to the end of the present Washington Boulevard. Crooks, *Politics*, 20. Greene, *Baltimore*, 164; Olson, *Baltimore*, 233.

7. Helen B. Pendleton, "Negro Dependence in Baltimore," *Charities: A Review of Local and General Philanthropy* 15 (October 7, 1905): 50–58; J. H. N. Waring, "Some Causes of Criminality Among Colored People," *Charities: A Review of Local and General Philanthropy* 15 (October 7, 1905): 45–49; Olson, *Baltimore*, 276.

8. Pendleton, "Negro Dependence," 50–58; Waring, "Some Causes," 45–49; Washington, "Law and Order," 547–48.

9. U.S. Census, *1900 Population Schedules, Baltimore, Maryland*, E.D. 216, vol. 19, sheet 4, line 79; B. R. Sheriff, *R. L. Polk and Company's Baltimore City Directory for 1902* (Baltimore: R. L. Polk, 1902), 1234.

10. U.S. Census, *1900 Population Schedules, Baltimore, Maryland*, E.D. 216, vol. 19, sheet 4, line 79; B. R. Sheriff, *R. L. Polk and Company's Baltimore City Directory for 1899* (Baltimore, R. L. Polk, 1899), 895. The 1900 census lists the following as members of the Ortwine household: William Ortwine, white, 80; Mary J. Ortwine, white, 80; Samuel Lewis, black, 40; Carrie Lewis, black, 38; George W. Lewis, black, 11; George Baker, black, 21; Julia Sisco, black, 21; Gwendoline Sisco, black, 6. George Baker listed his occupation as gardener, his birthdate as May 1879, his birthplace as Maryland, his father's birthplace as Maryland, and his mother's birthplace as Virginia. He was also recorded as single and literate. The 1900 census also shows that Samuel Lewis lived in a house on the Ortwine property without paying rent. The census also lists Lewis as a servant, while the 1899 city directory lists his occupation as coachman. These two sources imply that Lewis worked as Ortwine's driver. His wife, Carrie, was not employed and presumably stayed home and cared for their son George and Julia Sisco's daughter Gwendoline. Julia and Gwendoline Sisco were recorded as boarders, and Julia's occupation was listed as servant. Given the Ortwines' advanced age, it seems likely that Julia worked in their home. The Siscos were probably recorded as boarders since they did not live specifically in the Ortwines' house and did not share a familial relationship

with the Lewises but were provided with room and board by the Ortwines. However, George Baker was registered as a lodger, which suggests that he did not take meals with the household.

11. McKelway and Liebling, "Who Is This King?" pt. 1, 21. U.S. Census, *1900 Population Schedules, Baltimore, Maryland*, E.D. 216, vol. 19, sheet
4, line 79; *1910 Population Schedules, Baltimore, Maryland*, E.D. 60, vol. 6,
sheet 2, line 53. The 1910 census suggests that Baker was out of work for
twenty weeks between 1909 and 1910.

12. First spoken in the fall of 1931; reprinted in *ND,* September 7, 1974,
19. Crooks, *Politics,* 7; Olson, *Baltimore,* 234, 274–75.

13. A general discussion of African Americans in the labor movement
may be found in Philip Foner, *Organized Labor and the Black Worker 1619–
1973* (New York: Praeger, 1979). Olson, *Baltimore,* 234, 274–75.

14. Margaret Law Callcott, *The Negro in Maryland Politics: 1870–1912*
(Baltimore: Johns Hopkins University Press, 1969), vii–ix, 133–61; Crooks,
Politics, 41–71; Greene, *Baltimore,* 168; Mencken, *Newspaper,* 54–55; Olson,
Baltimore, 275; "Negro Segregation," 11–13.

15. For an examination of Washington's leadership, see Louis R. Har-
lan, *Booker T. Washington,* vol. 1, *The Making of a Black Leader* (New York:
Oxford University Press, 1972), and Louis R. Harlan, *Booker T. Washington,*
vol. 2, *The Wizard of Tuskegee, 1910–1915* (New York: Oxford University
Press, 1983). Greene, *Baltimore,* 166–68; W. E. B. Du Bois, *The Souls of Black
Folk* (Chicago: A. C. McClurg, 1903), 41–59; Richard Newman, *Black Power
and Black Religion* (West Cornwall, Conn.: Locust Hill Press, 1987), 65–72;
Baltimore Afro-American, January 6, 1906, 4. In 1906 Du Bois lectured on
John Brown in a Baltimore AME church to an audience of 300 people. The
article suggested that the crowd came "more to hear Mr. Du Bois than
hear of John Brown." E. Franklin Frazier, *The Negro Church in America* (1963;
reprint, New York: Schocken Books, 1974), 35–71; Benjamin Mays and
Joseph W. Nicholson, *The Negro's Church* (New York: Russell and Russell,
1933), 90–93, 278; Lawrence Levine, *Black Culture and Black Consciousness*
(New York: Oxford University Press, 1977), 174–77. For a discussion of
the changes in mainstream African-American denominations, see Gayraud S. Wilmore, *Black Religion and Black Radicalism: An Interpretation of the
Religious History of Afro-American People,* 2d. ed. (Maryknoll, N.Y.: Orbis
Books, 1983), 135–66.

16. Wilmore, *Black Religion,* 160–66; C. Eric Lincoln and Lawrence H.
Mamiya, *The Black Church in the African American Experience* (Durham, N.C.:
Duke University Press, 1990), 115–63.

17. Olson, *Baltimore,* 278; Seth Scheiner, "The Negro Church and the
Northern City, 1890–1930," in *Seven on Black: Reflections on the Negro Experience in America,* ed. William G. Shade and Roy C. Herrenkohl (Philadelphia: J. B. Lippincott, 1969), 92–116; Mays and Nicholson, *Negro's Church,*
94, 115, 223. Azzie Brisco Koger's *Negro Baptists of Maryland* (Baltimore:
Clark Press, 1946) traces the history of the black Baptist church in Baltimore from 1836 to 1946. Leroy Graham, *Baltimore, The Nineteenth Century*

Black Capital (Washington, D.C.: University Press of America, c.1982). Graham's work discusses the evolution of and divisions within the black churches in Baltimore during the nineteenth century.

18. Scheiner, "Negro Church," 100–103; Koger, *Negro Baptists*, 14.

19. B. R. Sheriff, *R. L. Polk and Company's Baltimore City Directory for 1903* (Baltimore: R. L. Polk, 1903), 1305; McKelway and Liebling, "Who Is This King?" pt. 1, 21; Hezekiah Craig and Eli Diana interview, September 8, 1986, Los Angeles, California. In his later years Isaac King roomed with Hezekiah Craig and reminisced about his early encounters with Father Divine. King claimed to have been born in 1869 in Georgia and moved to Alabama where he met Father Divine. He showed Hezekiah Craig several old pictures of himself and others with Father Divine.

20. Hezekiah Craig and Eli Diana interview, September, 8, 1986, Los Angeles, California. For an examination of the roots of New Thought, see Gail Thain Parker, *Mind Cure in New England: From the Civil War to World War I* (Hanover, N.H.: University Press of New England, 1973); Richard Weiss, *The American Myth of Success: From Horatio Alger to Norman Vincent Peale* (New York: Basic Books, 1969), 144–45, 172–88; Charles Samuel Braden, *These Also Believe: A Study of Modern American Cults and Minority Religious Movements* (New York: Macmillan, 1949), 128–40; Martin A. Larson, *New Thought or A Modern Religious Approach: The Philosophy of Health, Happiness, and Prosperity* (New York: Philosophical Library, 1985), 213–15. Charles Samuel Braden also produced a comprehensive study of New Thought in his *Spirits in Rebellion: The Rise and Development of New Thought* (Dallas, Tex.: Southern Methodist University Press, 1963).

21. Braden, *These Also Believe*, 133–38; Parker, *Mind Cure*, 15, 131–49; Weiss, *American Myth*, 133–36. Carl Jackson, in *The Oriental Religions and American Thought: Nineteenth-Century Explorations* (Westport, Conn.: Greenwood Press, 1981) explores the impact of Eastern philosophies on American intellectual traditions.

22. Leon Litwack, *Been in the Storm So Long: The Aftermath of Slavery* (New York: Vintage Books, 1979), 450–501. The presence of New Thought in the black community is documented in Robert Hill and Barbara Bair, eds., *Marcus Garvey: Life and Lessons* (Berkeley: University of California Press, 1987), xxviii–xxix.

23. Richard Weiss argues that during the Progressive period in U.S. history New Thought philosophy appealed to the white middle class fighting status anxiety resulting from the effects of industrialization. Weiss, *American Myth*, 3–15. For information on the general aspects of New Thought, see Parker, *Mind Cure*, 7–9, 70–73; Larson, *New Thought*, 291–92; and Braden, *These Also Believe*, 133–43. For a history of the early New Thought movement from the perspective of a follower, see Horatio Dresser, *History of the New Thought Movement* (New York: Thomas Y. Crowell, 1919).

24. In his master's thesis at Miami University, Ronald Moran White contends that Father Divine derived his theology from those New Thought sources that he later often cited during his sermons. However, most of the

works that White argues inspired Father Divine's teachings were published between 1916 and 1927, several years after Father Divine adopted New Thought concepts and terminology. The only New Thought works that George Baker could have read during his early years in Baltimore were those of Lynn, whom White cites, and Eddy and the Unity School, whom White does not cite. Religious curiosity probably drove Baker to study the works of Lynn and Eddy, but he made only rare references to Lynn's teachings and rejected outright those of Eddy. (Although he became a severe critic of Christian Science and claimed to have never read Mary Baker Eddy's works, his familiarity with her teachings suggests that he did read her books. Nevertheless, he later insisted that Mary Baker Eddy had derived her teachings from him.) Although Lynn and Eddy may have made some impact on George Baker, his later vocabulary, ideas, and the organization of his ministry most closely resemble those of the Unity School, and Charles Fillmore had the strongest influence over the young preacher. Mary Baker Eddy, *Science and Health* (Boston: Trustees under Will of Mary Baker G. Eddy, 1906); Ronald Moran White, "New Thought Influences on Father Divine," M.A. thesis, Miami University, 1980. For a general discussion of Unity School theology, see Charles Fillmore, *Jesus Christ Heals* (Kansas City, Mo.: Unity School of Christianity, 1909). H. Emilie Cady, *Lessons in Truth* (Kansas City, Mo.: Unity School of Christianity, 1926); Braden, *These Also Believe*, 144–79; Larson, *New Thought*, 345–54. Father Divine made direct mention of New Thought authors and works in the following: *ND*, November 2, 1939, 34–35; July 20, 1974, 20; July 6, 1974, 19; *Light*, January 24, 1935, 3. Elam J. Daniels, *Father Divine: The World's Chief False Christ* (Winter Garden, Fla.: Bible Echo Press, 1937), 40.

25. Braden, *These Also Believe*, 144–79; Larson, *New Thought*, 332–28; Marcus Bach, *They Have Found a Faith* (New York: Bobbs-Merrill, 1946), 222–30; Clarence Howell, "Father Divine: Another View," *Christian Century*, October 7, 1936, 1332–33.

26. In the early years of the Unity School movement, Fillmore's teachings were spread by Unity pamphlets, Unity periodicals, and the work of Dr. H. Emilie Cady, a homeopathic physician who composed a set of lessons for Unity School disciples. Cady, *Lessons in Truth*; Braden, *These Also Believe*, 144–79; Larson, *New Thought*, 345–54.

27. Larson, *New Thought*, 345–54.

28. Carey McWilliams, *Southern California, An Island on the Land*, 2d ed. (Santa Barbara, Calif.: Peregrine Smith, 1973), 256–57, 324–26. Hezekiah Craig and Eli Diana interview, September 8, 9, 1986, Los Angeles, California. Hezekiah Craig commented that during a banquet in Philadelphia in 1957, while guests greeted Father Divine as they passed behind him, Father Divine abruptly turned around with a look of recognition after hearing King's voice. King's assertion that Father Divine was in Los Angeles in 1906 is supported by an interview with Father Divine in 1940, which appeared in *ND*, December 12, 1940, 18. In later years, Father Divine commented on the massive interest in New Thought and metaphysics in Cal-

ifornia: "Now those persons are not supposed to be what the ordinary human mind would term as the ignorant and the fanatics. They would not even be termed as the radicals. They are the intellectuals studying in the highest colleges out in California, especially there in California; and from other countries they come to California as it is considered a great metaphysical center out there." First spoken February 7, 1933, reprinted in *ND*, October 25, 1986, 14. Letter: Mrs. M. J. Divine to Jill Watts, April 14, 1987; Dresser, *History of New Thought*, 242–43.

29. *ND*, December 12, 1940, 18. For a history of William Seymour and the origins of the Pentecostal church, see James J. Tinney, "William J. Seymour: Father of Modern-Day Pentecostalism," in *Black Apostles: Afro-American Clergy Confront the Twentieth Century*, ed. Randall K. Burkett and Richard Newman (Boston: G. K. Hall, 1978), 213–25. For a firsthand account of the Azusa Street revival by one of the participating ministers, see Frank Bartleman, *Another Wave of Revival* (1962; reprint, Springdale, Pa.: Whitaker House, 1982). There is a debate in Pentecostal circles concerning the true father of American Pentecostalism. While many favor Seymour, others argue that Charles F. Parham was the founder of the movement. Parham was a white minister who opened a bible college in Texas that Seymour attended before he moved to Los Angeles. For a work on the ministry of Parham, see James R. Goff, Jr., *Fields White Unto Harvest: Charles F. Parham and the Missionary Origins of Pentecostalism* (Fayetteville: University of Arkansas Press, 1988).

30. Father Divine stated, "I recall many years ago shortly after the HOLY GHOST fell in the demonstration or came into expression in My light of understanding, but when I say fell in the demonstration of speaking in tongues in Los Angeles in nineteen six and after then spread throughout this country." *ND*, December 12, 1940, 18.

31. Reprinted in Larson, *New Thought*, 353.

32. *ND*, December 12, 1940, 18.

33. McKelway and Liebling, "Who Is This King?" pt. 1, 22. U.S. Census, *1910 Population Schedules, Baltimore, Maryland*, E.D. 60, vol. 6, sheet 2, line 53, E.D.D. 58–63; *1880 Population Schedules, Rockville, Montgomery County, Maryland*, E.D. 113, vol. 15, sheet 20, line 33. Morris maintained that between 1906 and 1912, George Baker lived on Fairmount Avenue in East Baltimore in a boardinghouse run by Anna Snowden. The 1910 census shows one household that closely approximates Morris's description located at 1503 Fairmount Avenue. The household was headed by 45-year-old Harriette A. Snowden and included her grandchildren Herold W. Clark, 11, Sarah C. Clark, 5, and a boarder named Anderson Baker, 25, who worked as a gardener. It seems probable that Anderson and George Baker are the same person and that the discrepancies in name and age reflect the spiritual transition in George Baker's life. *Sanborn Fire Insurance Map: Baltimore, Maryland* (Baltimore: Sanborn Fire Insurance Company, 1901, 1910, 1914), Pratt Library, Baltimore. Snowden may have been an acquaintance of Baker's from Rockville. It is possible that Harriette Snowden may have

been related to Luther Snowden of Rockville since Snowden had a daughter named Harriet who was of the same age. If Harriette was Luther Snowden's daughter, then Baker may have learned of his father's death on December 15, 1904, of nephritis, in Rockville. *Montgomery County Board of Health* (Death Record) 1899–1906, [MdHR 20, 213-2], 97. Maryland State Archives, Annapolis, Md.; Greene, *Baltimore*, 162; Olson, *Baltimore*, 279–85.

34. McKelway and Liebling, "Who Is This King?" pt. 1, 21–22; B. R. Sheriff, *R. L. Polk and Company's Baltimore City Directory for 1904* (Baltimore: R. L. Polk, 1904), 764; B. R. Sheriff, *R. L. Polk and Company's Baltimore City Directory for 1906* (Baltimore: R. L. Polk, 1906), 830. Morris's contention that Baker worshiped in Reverend Henderson's Eden Street Baptist Church is corroborated by the Baltimore city directories. According to the city directories, a Reverend Thomas Henderson lived in Baltimore on Peabody Street in 1906. Henderson, who had lived at the Peabody address for several years, listed his occupation as laborer until 1904 when he was listed as a minister, which implies that he must have founded his church sometime in late 1904. The Eden Street Church was not recorded in the directory, which suggests that it was independent of the major Baptist denominations and a small church.

35. McKelway and Liebling, "Who Is This King?" pt. 1, 22–24. John Hoshor, *God in a Rolls-Royce: The Rise of Father Divine, Madman, Menace, or Messiah* (New York: Hillman-Curl, 1936), 32–33. Hoshor, who apparently also interviewed Morris, provides a different account of Morris and Baker's first encounter. In this version, Morris claimed to have operated a mission on Druid Hill Avenue. George Baker frequented the evening devotionals and adopted much of Morris's philosophy. Given the fact that it would have been unlikely that an unskilled laborer like Morris could have afforded a home in a black middle-class neighborhood, this account is probably inaccurate. The sensationalized and racist nature of Hoshor's work further undermines the credibility of this story.

36. Morris's wife, Callie, was a native of Maryland, and perhaps family ties drew Morris to Baltimore. The 1903 city directory listed a Samuel Morris, which indicates the possibility that Morris may have been in town a few years before he met George Baker in 1907. B. R. Sheriff, *R. L. Polk and Company's Baltimore City Directory for 1903* (Baltimore: R. L. Polk, 1903), 1237. U.S. Census, *1900 Population Schedules, Allegheny City, Pennsylvania,* E.D. 27, vol. 3, sheet 10A, line 7. The Morris household contained Samuel Morris, 32, born in Pennsylvania; Callie Morris, 32, born in Maryland; Arthur Morris, 4, born in Pennsylvania; and Verna Morris, 3, born in Pennsylvania. Samuel Morris listed his occupation as teamster, and his wife, Callie, listed her occupation as laundress.

37. McKelway and Liebling, "Who Is This King?" pt. 1, 23.

38. Ibid.

39. McKelway and Liebling state that Hickerson was an assistant minister in Elder Warien Roberson's Live Ever and Die Never Church in Bos-

ton. However, Roberson's church headquartered in New York City was not organized until after the outbreak of World War I. Perhaps Hickerson may have come into contact with Roberson earlier when the elder toured the country as an itinerant minister or later may have been involved with Roberson's church in the 1920s. McKelway and Liebling, "Who Is This King?" pt. 1, 23–24. The 1900 census lists the following: R. H. Bradshaw, 53, head of household; John A. Hickerson, 23, boarder; Sarah Hickerson, 24, boarder; Hessie Hickerson, 2, boarder; and Eugene Hickerson, 2, boarder. The census taker recorded that the Hickersons had only one child, which implies that either Hessie or Eugene may have been a child of a relative. U.S. Census, *1900 Population Schedules, Alexandria, Virginia,* E.D. 92, vol. 5, sheet 8, line 13. Hoshor claims that John A. Hickerson (Reverend Bishop Saint John the Vine) was arrested on a statutory charge. However, Hoshor confused Hickerson with Elder Roberson, who was convicted of transporting female minors across state lines for sexual purposes. Hoshor, *Rolls-Royce,* 34–35; Joseph R. Washington, *Black Sects and Cults: The Power Axis in an Ethnic Ethic* (New York: Anchor Press/Doubleday, 1973), 116; Maurice R. Davie, *Negroes in American Society* (New York: McGraw-Hill, 1949), 183; B. R. Sheriff, *R. L. Polk and Company's Baltimore City Directory for 1905* (Baltimore: R. L. Polk, 1905), 802.

40. *New York Amsterdam News,* November 23, 1932, 1. For a discussion of Ethiopianism, its impact on African-American thought, and its influence on the rise of the Rastafarians, see Leonard D. Barrett, *The Rastafarians: Sounds of Cultural Dissonance* (Boston: Beacon Press, 1977), 70–76. Although organized sects of black Jews did not appear until 1915, Hickerson probably learned of Ethiopianism from the numerous traveling preachers who taught the philosophy in the United States or in the ports of the West Indies where Ethiopianism had been thriving. Interestingly, a 1932 picture shows Hickerson in ceremonial robes identical to those of Rastafarian priests. Since Rastafarianism developed about 1932, it seems plausible that the styles evolved independently but may have shared common roots. Hickerson apparently preached in robes while in Baltimore, for in later years Father Divine commented, "There was another that happened to be in Baltimore . . . and he caught the formality of robes and ran up here New York City with it." The person that Father Divine referred to was probably Hickerson, who at the time was living and preaching in New York City. First spoken March 8, 1933, reprinted in *ND,* September 9, 1978, 3. For an examination of the origins of Ethiopian Judaism in America, see Howard M. Brotz, *The Black Jews of Harlem: Negro Nationalism and the Dilemmas of Negro Leadership* (London: Free Press of Glencoe, 1964), 1–14; *Baltimore Sun,* August 25, 1911, 8. The *Sun* article tells of a black preacher who claimed that his name was Calvary and that he was Abyssinian. The preacher was banished from Charlottesville, Virginia, for preaching racial equality.

41. McKelway and Liebling, "Who Is This King?" pt. 1, 23.

42. *New York Amsterdam News,* November 23, 1932, 1; McKelway and Liebling, "Who Is This King?" pt. 1, 23; Theodore Schroeder, "Living Gods,"

Azoth: The Occult Magazine of America, October 1918, 202–5; Theodore Schroeder, "Psychology of One Pantheist," *Psychoanalytic Review* 20 (July 1921): 314–25. Although Father Jehovia, the Bishop, and the Messenger each claimed to have influenced the other, it seems likely that the Messenger had the most direct link to New Thought philosophy. They all internalized New Thought ideas independently and from different sources, but only the Messenger admitted familiarity with New Thought literature. The Messenger was probably instrumental in advancing Father Jehovia's and the Bishop's knowledge of New Thought philosophy and introducing the men to the specific vocabulary used by New Thought disciples. As early as 1918, Theodore Schroeder, a psychiatrist who studied members of the Bishop's sect in New York, compiled a sample sermon from notes he had taken during a service in the Bishop's church. The messages not only strongly espoused New Thought philosophy but also utilized New Thought terminology. Furthermore, most of the content and vocabulary of the sermons were identical to messages delivered by Father Divine. Even though the earliest recorded sermons of Father Divine date from 1931, an incident in Valdosta, Georgia, indicates that the Messenger preached a version of New Thought as early as 1913. Therefore, the inferences made by other authors that the Messenger sat in on the Bishop's services in New York and mimicked the Bishop's style and theology are questionable. It seems much more likely that the Messenger and the Bishop preached different versions of a common philosophy. For a sample of Father Divine's later messages, see any issue of the *New Day.* Many of the terms and phraseology found in Father Divine's later sermons are included and defined in Ernest Shurtleff Holmes, *New Thought Terms and Their Meanings* (New York: Dodd, Mead, 1942).

43. McKelway and Liebling, "Who Is This King?" pt. 1, 21–26.

44. *New York News,* October 1, 1932, 8; U.S. Census, *1910 Population Schedules, Baltimore, Maryland,* E.D. 60, vol. 6, sheet 2, line 53; B. R. Sheriff, *R. L. Polk and Company's Baltimore City Directory for 1911* (Baltimore: R. L. Polk, 1911), 257.

45. Daniels, *Father Divine,* 39.

46. McKelway and Liebling, "Who Is This King?" pt. 1, 23–24; *New York Amsterdam News,* November 23, 1932, 1; *ND,* June 15, 1974, 15. Although McKelway and Liebling do not specify the Messenger's stand during the breakup, other sources suggest that at this time the Messenger established his sole claim to divinity. The Bishop claimed, "It was I who pronounced the theory that God was within man. [The Messenger] . . . grabbed it and started out preaching that it had come to him from Heaven." The Messenger's later recollections, reprinted in the *New Day,* reveal that by 1914, he definitely considered himself divine.

CHAPTER THREE

1. First spoken on March 8, 1933, reprinted in *ND,* December 9, 1978, 3.
2. For another interpretation of this period of Father Divine's life, see

Robert Weisbrot, *Father Divine and the Struggle for Racial Equality* (Urbana: University of Illinois Press, 1983), 17. First spoken on March 8, 1933, reprinted in *ND*, December 9, 1978, 3.

3. First spoken on March 8, 1933, reprinted in *ND*, December 9, 1978, 3. In a November 1939 message, Father Divine proclaimed that a street preacher exhibited "the characteristics and the nature of a thief and of a robber." He compared these ministers to beggars and declared, "I got after them about begging and holding up the people." *ND*, November 2, 1939, 52; Weisbrot, *Father Divine*, 17.

4. First spoken on March 8, 1933, reprinted in *ND*, December 9, 1978, 3; Weisbrot, *Father Divine*, 17.

5. First spoken on March 8, 1933, reprinted in *ND*, December 9, 1978, 3.

6. Weisbrot, *Father Divine*, 17. First spoken on March 8, 1933, reprinted in *ND*, December 9, 1978, 3. For information on Reverend Arthur Penrhyn Stanley, who was born in 1815 and died 1881, see George John Stevenson, *The Methodist Hymn-Book* (London: S. W. Partridge, 1883), 404–5. At a 1986 luncheon followers played a tape of one of Father Divine's messages. Father Divine concentrated on eternal life on earth for all those who closely followed his teachings. After the message finished, Mother Divine explained to diners that the message was a reaction to a visiting church choir that had sung several hymns focusing on salvation and eternal life in heaven. Mrs. M. J. Divine's comments, luncheon at Woodmont Estate, Gladwyne, Pennsylvania, October 15, 1986.

7. First spoken on September 30, 1931, reprinted in *ND*, June 29, 1974, 19. St. Clair McKelway and A. J. Liebling, "Who Is This King of Glory?" *New Yorker*, pt. 1, June 13, 1936, 24. Anderson K. Baker is recorded on Fairmount Avenue in the 1911 directory but does not appear in subsequent directories. B. R. Sheriff, *R. L. Polk and Company's Baltimore City Directory for 1911* (Baltimore: R. L. Polk, 1911), 257; B. R. Sheriff, *R. L. Polk and Company's Baltimore City Directory for 1912* (Baltimore: R. L. Polk, 1912); *ND*, August 13, 1974, 19. Father Divine told an undercover investigator that he was an itinerant and that the poor people fed and sheltered him. *SCN*, April 25, 1930, 1, 7.

8. Testimony from banquet on February 28, 1937, reprinted in *ND*, March 1, 1980, 1; Edna Mae Claybrooke interview, October 15, 1986, Gladwyne, Pennsylvania. Claybrooke, one of Father Divine's secretaries and later Mother Divine's personal secretary, commented that even in the 1930s and 1940s Father Divine held services in homes of poor families and gladly served what the family had to offer.

9. Testimony from banquet on February 28, 1937, reprinted in *ND*, March 1, 1980, 1. Several outside observers recorded the banquet rituals in the 1930s and 1940s. See Claude McKay, *Harlem: Negro Metropolis* (New York: E. P. Dutton, 1940), 38–44; Samuel Braden, *These Also Believe: A Study of Modern American Cults and Minority Religious Movements* (New York: Macmillan, 1949), 1–6; Marcus Bach, *They Have Found a Faith* (New York: Bobbs-Merrill, 1946), 175–77; *SCN*, April 25, 1930, 7.

10. First spoken fall 1931, reprinted in *ND*, August 20, 1974, 18.

11. *Valdosta Daily Times,* February 6, 1914.

12. Ibid., February 5, 1914.

13. Ibid., February 5, 1914; February 6, 1914.

14. Benjamin Mays and Joseph Nicholson, *The Negro's Church* (New York: Russell and Russell, 1933), 100–101.

15. "GOD requires a wide open, consecreated heart and mind and soul and body. Those who call themselves men do not bring themselves into subjection to the CHRIST as readily, apparently, as those who call themselves women. Women have developed an obedient and submissive spirit and have obeyed their husbands. If they wanted to come down here for instance, they asked their husbands if they could come. But those who call themselves men, when they want to go anywhere, they just say 'I'm going.' It is comparatively easy for a woman to exchange submission to her husband for submission for ME, but it is hard for a so-called man to recognize in another something superior to his own estimate of himself." First spoken October 1931, reprinted in *ND,* August 13, 1974, 19. First spoken September 20, 1931; reprinted in *ND,* June 22, 1974, 20.

16. *Valdosta Daily Times,* February 27, 1914.

17. Ibid., February 6, 1914; February 17, 1914.

18. Ibid., February 6, 1914.

19. *Valdosta Daily Times,* February 6, 1914; February 17, 1914. For secondary accounts of the Valdosta incident, see Fred Lamar Pearson and Joseph Aaron Tomberlin, "John Doe, Alias God: A Note on Father Divine's Georgia Career," *Georgia Historical Quarterly* 60 (1976): 43–48; McKelway and Liebling, "Who Is This King?" pt. 1, 24–26.

20. *Valdosta Daily Times,* February 21, 1914.

21. J. R. Moseley, *Manifest Victory: A Quest and Testimony* (New York: Harper and Brothers, 1947), 106–7. In later years, after the Messenger had become Father Divine, Moseley visited him in New York City. Father Divine warmly received Moseley, showed his old friend around one of the Peace Missions, and invited the Georgia minister to speak at a banquet.

22. Pearson and Tomberlin, "John Doe," 46. Pearson and Tomberlin interviewed J. B. Copeland's son James, who recalled several details of the Messenger's case and his father's involvement. Moseley, *Manifest Victory,* 106–7.

23. *Valdosta Daily Times,* February 27, 1914; March 2, 1914. McKelway and Liebling, "Who Is This King?" pt. 1, 24–26.

24. *Valdosta Daily Times,* February 27, 1914; February 28, 1914; March 2, 1914. Pearson and Tomberlin, "John Doe," 46.

25. *Valdosta Daily Times,* February 27, 1914.

26. Ibid.

27. Ibid., March 2, 1914.

28. McKelway and Liebling, "Who Is This King?" pt. 1, 25–26.

29. *Valdosta Daily Times,* February 27, 1914; February 28, 1914. Moseley, *Manifest Victory,* 107.

30. *Valdosta Daily Times,* February 28, 1914.

31. Moseley, *Manifest Victory*, 107–9.

32. *ND*, December 12, 1940, 18–19; Moseley, *Manifest Victory*, 107–9.

33. *ND*, July 13, 1974, 19; McKelway and Liebling, "Who Is This King?" pt. 1, 26.

34. *ND*, July 6, 1974, 17; June 15, 1974, 20. Hezekiah Craig interview, August 27, 1986, Los Angeles, California. Mother Divine explained in an interview with a television reporter that the scars traversing the back of Father Divine's head resulted from lynchings. Followers who have met Father Divine confirm that he did have scars on the back of his head. *ND*, December 25, 1982, 21.

35. Theodore Schroeder, "A 'Living God' Incarnate," *Psychoanalytic Review* 19 (January 1932): 40–41. Schroeder, a research psychologist, attended many services conducted by the Bishop and produced several studies on the church and its followers. See also Theodore Schroeder, "Living Gods," *Azoth: The Occult Magazine of America*, October 1918, 202–5, "Psychology of One Pantheist," *Psychoanalytic Review* 20 (July 1921): 314–25; McKelway and Liebling, "Who Is This King?" pt. 1, 26; John Hoshor, *God in a Rolls-Royce: The Rise of Father Divine, Madman, Menace, or Messiah* (New York: Hillman-Curl, 1936), 34–35. Joseph R. Washington, *Black Sects and Cults: The Power Axis in an Ethnic Ethic* (Garden City, N.Y.: Anchor Press, 1973), 116; Maurice R. Davie, *Negroes in American Society* (New York: McGraw-Hill, 1949), 183; Robert Allerton Parker, *Incredible Messiah: The Deification of Father Divine* (Boston: Little, Brown, 1937), 93–101; *New York Amsterdam News*, November 23, 1932, 1.

36. *ND*, June 15, 1974, 15. The Messenger's recollections contradict the common belief that when the evangelist first arrived in New York, he renewed his friendship with the Bishop and adopted many of the Bishop's rituals and practices. After the breakdown of the Fairmount Avenue ministry, the two preachers never again shared a good relationship and continued to bicker over theological principles. See the Bishop's attack on the Messenger in *New York Amsterdam News*, November 23, 1932, 1. McKelway and Liebling in their article and Hoshor in his book were the first to claim that the Messenger and the Bishop reestablished friendly ties. See McKelway and Liebling, "Who Is This King?" pt. 1, 26; Hoshor, *Rolls-Royce*, 34–35.

37. *ND*, June 22, 1974, 17.

38. First spoken on September 26, 1931, reprinted in *ND*, June 29, 1974, 18. Followers interpret this passage as a prediction of the rise of the U.S. space program. First spoken March 3, 1933, reprinted in *ND*, December 9, 1978, 4. In 1933 Father Divine declared, "I came back here to New York in 1917. Of course I did travel backwards and forth, but I happened to stop right over here on Broome Street." Broome Street, which is in Manhattan, may have been a temporary location before the flock moved to Brooklyn. For estimate on the size of the Messenger's flock, see Hoshor, *Rolls-Royce*, 33; McKelway and Liebling, "Who Is This King?" pt. 1, 26.

39. McKay, *Negro Metropolis*, 15–31; Florette Henry, *Black Migration* (New

York: Anchor Press, 1975), 87–90, 122–24; Jervis Anderson, *This Was Harlem: A Cultural Portrait* (New York: Farrar Straus Giroux, 1981), 59–133; Edwin R. Lewinson, *Black Politics in New York City* (New York: Twayne, 1974), 161–74.

40. *ND*, November 2, 1939, 52–53. For a survey of several of the early sects in Harlem, see Washington, *Black Sects*, 36–139. McKay, *Negro Metropolis*, 32–85; Mays and Nicholson, *Negro's Church*, 94–103; Howard Brotz, *The Black Jews of Harlem: Negro Nationalism and the Dilemmas of Negro Leadership* (London: Free Press of Glencoe, 1964), 9–14.

41. First spoken September 30, 1931, reprinted in *ND*, June 29, 1974, 19; *ND*, November 2, 1939, 52–53.

42. First spoken September 30, 1931, reprinted in *ND*, June 29, 1974, 19.

43. First spoken March 3, 1933, reprinted in *ND*, December 9, 1978, 4; *ND*, August 28, 1954, 15. Claude McKay interviewed a Mrs. Deanne who claimed to have lived in the Brooklyn collective in 1914. Perhaps the Messenger organized the home in 1914 but did not settle permanently in New York until 1917. It is also possible that the woman, interviewed in the late 1930s, may have forgotten the exact date. McKay, *Negro Metropolis*, 33–34; Mrs. M. J. Divine, *The Peace Mission Movement* (Philadelphia: Imperial Press, 1982), 23–25.

44. *ND*, August 28, 1954, 15; McKay, *Negro Metropolis*, 33–34; McKelway and Liebling, "Who Is This King?" pt. 1, 26, 28.

45. McKay claimed that the household was composed only of women, but at least one male follower and perhaps more lived in the Brooklyn collective. McKay, *Negro Metropolis*, 33–34; Hezekiah Craig and Eli Diana interview, September 8, 1986, Los Angeles, California. First spoken February 7–8, 1939, reprinted in *ND*, March 5, 1983, 13.

46. Hezekiah Craig and Eli Diana interview, September 8, 1986, Los Angeles, California. Hezekiah Craig and Eli Diana were acquainted with Gabriel, who died in 1971, reportedly at the age of 125. First spoken February 7–8, 1939, reprinted in *ND*, March 5, 1983, 13; McKelway and Liebling, "Who Is This King?" pt. 1, 26; *SCN*, July 1, 1932, 7.

47. Although no evidence on Peninniah's early life exists, most authors agree that the Messenger recruited Peninniah in Macon, Georgia, which is possible since it was probably Peninniah whom Moseley encountered. Peninniah only once made any reference to her history. Hospitalized in 1937, she gave her name as Anna Brown and listed her age as 63. However, probably neither the name nor age were accurate, and Peninniah gave such data to avoid publicity and appease the hospital admitting staff. Moseley, *Manifest Victory*, 107. Moseley mistakenly identified Peninniah as Faithful Mary, a follower who resembled Peninniah but did not join the movement until the 1930s. Faithful Mary, *"God," He's Just a Natural Man* (New York: Gailliard Press, 1936), 3–10; Hoshor, *Rolls-Royce*, 33; *Literary Digest*, May 1, 1937, 7; *SCN*, April 25, 1930, 7. First spoken February 7–8, 1939, reprinted in *ND*, March 5, 1983, 13. Interestingly, Peninniah was the

name of a minor Old Testament biblical character: a wife of Elkanah, Peninniah bore several children during a period of time when his other wife, Hannah, was barren. Later Hannah gave birth to Samuel (1 Samuel 1:2). *ND*, November 5, 1942, 38.

48. First spoken February 7–8, 1939, reprinted in *ND*, March 5, 1983, 13.

49. Mrs. M. J. Divine, *Peace Mission Movement*, 56.

50. First spoken October 1931, reprinted in *ND*, August 13, 1974, 18.

51. *ND*, June 22, 1974, 20; *SCN*, April 29, 1932, 1; Edna Mae Claybrooke interview, October 15, 1986, Gladwyne, Pennsylvania. Although some authors contend that a distinction existed between Father Divine's "children" and his "angels," according to Claybrooke, both categories denote followers of Father Divine.

52. Although few of the early hymns have survived, it is possible the Brooklyn household sang this one or a similar composition. The song appears on the introduction to a cassette recording of Father Divine's sermons read by his second wife, Mrs. M. J. Divine. Reverend M. J. Divine, *The Word of God Revealed*, audiocassette (Philadelphia: Peace Mission Movement, n.d.); *SW*, July 21, 1936, 25; Mrs. M. J. Divine, *Peace Mission Movement*, 105–8.

CHAPTER FOUR

1. Nathan Irvin Huggins, *Harlem Renaissance* (New York: Oxford University Press, 1971), 54–56; David Levering Lewis, *When Harlem Was in Vogue* (New York: Vintage Books, 1982), 3–5.

2. Huggins, *Harlem Renaissance*, 3–12. Huggins's work focuses primarily on the literary aspect of the Renaissance, and he argues that the Renaissance was both an African-American and Euramerican awakening. Huggins contends that the black experience is so intimately bound to American culture that a phenomenon like the Renaissance cannot be analyzed isolated from white American culture and that the white participants in the Renaissance provided the impetus for the cultural awakening. Huggins argues that blacks struggled to assert their equality through the white literary tradition. As a result, black literature became increasingly artificial and, Huggins concludes, the Renaissance was in many ways a failure. For another work on the Harlem Renaissance, see Lewis, *When Harlem*, 20–21, 34–44. Lewis offers a broader view of the Harlem Renaissance. Moving beyond the literary crowd, Lewis explores African-American music, the entertainment industry, political leadership, and some religious movements. See also Theodore G. Vincent, *Voices of a Black Nation: Political Journalism in the Harlem Renaissance* (San Francisco: Ramparts Press, 1973); Houston Baker, *Modernism and the Harlem Renaissance* (Chicago: University of Chicago Press, 1978); Victor Kramer, ed., *The Harlem Renaissance Reexamined* (New York: AMS Press, 1987).

3. A variety of works investigate Marcus Garvey and the UNIA.

E. David Cronon, *Black Moses: The Story of Marcus Garvey and the Universal Negro Improvement Association* (Madison: University of Wisconsin Press, 1955); Judith Stein, *The World of Marcus Garvey: Race and Class in Modern Society* (Baton Rouge: Louisiana State University Press, 1986). For an overview of Garvey's life, activities, and philosophy, see Robert A. Hill and Barbara Bair, eds., *Marcus Garvey: Life and Lessons* (Berkeley: University of California Press, 1987), xv–lxviii. For information on Reverend Bishop Saint John the Vine's participation in the Garvey movement, see *New York Amsterdam News*, November 23, 1932, 1.

4. Florette Henri, *Black Migration: Movement North* (Garden City, N.Y.: Anchor Press/Doubleday, 1975), 184–85. For a discussion of the increase of religious alternatives, see Benjamin Mays and Joseph W. Nicholson, *The Negro Church* (New York: Russell and Russell, 1933), 94–99, 200; Seth Scheiner, "The Negro Church and the Northern City, 1890–1930," in *Seven on Black: Reflections on the Negro Experience in America*, ed. William G. Shade and Roy C. Herrenkohl (Philadelphia: J. B. Lippincott, 1969), 92–116; Gayraud S. Wilmore, *Black Religion and Black Radicalism*, 2d ed. (Maryknoll, N.Y.: Orbis Books, 1983), 135–63.

5. Howard Brotz, *The Black Jews of Harlem: Negro Nationalism and the Dilemmas of Negro Leadership* (London: Free Press of Glencoe, 1964), 1–45. For information on Elder Warien K. Roberson, see *NYT*, February 17, 1926, 20; April 16, 1926, 12; May 20, 1926, 27; *New York Age*, April 17, 1926, 1; May 29, 1926, 1. A brief examination of Prophet Noble Drew Ali is in Joseph R. Washington, *Black Sects and Cults: The Power Axis in an Ethnic Ethic* (Garden City, N.Y.: Anchor Press/Doubleday, 1973), 128.

6. Washington, *Black Sects*, 36–107. For an overview of George Wilson Becton's ministry, see Jervis Anderson, *This Was Harlem: A Cultural Portrait* (New York: Farrar Straus Giroux, 1981), 248–50, and Claude McKay, *Harlem: Negro Metropolis* (New York: E. P. Dutton, 1940), 84–85.

7. Charles P. Dickerson, *A History of the Sayville Community* (Sayville, N.Y.: Suffolk County News, 1975); St. Clair McKelway and A. J. Liebling, "Who Is This King of Glory?" *New Yorker*, pt. 1, June 13, 1936, 28.

8. McKelway and Liebling, "Who Is This King?" pt. 1, 28; Sara Harris, *Father Divine: Holy Husband* (New York: Doubleday, 1953), 22; Robert Allerton Parker, *The Incredible Messiah: The Deification of Father Divine* (Boston: Little, Brown, 1937), 3–4.

9. *ND*, November 2, 1939, 34. Weisbrot characterizes Father Divine's relocation in Sayville as "a continuation, indeed a heightening of his creative withdrawal from the bustling evangelical life of his earlier years." According to Weisbrot, disappointed by his failure as an itinerant, Father Divine retired from evangelism. Robert Weisbrot, *Father Divine and the Struggle for Racial Equality* (Urbana: University of Illinois Press, 1983), 28.

10. *ND*, November 2, 1939, 34.

11. Kenneth Burnham, *God Comes to America: Father Divine* (Boston: Lambeth Press, 1979), 6.

12. First spoken on March 8, 1933, reprinted in *ND*, December 9, 1978, 3; *SCN*, April 25, 1930, 1; *Sunday News*, May 15, 1931, reprinted in *ND*, August 17, 1974, 19.

13. St. Clair McKelway and A. J. Liebling, "Who Is This King of Glory?" *New Yorker*, pt. 2, June 20, 1936, 22; Mrs. M. J. Divine interview, October 14, 1986, Gladwyne, Pennsylvania.

14. McKelway and Liebling, "Who Is This King?" pt. 2, 22; *SCN*, July 21, 1922, 1; April 25, 1930, 1; *Sunday News*, May 15, 1931, reprinted in *ND*, August 17, 1974, 19; *ND*, June 22, 1974, 20.

15. *SCN*, April 25, 1930, 7; Mrs. M. J. Divine interview, October 14, 1986, Gladwyne, Pennsylvania; Edna Mae Claybrooke interview, October 15, 1986, Gladwyne, Pennsylvania.

16. McKelway and Liebling, "Who Is This King?" pt. 2, 22; *SCN*, April 25, 1930, 1.

17. *SNC*, March 28, 1924, 4. For analysis of the race riots of 1919, see William M. Tuttle, Jr., *Race Riot: Chicago in the Red Summer of 1919* (New York: Atheneum, 1970), 23; *SCN*, March 28, 1924, 4; Dickerson, *History of Sayville*; Kenneth Jackson, *The Ku Klux Klan in the City, 1915–1930* (New York: Oxford University Press, 1967), 178. In Jackson's examination of the resurgence of the Klan, he notes that in 1923 several Klan members were elected to public office on Long Island and in 1924 the Klan briefly dominated the Suffolk County Republican Committee.

18. First spoken in December 1931, reprinted in *ND*, September 7, 1974, 17.

19. *SCN*, April 25, 1930, 1; Edna Mae Claybrooke interview, October 14, 1986, Gladwyne, Pennsylvania. Claybrooke, who described the private side of Father Divine, was one of his secretaries for 20 years. *New York Age*, May 16, 1931, 1–2; *ND*, December 9, 1978, 3. Father Divine believed that robes were unnecessary attire and wore suits for both business appointments and preaching. *SCN*, April 25, 1930, 1; McKelway and Liebling, "Who Is This King?" pt. 2, 22.

20. *SCN*, July 21, 1922, 1.

21. Ibid., March 31, 1922, 4.

22. *ND*, June 22, 1974, 20; December 28, 1974, 19. Father Divine mentioned in 1924 that he "had gone south and I came back."

23. Ibid., July 13, 1974, 20.

24. *SCN*, April 25, 1930, 1; Edna Mae Claybrooke interview, October 15, 1986, Gladwyne, Pennsylvania.

25. Bruce Barton, *The Man Nobody Knows: The Discovery of the Real Jesus* (Indianapolis: Bobbs-Merrill, 1925). Father Divine also praised Barton's *The Book Nobody Knows* (New York: Gosset and Dunlap, c. 1926). In several sermons Father Divine cited New Thought and religious works. *ND*, November 2, 1939, 34–35; July 6, 1974, 19; July 20, 1974, 20; *Light*, January 24, 1935, 3.

26. *Christ in You* (New York: Dodd, Mead, 1918), 6, 132; Robert Collier, *The Secret of Gold* (New York: Robert Collier, 1927).

27. Jeddu Krishnamurti, *The Kingdom of Happiness* (New York: Liverlight, 1927), 13.

28. Ibid., 29–31.

29. Baird T. Spalding, *The Life and Teaching of the Masters of the Far East,* vol. 1 (Los Angeles: Devorss, 1924), 7.

30. Ibid., 156.

31. Martin A. Larson, *New Thought or A Modern Religious Approach* (New York: Philosophical Library, 1985), 327–34; Marcus Bach, *They Have Found a Faith* (New York: Bobbs-Merrill, 1946), 222–53.

32. Weisbrot speculates that the New Thought literature of the 1920s "may also have done much to shape Divine's religious focus." Weisbrot, *Father Divine,* 28; McKelway and Liebling, "Who Is This King?" pt. 1, 23. Studies that contend that Father Divine presented coherent sermons and was influenced by New Thought authors are Ronald Moran White, "New Thought Influences on Father Divine," M.A. thesis, Miami University, 1980, and Charles Samuel Braden, *These Also Believe: A Study of Modern Religious Cults and Minority Religious Movements* (New York: Macmillan, 1949), 1–76.

33. *ND,* November 2, 1939, 34–35; July 6, 1974, 19; July 20, 1974, 20; *Light,* January 24, 1935, 3. Father Divine's extensive reading list also included Joseph Sieber Benner, *The Impersonal Life* (San Diego: Sun Publishing, 1916); Lillian DeWaters, *The Christ Within* (Stamford, Conn.: Lillian DeWaters, 1925); Baird T. Spalding, *The Life and Teaching of the Masters of the Far East,* vol. 2 (Los Angeles: Devorss, 1927). In an interview with Charles Braden in the 1940s, Father Divine admitted that he had at one time passed out Unity School literature, but earlier he had denied distributing any of Fillmore's works. Most likely, at one point he did hand out Unity publications but stopped when Unity began printing a price on their works. He insisted that he feared that people would want to pay for the books, which was a violation of his teachings. Perhaps his exclusion of Unity School writings resulted from the close similarities between his theology and Fillmore's philosophy. However, Father Divine passed out other books that resembled his teachings. Braden, *These Also Believe,* 75–76.

34. *Light,* January 24, 1935, 3; *SCN,* April 25, 1930, 1; *ND,* November 2, 1939, 35. Father Divine dated the expansion of his following to 1927 and 1928: "When I got up to that place where I was willing to give out a thousand dollars' worth [of books] a month, why, we were caught up in the SPIRIT and the way it was found out, the people flooded out to Sayville and swamped the place, and so from that time, around nineteen twenty-eight, twenty-seven or twenty-eight . . . it has been spreading publicly."

35. The FBI compiled several files of newspaper clippings on the movement that contain the name of the newspaper and date of the article but no page numbers. FBI 31-46627-A; *New York Evening Journal,* May 6, 1937. Many studies have concluded that all the new disciples were Long Island domestics with substantial incomes. Consequently, most investigators

conjecture that Father Divine derived his wealth from his financially secure new converts. Such assumptions distort both the position of blacks
in the work force and the composition of Father Divine's congregation.
For an example of speculation along these lines, see McKelway and Liebling, "Who Is This King?" pt. 2, 22.

36. Weisbrot, *Father Divine*, 34–37.

37. *ND*, July 13, 1974, 17; Mays and Nicholson record the presence of
Unity churches in the black communities; *Negro's Church*, 222.

38. Louis R. Harlan, *Booker T. Washington*, vol. 1, *The Making of a Black
Leader* (New York: Oxford University Press, 1972), 95; Robert Hill, "General Introduction," in *The Marcus Garvey and Universal Negro Improvement
Association Papers*, vol. 1, *1826–August 1919*, ed. Robert Hill and Carol Rudisell (Berkeley, Calif.: University of California Press, 1983), xxxv–xc; Hill
and Bair, *Marcus Garvey*, xxviii–li.

39. Hill and Bair, *Marcus Garvey*, lxv–lxvi; Cronon, *Black Moses*, 103–43;
Stein, *World of Marcus Garvey*, 186–208.

40. FBI File 31-46627-A; *New York Evening Journal*, April 15, 1937; *Sunday
News*, April 27, 1930, reprinted in *ND*, August 17, 1974, 19; *SCN*, April 25,
1930, 7; John Hoshor, *God in a Rolls-Royce: The Rise of Father Divine, Madman, Menace, or Messiah* (New York: Hillman-Curl, 1936), 38. Hoshor claims
that the first white follower joined in 1926. According to Hoshor, this follower, a white man, had come to Father Divine after losing his job, and
the minister found him a live-in position in a home on Long Island. At the
end of the summer when his employers returned to the city, he moved
into Father Divine's Macon Street home. The inaccuracies and racism in
Hoshor's biography of Father Divine detract from the credibility of his
claims. However, by the late 1920s, Father Divine clearly had a significant
number of white followers. Albert C. Grier et al., *Father Divine: An Intepre-
tation with Appreciations and Comments* (Santa Barbara: Red Rose Press, n.d.)
discusses the presence of white followers during this period of Father Divine's ministry.

41. *ND*, June 22, 1974, 18; *SCN*, April 25, 1930, 1; *Sunday News*, April
27, 1930, reprinted in *ND*, August 17, 1974, 19.

42. *ND*, June 22, 1974, 18; *SCN*, April 25, 1930, 1, 7.

43. *SCN*, April 25, 1930, 7; Bart Bing, "Sayville Religious Teaching Draws
Big Crowds," *Island News*, October 1, 1931, reprinted in *ND*, June 15, 1974,
18–19; Braden, *These Also Believe*, 1–6; luncheon at Woodmont in Gladwyne, Pennsylvania, October 14 and 15, 1986. The similarity between the
earliest and later accounts and present banqueting practices suggests that
the Holy Communion banquets have remained structurally the same
throughout the years.

44. *SCN*, April 25, 1930, 1, 7; *Sunday News*, April 27, 1930, reprinted in
ND, August 17, 1974, 19.

45. *SCN*, April 25, 1930, 1, 7.

46. Ibid.

47. *SCN*, April 25, 1930, 7; *Sunday News*, April 27, 1930, reprinted in *ND*, August 17, 1974, 19; *ND*, September 21, 1974, 22; Bing, "Sayville Religious Teaching," 19.

48. *SCN*, April 25, 1930, 7.

49. Ibid.

50. *ND*, September 21, 1974, 19; *SCN*, April 25, 1930, 1, 7; *Sunday News*, April 27, 1930, reprinted in *ND*, August 17, 1974, 19. Samuel Braden, who interviewed Father Divine in the 1940s, compared the Peace Mission's moral code with Roman Catholic monasticism; Braden, *These Also Believe*, 76.

51. *ND*, August 13, 1974, 18. "A child should be trained hereditively or prenatally. I have also said, train a child seven years before it is born and then train him seven years after it is born, in the right way, whatsoever way it may be that is deemed right by the parent, and that child will be bent in the way it will go when it is old." First spoken on September 5, 1942, reprinted in Reverend M. J. Divine, *A Treatise on Overpopulation Taken from Interviews, Sermons and Lectures of Father Divine* (Philadelphia: New Day Publishing, 1967), 1. *SCN*, April 25, 1930, 7.

52. *SCN*, April 25, 1930, 7.

53. Ibid.

54. Ibid.

55. Ibid.

56. *SCN*, April 25, 1930, 1, 7; *Sunday News*, April 27, 1930, reprinted in *ND*, August 17, 1974, 19. Hadley reported that the household had 30 permanent residents and directly mentioned 10 other followers and sympathizers who visited Father Divine during the course of her investigation. However, she curiously neglected to enumerate the visitors on the weekends. At least 40 people attended services regularly and probably more on holidays.

57. *SCN*, April 25, 1930, 7.

58. *SCN*, April 25, 1930, 7; *Sunday News*, April 27, 1930, reprinted in *ND*, August 17, 1974, 19. Later, some charged that Hadley under Father Divine's mysterious powers had joined the cult and reported what Father Divine wanted the authorities to know.

59. *SCN*, April 25, 1930, 1.

60. *Sunday News*, April 27, 1930, reprinted in *ND*, August 17, 1974, 19.

61. *SCN*, April 17, 1931, 1, 8; May 8, 1931, 1; May 15, 1931, 1.

62. *ND*, July 17, 1974, 17–18, August 10, 1974, 19–20.

63. Heavenly Rest interview, December 15, 1986, Los Angeles, California.

64. Walter Clemow Lanyon, *The Eyes of the Blind* (Los Angeles: Inspiration House, 1959), 8; *ND*, August 10, 1974, 19–20; September 28, 1974, 19.

65. *ND*, August 17, 1974, 17; August 10, 1974, 19–20.

66. *Sunday News*, May 15, 1931, reprinted in *ND*, August 17, 1974, 19; *SCN*, April 17, 1931, 1, 8.

67. *SCN*, April 24, 1931, 1; April 17, 1931, 1, 8; May 1, 1931, 1.

68. Ibid., May 8, 1931, 1. Previous studies date Father Divine's legal clashes to the fall of 1931. Actually the Suffolk County Grand Jury handed down a secret indictment on May 5, 1931, paving the way for Father Divine's first arrest in Sayville on May 8, 1931.

CHAPTER FIVE

1. *SCN*, May 8, 1931, 1; May 15, 1931, 1; *NYT*, November 17, 1931, 3. Michael St. John may have been the follower named Michael that J. R. Moseley met in Georgia in 1913. J. R. Moseley, *Manifest Victory: A Quest and Testimony* (New York: Harper and Brothers, 1947), 107–9.

2. According to Robert Allerton Parker, Ellee Lovelace had learned of Father Divine through Susan Hadley's investigation and had traveled to Sayville where he was cured of painful arthritis. Attributing his recovery to Father Divine, Lovelace dedicated himself to the movement. Robert Allerton Parker, *Incredible Messiah: The Deification of Father Divine* (Boston: Little, Brown, 1937), 13–14; *SCN*, May 8, 1931, 1; May 15, 1931, 1.

3. *SCN*, May 8, 1931, 1; May 15, 1931, 1; June 19, 1931, 1.

4. Bart Bing, "Sayville Religious Teaching Draws Big Crowds," *Island News*, October 1, 1931, reprinted in *ND*, June 15, 1974, 18–19; July 27, 1974, 17.

5. *SCN*, October 9, 1931, 4.

6. Bing, "Sayville Religious Teaching," reprinted in *ND*, June 15, 1974, 19; *SCN*, May 27, 1932, 1, 3.

7. *ND*, June 22, 1974, 20; August 10, 1974, 19, 20.

8. *SCN*, October 9, 1931, 7; *ND*, July 13, 1974, 17. Father Divine condemned those who charged to transport people to his worship services: "I have heard of those that were coming out here in their cars with extra seats and would not bring another along unless he paid. Do you call that Christianity? Is that what I do? You can not sell religion. You've got to give freely and freely it will be given to you." For estimates on the growth of Father Divine's following, see Bing, "Sayville Religious Teaching," reprinted in *ND*, June 15, 1974, 19; *Suffolk Citizen*, October 2, 1931, reprinted in *ND*, August 17, 1974, 20.

9. In the fall of 1931, John Lamb began keeping a journal, which the movement reprinted in the *New Day* in 1974–1975 and 1986–1989. Lamb's journal serves as the earliest internal record of Peace Mission movement activities. *ND*, August 13, 1974, 18.

10. *ND*, August 13, 1974, 18; August 20, 1974, 19; Edna Mae Claybrooke interview, October 15, 1986, Gladwyne, Pennsylvania.

11. Bing, "Sayville Religious Teaching," reprinted in *ND*, June 15, 1974, 19; *Suffolk Citizen*, October 2, 1931, reprinted in *ND*, August 17, 1974, 20.

12. Both Bing and Lamb refer to the banquets as sittings, but the reporter from the *Suffolk County Citizen* called the services "tables." Father Divine may have used the two terms interchangeably to refer to the continuous Holy Communion banquets he served on Saturday and Sunday.

Bing, "Sayville Religious Teaching," reprinted in *ND*, June 15, 1974, 18–19; *Suffolk Citizen*, October 2, 1931, reprinted in *ND*, August 17, 1974, 19–20; *ND*, June 22, 1947, 17–18.

13. *ND*, July 13, 1974, 19; Bing, "Sayville Religious Teaching," reprinted in *ND*, June 15, 1974, 18; *SCN*, August 7, 1931, 1, 3; October 2, 1931, 1, 3.

14. *ND*, June 29, 1974, 17.

15. *SCN*, September 25, 1931, 1, 8; October 2, 1931, 1; *ND*, June 29, 1974, 18; Reverend Albert C. Grier et al., *Father Divine: An Interpretation with Appreciations and Comments* (Santa Barbara, California: Red Rose Press, n.d.), 20; *Suffolk Citizen*, October 2, 1931, reprinted in *ND*, August 17, 1974, 20.

16. Even more shocking to the general public were followers' unsympathetic attitudes toward the deaths that occurred at Father Divine's home. After a worshiper named Roger Caroline died of a stroke, Michael St. John explained to police that Caroline had been drinking and playing cards the previous night. "It is only natural that when a man approaches the presence of God in such a condition death should be instantaneous." St. John further commented, "It should force home a lesson to others." *SCN*, October 23, 1931, 1, 8; October 16, 1931, 1; August 7, 1931, 1, 3; October 2, 1931, 1, 3; October 9, 1931, 1, 7; *ND*, July 13, 1974, 17.

17. *ND*, July 27, 1974, 17.

18. *SCN*, November 20, 1931, 1, 6; *ND*, July 27, 1974, 17; August 24, 1974, 17; *NYT*, November 17, 1931, 3.

19. *ND*, July 27, 1974, 17; August 24, 1974, 17; *SCN*, November 20, 1931, 1, 6; *NYT*, November 17, 1931, 3; *New York Amsterdam News*, November 18, 1931, 2.

20. *SCN*, November 20, 1931, 1, 6; *ND*, July 27, 1974, 17; August 31, 1974, 17.

21. The *Suffolk County News* published a list of the followers arrested in the raid. "The following pleaded guilty. Unless another address is given, it will be assumed that they reside at the Divine home, 72 Macon street: Mary Willis, 60 Macon Street, Ethel Matthews [John Lamb's wife], Mary Templeton, Canada, Molly Bean, Racheal Weatherfield, Hannah James, Ester Grace, John Divine, Virtue Bloom, J. Maynard Matthews [John Lamb], 401 Washington Street Brookline Mass.; Alice Thibow, 37, Macon Street; Hazel Crosby, Rachael Blum, Florence Richardson, Susan James, Francis Kharas, Mable Lewis, 104 West 144th Street, Manhattan; Faith Victoria, Lillian Divine, Moserrat, West Indies; Patience Tinsely, Port Jefferson; Jessie Mauel, 5 James Place, Inwood; Mary Brown, Wonderful Wisdom, Glory King, Sarah Cook, Cora Watson, Silvester Bowan, Edna Crosby, Hatter Davis, Grace Dorset, Priscilla Paul, Helen Washington, Blanch Hanshaw, Joseph Gabriel, John Ridgeway, 153 East 51st Street, Manhattan; Elizabeth Jones, Margaret Jones, Olive Morse, 51 Macon Street; Rachael Fredrick, Stella Henson, Dorkis Divine, Julia Arras, a Spaniard and not an American citizen; Clara Burton, Blanche Cramer, James Strong, Brazil and not yet a citizen; James Banks, Petersburg, Virginia. Those pleading not guilty: Martha

Messinger, Emma Williams, Lubelle Blakely, Bessie Lovejoy, Johanna Jenkins, Helen Brown, Alitha Burrell, a West Indian; Elenor Banks, Sarah Moskin, Kensington Hotel, Sayville; Katherina Welsh, 166 16th street, Buffalo; Sarah Mantigut, Martha Rose, Onward Universe [Thomas Brown], who pressed onward to Sayville from Abico, Bahama Islands, British West Indies; Celestial Divine, Charles Jenkins, Mary Davis, Betty Edwards, 176-07 Brinkerhoff Avenue Jamaica; Annie Mowe, 320 East 42nd street, Manhattan; Helen Faust [Heavenly Rest], 6 Prospect Place, Manhattan; John Armstrong, Lillian Cooper, Michael St. John, David Hadnot, 18 Henry Street, Eugene Del Mar, John Merk, Jamaica, British West Indies and not a citizen; Faith Moore, Mary Jones, 37 Macon Street; Clarence Willis, Betty Hamlin, Francis Lander, Birmingham England, Mary Orr and Penniniah Divine." *SCN*, November 20, 1931, 1, 6; *NYT*, November 21, 1931, 11.

22. *SCN*, November 27, 1931, 1; *ND*, July 27, 1974, 19.

23. *ND*, August 10, 1974, 17.

24. *SCN*, November 27, 1931, 1, 2.

25. *New York Age*, December 5, 1931, reprinted in *ND*, August 24, 1974, 17–18; *ND*, August 10, 1974, 17; *SCN*, November 27, 1931, 1, 2; *NYT*, November 22, 1931, 11.

26. *New York Age*, December 5, 1931, reprinted in *ND*, August 24, 1974, 17–18; *ND*, August 10, 1974, 17; *SCN*, November 27, 1931, 1, 2; *NYT*, November 22, 1931, 11.

27. *ND*, August 10, 1974, 17.

28. Born in 1864 in New York City and educated at the University of California, Eugene Del Mar was a lawyer and businessman. Fascinated with New Thought and metaphysics, Del Mar served as an associate editor for several metaphysical magazines. He lectured extensively around the nation and wrote several books on metaphysical topics. Impressed by his first visit to Father Divine's home on October 30, 1931, Del Mar decided to continue attending worship services and study New Thought under the Sayville minister. Albert Nelson Marquis, ed., *Who's Who in America*, vol. 17, *1932–33* (Chicago: Marquis Who's Who, 1932), 685; *NYT*, November 21, 1931, 11. Millard J. Bloomer was a retired newspaper publisher who owned Bloomer Estates Incorporated in Harlem. Bloomer reportedly was a member of the press corp that accompanied President Woodrow Wilson to Paris at the end of World War I. In the spring of 1931, he conducted a private investigation into Father Divine's activities. After residing at Father Divine's home for several days, Bloomer became convinced that Father Divine was a legitimate religious leader. A strong supporter of Father Divine, Bloomer solicited funds for his ministry from the Hoover campaign only to find that the clergyman refused Hoover's donation. *ND*, August 17, 1974, 18–19.

29. *SCN*, November 27, 1931, 1, 8; *New York Age*, December 5, 1931, reprinted in *ND*, August 24, 1974, 17–18; *ND*, August 10, 1974, 17; August 17, 1974, 18–19; *NYT*, November 21, 1931, 11.

30. *NYT*, November 29, 1931, 31; *New York Amsterdam News*, December 2, 1931, 2.

31. Warren Susman, "Piety, Profits and Play," in *Men, Women and Issues in American History*, ed. Howard Quint and Milton Cantor (Homewood, Ill.: Dorsey Press, 1980), 202–27.

32. *ND*, August 24, 1974, 20; September 7, 1974, 20; September 18, 1974, 18–19.

33. *SCN*, December 25, 1931, 1; *ND*, September 28, 1974, 18.

34. *ND*, September 28, 1974, 18; *New York Amsterdam News*, December 23, 1931, 1, 11.

35. *New York Amsterdam News*, December 23, 1931, 1, 11; *ND*, September 28, 1974, 18. Father Divine consistently ended his sermons with "I thank you." See sermons reprinted in the *Spoken Word* or the *New Day*.

36. *ND*, September 28, 1974, 18; *New York Amsterdam News*, December 23, 1931, 1, 11.

37. *ND*, September 28, 1974, 18.

38. Righteous Endeavor interview, September 13, 1986, Los Angeles, California.

39. *ND*, October 19, 1974, 17; October 26, 1974, 20; November 23, 1974, 19. In one message Father Divine admitted to feeling a little run-down but insisted that he was never sick and was only taking on another's illness.

40. Del Mar's letter dated November 23, 1931, was reprinted in various issues of the *New Day*. For a complete text of the letter, see *ND*, January 16, 1954, s.12–s.13. In 1956, one of Father Divine's followers, Miss Deborah Newmind, testified before a Philadelphia congregation that she had first learned of Father Divine through Del Mar's letter, which was brought to a Seattle "Truth Centre" by visiting lecturers. *ND*, April 28, 1956, s.56–s.60.

41. Grier, *Father Divine*, 5; *ND*, November 16, 1974, 20. Reverend Grier's daughter toured the metaphysical lecture circuit and was also instrumental in spreading Father Divine's teachings. *ND*, April 28, 1956, s.57.

42. Although the *Metaphysical News* contained a national directory of "Truth Centers," most of the listings were located in California and the Pacific Northwest, which indicates that the readership was probably concentrated in these areas. For example, see *MN*, March 16, 1932, 7. Before Father Divine's rise to prominence in the metaphysical community, messages from Krishnamurti, Ojai's Indian Theosophist and one of the authors that Father Divine referred to in his messages, dominated the publication. See the *Metaphysical News*, 1929–1932. Charles P. LeWarne, "Vendovi Island: Father Divine's 'Peaceful Paradise of the Pacific,' " *Pacific Northwest Historical Quarterly* 75 (January 1984): 2–12.

43. *MN*, March 16, 1932, 1, 3; December 1931 to April 1932; LeWarne, "Vendovi Island," 6.

44. *ND*, November 30, 1974, 18; October 19, 1974, 17.

45. *ND*, March 8, 1975, 17; December 7, 1974, 20.

46. Father Divine's new home was provided by follower Charles Cal-

loway. Calloway, a retired railroad employee, had become involved in the movement in the fall of 1931 and was attracted to Father Divine's work with the poor. Desiring to assist Father Divine's ministry, Calloway on several occasions attempted to give the clergyman contributions, all of which Father Divine refused. Once Father Divine began to spend more time in New York City, Calloway offered his home to the minister, his wife, and their staff. Father Divine accepted Calloway's invitation and moved into Calloway's leased apartment located on West 135th Street in Harlem. *ND*, August 17, 1974, 18.

47. *ND*, August 17, 1974, 18; December 7, 1974, 20; April 19, 1975, 20.

48. *ND*, February 8, 1975, 20; June 22, 1974, 18.

49. The messages recorded in John Lamb's journal contained few references to politics. The absence possibly reflected Lamb's disinterest in politics. However, since Lamb believed Father Divine was God and that all of the clergyman's statements were holy, it seems unlikely that he would have omitted anything Father Divine said. *ND*, July 27, 1974, 20.

50. Ibid., March 1, 1975, 20.

51. Ibid., June 22, 1974, 20.

52. Ibid., September 7, 1974, 18; July 7, 1938, 38.

53. Ibid., July 13, 1974, 17.

54. Ibid., May 24, 1975, 17.

55. Ibid., October 26, 1974, 18.

56. Ibid., June 29, 1974, 18.

57. *Baltimore Afro-American*, July 9, 1932, 1.

58. *ND*, November 15, 1975, 18; June 29, 1974, 19; *SW*, January 14, 1936, 18.

59. Robert Weisbrot, *Father Divine and the Struggle for Racial Equality* (Urbana: University of Illinois Press, 1983), 5–6.

60. *New York Amsterdam News*, March 30, 1932, 11.

61. Ibid.

62. Ibid.

63. *New York Amsterdam News*, February 3, 1932, 3; February 10, 1932, 2; *New York Age*, January 30, 1932, 2, 11; July 25, 1931, 1.

64. *ND*, December 28, 1974, 18; *New York Age*, February 6, 1932, reprinted in *ND*, May 3, 1975, 20; *ND*, November 30, 1974, 17–18; December 28, 1974, 18; Weisbrot, *Father Divine*, 45–46.

65. *MN*, May 5, 1932, 8; *ND*, March 3, 1975, 19; November 30, 1974, 17; Joseph R. Washington, Jr., *Black Sects and Cults: The Power Axis in an Ethnic Ethic* (New York: Anchor Press/Doubleday, 1973), 67–70.

66. For another discussion of the conflict between Father Divine and Lawson, see Weisbrot, *Father Divine*, 45–46.

67. Branch was hospitalized for three weeks. After her release she was prohibited from returning to Father Divine's home. She eventually rejoined the movement and remained an active member into the 1970s. *SCN*, November 20, 1931, 1, 7; *ND*, October 12, 1974, 17–18.

68. *SCN*, April 29, 1932, 1.

69. *SCN*, April 8, 1932, 1, 8; April 22, 1932, 7; May 20, 1932, 1; *New York Amsterdam News*, May 4, 1932, 1.

70. *SCN*, May 27, 1932, 1, 3.

71. Ibid., May 27, 1932, 3.

72. Ibid.

73. *ND*, August 2, 1975, 20; *SCN*, May 27, 1932, 3.

74. *ND*, June 21, 1975, 17–20.

75. Ibid., June 21, 1975, 20.

76. *SCN*, May 27, 1932, 3.

77. *SCN*, June 10, 1932, 1; *NYT*, June 5, 1932, 12; *New York Amsterdam News*, June 8, 1932, 8. When arrested, Father Divine admitted to being 52 years old and claimed to have no formal education. He listed his occupation as minister and told the clerk that he had done evangelical work in Boston and Baltimore. When pressed, he gave his birthplace as Providence, which the clerk recorded as being in Rhode Island. Justice Smith's investigation resulted from Father Divine's refusal to divulge any additional personal information to the court clerk. *SCN*, May 27, 1932, 3; *ND*, December 25, 1982, 21.

78. *SCN*, June 10, 1932, 1; *Nassau Daily Review*, June 9, 1932, reprinted in *ND*, August 31, 1974, 17.

CHAPTER SIX

1. *Baltimore Afro-American*, June 18, 1932, 6; *SCN*, June 10, 1932, 1; *Nassau Daily Review*, June 9, 1932, reprinted in *ND*, August 31, 1974, 17; *Negro World*, June 18, 1932, 1, 2.

2. Father Divine specifically instructed Mother Divine to read Luke 22:54–71, describing Peter's betrayal of Jesus Christ; Mark 14:53–72, chronicling the sentencing of Jesus Christ to death for blasphemy; Mark 16:9–14, recounting Christ's resurrection; and Isaiah 42 and 43, enumerating God's promises to his chosen servants and predicting Babylon's doom. Father Divine's letter to Peninniah was reprinted in *ND*, June 28, 1974, 19–20; July 5, 1975, 17–20; *Negro World*, July 2, 1932, 1, 2.

3. *ND*, July 19, 1975, 18; July 26, 1975, 19. In March 1931, Alabama authorities arrested nine black youths and charged them with the rape of two white female teenagers in a boxcar. An all-white jury found the youths guilty on the basis of questionable testimony by the two girls. Eight of the nine received death sentences, and as news of their plight reached the nation, they became a cause célèbre in the African-American community. For a study of the case, see Dan T. Carter, *Scottsboro: A Tragedy of the American South* (New York: Oxford University Press, 1969). Returning to his New York City headquarters on the train after his release, Father Divine discussed the Scottsboro case with passengers. *New York Amsterdam News*, June 29, 1932, 2.

4. *SCN*, July 1, 1932, 7; *ND*, July 19, 1932, 19–20; *Negro World*, July 2,

1932, 1, 2; July 26, 1932, 17–18. Before Father Divine was sentenced, he sold his Sayville home to Joseph Gabriel. *SCN*, June 10, 1932, 1.

5. *SCN*, July 1, 1932, 7.

6. *ND*, July 26, 1932, 17–18. Although evidence suggests that Father Divine never claimed direct responsibility for Smith's death, most studies assert that when he first heard of the judge's demise, he responded, "I hated to do it." This quotation first appeared in John Hoshor, *God in a Rolls-Royce: The Rise of Father Divine, Madman, Menace, or Messiah* (New York: Hillman-Curl, 1936), 84–86. Nothing documents Hoshor's assertion.

7. First spoken October 5, 1932, reprinted in *ND*, September 26, 1987, 15.

8. *New York News*, August 6, 1932, 1; October 8, 1932, 1, 3.

9. *ND*, August 9, 1975, 17–20; August 16, 1975, 17–20; *Baltimore Afro-American*, July 9, 1932, 1.

10. *Baltimore Afro-American*, July 16, 1932, 1.

11. Faithful Mary, *"God," He's Just a Natural Man* (New York: Gailliard Press, 1937), 9, 10; *New York News*, October 1, 1932, 1; *ND*, August 17, 1974, 18; Claude McKay, " 'There Goes God!' The Story of Father Divine and His Angels," *Nation*, February 6, 1935, 151–53.

12. Faithful Mary, *"God,"* 3–10.

13. Ibid.; McKay, " 'There Goes God!' " 155; *SCN*, March 8, 1935, 1, 8; *New York News*, October 28, 1933, 8.

14. Hezekiah Craig interview, August 27, 1986, February 3, 1987, August 24, 1987, Los Angeles, California.

15. *MN*, July 20, 1932, 1; November 9, 1932, 1; December 7, 1932, 2; January 18, 1933, 2; April 19, 1933, 5; Charles P. LeWarne, "Father Divine's 'Peaceful Paradise of the Pacific,' " *Pacific Northwest Quarterly* 75 (January 1984): 2–12.

16. *WE*, February 3, 1934, 3; FBI File 31-46627: Delight Jewett deposition, March 22, 1937.

17. George Corey interview, December 15, 1986, Los Angeles, California.

18. First spoken January 19, 1933, reprinted in *ND*, October 11, 1986, 7. For other references to early Peace Mission businesses, see *ND*, November 2, 1939, 28–29; August 17, 1974, 18.

19. *ND*, October 11, 1986, 7. First spoken January 19, 1933, reprinted in *ND*, October 11, 1986, 7; *ND*, November 2, 1939, 28–29; August 17, 1974, 18.

20. *SW*, August 22, 1936, 29; *ND*, November 2, 1939, 28–29; August 2, 1986, 4; August 15, 1987, 14; June 21, 1986, 16–18; August 17, 1974, 18.

21. *ND*, July 25, 1940, 61; *Light*, January 24, 1935, 3.

22. *ND*, December 6, 1986, 8; Hezekiah Craig and Eli Diana interview, December 14, 1986, Los Angeles, California.

23. McKay, " 'There Goes God!' " 152.

24. *New York News*, October 15, 1932, 1, 3; Hezekiah Craig interview, August 27, 1986, Los Angeles, California.

25. The UNIA purchased the SS *Shadyside* and offered excursions on the Hudson in the summer of 1920. Built in 1873, the ship incurred numerous expenses and proved to be a financial loss for the UNIA. After only a few months of service, the ship was retired, docked in New Jersey, and sank in a winter storm in 1921. E. David Cronon, *Black Moses: The Story of Marcus Garvey and the Universal Negro Improvement Association* (Madison: University of Wisconsin Press, 1955), 85; Marcus Garvey, *The Marcus Garvey and Universal Negro Improvement Association Papers*, vol. 2, *27 August 1919– 31 August 1920*, ed. Robert A. Hill, Emory J. Tolbert, and Deborah Forczeh (Berkeley: University of California Press, 1983), 283, 318, 356.

26. *Reporter*, August 2, 1932, 5.

27. *Baltimore Afro-American*, June 25, 1932, 6.

28. *New York Amsterdam News*, November 23, 1932, 1.

29. First spoken November 6, 1932, reprinted in *ND*, May 23, 1987, 4– 5; *NYT*, November 7, 1933, 13.

30. First spoken March 6, 1933, reprinted in *ND*, June 21, 1986, 16–18; Harvard Sitkoff, *A New Deal for Blacks* (New York: Oxford University Press, 1978), 40–43. For an examination of Roosevelt's plans for economic recovery, see William E. Leuchtenburg, *Franklin Roosevelt and the New Deal* (New York: Harper Colophon Books, 1963).

31. *SCN*, January 13, 1933, 1; *New York Amsterdam News*, November 23, 1932, 2; *NYT*, January 10, 1933, 17.

32. First spoken December 21, 1932, reprinted in *ND*, February 5, 1983, 26; *MN*, December 7, 1932, 2; *New York News*, December 31, 1932, 1. Joerns was also a practitioner who offered his services as a healer in his paper. One of his advertisements read: "Divine Healing Now a Scientific Fact: Henry A. Joerns, Practitioner (If you are in difficulty, phone, write or call on). Mr. Joerns is recognized as possessing a clear spiritual consciousness and for many years has demonstrated the divine Laws to the satisfaction of all who come to him." *MN*, July 6, 1932, 4.

33. *MN*, February 1, 1932, 2.

34. Ibid., May 17, 1933, 1.

35. For a detailed study of the Peace Mission on Vendovi Island, see LeWarne, "Father Divine's 'Peaceful Paradise,' " 2–12 (the quote appears on p. 8). *MN*, October 5, 1932, 2; January 18, 1933, 2; May 17, 1933, 5.

36. *MN*, October 5, 1932, 2; January 18, 1933, 2; April 19, 1933, 5. A comparison of the itinerary of Humble and Hampton and a later list of Peace Missions reveals that extensions appeared along the routes pursued by the two lecturers. For example, see *ND*, October 20, 1938, 100. Carey McWilliams, *Southern California, An Island on the Land*, 2d ed. (Santa Barbara, Calif.: Peregrine Smith, 1973), 249–313.

37. McWilliams notes that most sects in Los Angeles area drew directly from New Thought. *Southern California*, 249–313; Kevin Starr, *Inventing the Dream: California Through the Progressive Era* (New York: Oxford University Press, 1985), 47–48, 211–18, 248, 284; Gregory Singleton, *Religion in the City of Angels: American Protestant Culture and Urbanization, Los Angeles* (Ann

Arbor: UMI Research Press, 1979), 159–71; Charles Samuel Braden, *Spirits in Rebellion: The Rise and Development of New Thought* (Dallas: Southern Methodist University Press, 1963), 187, 206, 261–98, 304–11. For an examination of the attraction of Southern California for the infirm, see John E. Baur, *The Health Seekers of Southern California, 1870–1900* (San Marino, Calif.: Huntington Library Press, 1959).

38. Although the lecturers who visited Los Angeles are not mentioned by name, Humble's itinerary indicates that he was the white lecturer who brought Father Divine's teachings to the city. *SW*, August 15, 1936, 26–27; October 13, 1936, 21.

39. *SCN*, October 20, 1933, 7; *NYT*, November 7, 1933, 13; *ND*, December 25, 1982, 22; letter: Miss Veri Sweete to Jill Watts, March 7, 1983.

40. *SCN*, October 20, 1933, 7.

41. First spoken December 2, 1933, reprinted in *ND*, November 8, 1986, 14.

42. *ND*, November 2, 1939, 28–29; *New York News*, August 20, 1932, 2.

43. *NYT*, December 13, 1933, 7; *SCN*, June 16, 1933, 1; October 20, 1933, 1, 7; October 27, 1933, 1, 2.

44. *NYT*, November 7, 1933, 13; *New York News*, April 22, 1933, 3.

45. *NYT*, November 6, 1933, 3; November 7, 1933, 13; December 13, 1933, 7.

46. *NYT*, November 7, 1933, 13.

47. De Mena was born about 1892 in Nicaragua. She emigrated to the United States in 1913 and worked as a secretary and an interpreter. She was appointed the UNIA's assistant international organizer in 1926 and was on the staff of the *Negro World* in the early thirties. The alarm expressed by the leaders of the UNIA over Father Divine's growing influence and the defection of former Garveyites indicates that the crossover was significant. Marcus Garvey, *The Marcus Garvey and Universal Negro Improvement Association Papers*, vol. 5, *September 1922–August 1924*, ed. Robert A. Hill, Deborah Forczek, and Devra Weber (Berkeley: University of California Press, 1986), 659, 786. The migration from the UNIA to the Peace Mission movement was first noted by Roi Ottley, *'New World A-Coming': Inside Black America* (New York: Houghton Mifflin, 1943), 82–83.

48. *WE*, January 6, 1934, 1; February 13, 1934, 1. Randall Burkett points out that the format of the *World Echo* was identical to that of the *Negro World*. De Mena continued to print both the old series numbers from the *Negro World* along with the new numbers of the *World Echo*. Randall Burkett, *Garveyism as a Religious Movement: The Institutionalization of a Black Civil Religion* (Metuchen, N.J.: American Theological Library Association, Scarecrow Press, 1978), 42.

49. *WE*, January 27, 1934, 1.

50. Ibid., January 6, 1934, 1; January 27, 1934, 11.

51. Ibid., January 6, 1934, 3; January 27, 1934, 12; January 13, 1934, 7; Robert Hill and Barbara Bair, eds., *Marcus Garvey: Life and Lessons* (Berkeley: University of California Press, 1987), iii–iv.

52. *Negro World*, July 2, 1932, 2; Reverend M. J. Divine, *The Peace Mission Movement as Explained by Father Divine* (Philadelphia: New Day Publishing, n.d.), 51. Faithful Mary later charged that Father Divine borrowed extensively from Garvey. The UNIA could have influenced the organization of the Peace Mission movement and may have inspired Peace Mission parades, cruises, and journalistic endeavors. But Garvey and Father Divine were contemporaries whose philosophies evolved simultaneously. Faithful Mary, "God," 17.

53. *Black Man*, September–October, 1936, 11; Burkett, *Garveyism*, 56–60. Burkett discusses Garvey's conceptions of God.

54. For favorable articles on Father Divine, see *Negro World*, June 18, 1932, 1, 2; July 2, 1932, 1, 2. For examples of the editors' interest in New Thought and metaphysical topics, see *Negro World*, June 6, 1931, 2; December 12, 1931, 2; October 17, 1933, 2, 6. Robert Weisbrot, *Father Divine and the Struggle for Racial Equality* (Urbana: University of Illinois Press, 1983), 190–96. Robert Hill has done pioneering work on Garvey and New Thought; see "General Introduction," in *The Marcus Garvey and Universal Negro Improvement Association Papers*, vol. 1, *1826–August 1919*, ed. Robert Hill and Carol A. Rudisell (Berkeley: University of California Press, 1983), xlix–l; Hill and Bair, *Marcus Garvey*, xxviii–xxix; xlix–li.

55. *SW*, August 18, 1936, 10, 11–15; Ottley, "*New World A-Coming*," 82; Emory Tolbert, *The UNIA and Black Los Angeles* (Los Angeles: UCLA Afro-American Studies Center, 1980), 31, 51; Hezekiah Craig interview, August 24, 1987, Los Angeles, California; Garvey, *Universal Negro Improvement Association Papers*, vol. 5, 659; *Black Man*, late December 1935, 12; September–October 1936, 10–12.

56. *SW*, August 18, 1936, 10; Universal Negro Improvement Association, *Official Minutes of Second Regional Conference* (Toronto: UNIA, 1937), 6.

57. *Black Man*, late July 1935, 11–13.

58. *Daily Gleaner*, September 4, 1936, 11; *Black Man*, September–October 1936, 9–12.

59. *Black Man*, September–October 1936, 9–12 (quotation appears on p. 11).

60. John Peer Nugent, *The Black Eagle* (New York: Stein and Day, 1971), 21–22, 35–47, 74–81, 106–10; *WE*, February 24, 1934, 6; March 3, 1934, 8.

61. *NYT*, November 7, 1933, 13; Nugent, *Black Eagle*, 107.

62. Weisbrot, *Father Divine*, 132–36, 145–47; William Muraskin, "Harlem Boycott of 1934," *Labor History* 13 (Summer 1972): 361–73; *Spokesman*, November 9, 1934, 5.

63. *WE*, April 1934, 1; McKay, " 'There Goes God!' " 154; *WE*, April 7, 1934, 1, 3.

64. For an examination of the various alliances the Peace Mission forged during this period, see Weisbrot, *Father Divine*, 132–36, 145–47; Muraskin, "Harlem Boycott."

65. For a comprehensive study of the Communist party in Harlem during this period, see Mark Naison, *Communists in Harlem during the Depres-*

sion (Chicago: University of Illinois Press, 1983). See especially Naison's discussion of Father Divine and the party on pp. 129–30, 151. For another excellent discussion of the Peace Mission movement and the Communists, see Weisbrot, *Father Divine*, 147–52.

66. George Corey interview, December 15, 1986, Los Angeles, California; Weisbrot, *Father Divine*, 149; Naison, *Communists in Harlem*, 129–30.

67. FBI File 62-32932, vol. 2: George Baker File 100-81748, October 3, 1946, 6–7; Naison, *Communists in Harlem*, 129–30.

68. McKay, " 'There Goes God!' " 155.

69. *NYT*, May 3, 1935, 18; Weisbrot, *Father Divine*, 149.

70. *New York News*, September 29, 1934, 1, 6; Naison, *Communists in Harlem*, 129–30.

71. *New York News*, October 18, 1932, 3.

72. Hubert Kelley, "Heaven Incorporated," *American Magazine*, January 1936, 40–41, 106–8; *SCN*, April 19, 1935, 1, 8.

CHAPTER SEVEN

1. *SW*, November 3, 1934, 6; November 10, 1934, 4; Claude McKay, "Father Divine's Rebel Angel," *American Mercury*, February 1940, 73–80.

2. McKay, "Rebel Angel," 75; *SCN*, March 8, 1935, 1, 8; March 22, 1935, 1, 3; Claude McKay, " 'There Goes God!' The Story of Father Divine and His Angels," *Nation*, February 5, 1935, 151–53; *SW*, November 3, 1934, 6. McKay was fascinated by Father Divine and in an unfinished novel featured a religious leader, Glory Savior, based on Father Divine. See Claude McKay, *Harlem Glory: A Fragment of Afro-American Life* (Chicago: Charles H. Kerr, 1990).

3. *SW*, October 20, 1934, 6; August 15, 1936, 26; *LAT*, August 23, 1987, pt. 2, 1–2.

4. The FBI records show that Florence Wuest Hunt came from Cleveland, Ohio, and had inherited the Wuest dairy fortune. FBI File 31-46627: Florence W. Hunt, File 87-27, March 27, 1937, 1–5; Delight Jewett deposition, March 22, 1937; letter: John W. Hunt to Alpha Tau Omega Fraternity, February 6, 1936, 4–5; *SW*, November 3, 1934, 21; August 15, 1936, 26–27; October 13, 1936, 21.

5. *SW*, October 20, 1934; November 10, 1934, 13; August 25, 1936, 22–24; Hubert Kelley, "Heaven Incorporated," *American Magazine*, January 1936, 40–41, 106–8; letter: Veri Sweete to Jill Watts, March 7, 1983.

6. The front-page caption appeared on each issue of the *Spoken Word*. For an example of the format, see *SW*, November 10, 1934.

7. *SW*, August 25, 1936, 23–24; Library of Congress, *Newspapers in Microform: United States, 1948–1972* (Washington, D.C.: Library of Congress, Catalogue Division, 1973), 489.

8. *SW*, May 4, 1935, 15.

9. *SW*, May 20, 1935, 12; August 18, 1936, 15; August 24, 1936, 23–24.

10. Weisbrot contends that a contradiction in ideologies existed between Father Divine, who praised Ford and Carnegie, and the *Spoken Word*'s staff, who criticized Morgan and Mellon. But actually the gap between the two was not so great. Father Divine admired Ford and Carnegie for their business sense and ingenuity. Morgan and Mellon were different types of corporate leaders who derived their wealth from the banking industry. Undoubtedly Father Divine, with his mistrust of banks and the lending system, would have joined his disciples in their condemnation of such businessmen. Robert Weisbrot, *Father Divine and the Struggle for Racial Equality* (Urbana: University of Illinois Press, 1983), 66.

11. *SW*, June 29, 1935, 4.

12. Ibid.

13. William E. Leuchtenburg, *Franklin D. Roosevelt and the New Deal* (New York: Harper Colophon Books, 1963), 103–4, 114–15. For an examination of Townsend, see Abraham Holtzman, *The Townsend Movement: A Political Study* (New York: Octagon Books, 1975). For Sinclair, see William Bloodworth, *Upton Sinclair* (Boston: Twayne, 1977). Information on the New Deal may also be found in Kenneth Davis, *FDR, the New Deal Years: 1933–1937* (New York: Random House, 1986).

14. Newton Van Dalsem, *History of the Utopian Society of America* (Los Angeles: Utopian Society, 1942), 10, 11–19. *Utopian News*, September 13, 1934, 2, 8; February 18, 1935, 3; *SW*, October 20, 1934, 3, 4; June 29, 1935, 4; April 7, 1936, 5; August 25, 1936, 24.

15. *SW*, January 14, 1936, 30. Van Dalsem mentioned the defection of one of the founding members who could not compromise his religious beliefs with the society's demands. This individual was probably Roy Owens, whom the *Spoken Word* identified as a former member of the Utopian Society board of directors. Van Dalsem, *History*, 18; *SW*, November 3, 1934, 12; October 20, 1934, 5; Carey McWilliams, *Southern California, An Island on the Land*, 2d ed. (Santa Barbara, Calif.: Peregrine Smith, 1973), 306. John Roine initially resided in Ojai, California, and later moved to Los Angeles. *Utopian News*, January 12, 1935, 9; July 21; 1936, 21; December 15, 1936, 5. Hugh MacBeth, born in 1884 in Charleston, South Carolina, was a graduate of Harvard Law School who migrated to Los Angeles in 1913. He served as Los Angeles Deputy District Attorney in 1915. Charles J. Long, ed., *Who's Who: Los Angeles County: 1932–1933* (Los Angeles: Who's Who in Los Angeles County, 1933), 167; *Utopian News*, February 5, 1934, 1; February 11, 1935, 1, 2; *SW*, August 15, 1936, 15; October 13, 1936, 6; Emory J. Tolbert, *The UNIA and Black Los Angeles* (Los Angeles: UCLA Center for Afro-American Studies, 1980), 31, 39, 66–67.

16. *Utopian News*, December 27, 1934, 11; December 27, 1934, 7; January 14, 1935, 8; Van Dalsem, *History*, 24–25, 28–35.

17. Van Dalsem, *History*, 10–11. Richard Hofstadter first proposed the status-anxiety thesis and argued that Americans fearing displacement by forces resulting from industrialization founded the Progressive movement and undertook reform movements to protect their class rank. Richard Hof-

stadter, *Age of Reform: from Bryan to F.D.R.*, 12th ed. (New York: Alfred A. Knopf, 1977). In 1919 MacBeth wrote to W. E. B. Du Bois, requesting "for the good of the cause of law and order may I suggest that you quietly refer to us for deportation to Lower California, such rioting Negroes as may be causing the government trouble in Washington, Chicago and elsewhere? I might suggest that in Lower California we have enough good land to support five million of these Negro malcontents." Du Bois's contacts in the Los Angeles NAACP alleged that the company was a scheme to bilk the community out of money and reported that MacBeth and his associates had previously been involved in a mining project that resulted in drastic financial loss for investors. MacBeth maintained his membership in the Utopian Society while working with the Peace Mission movement. W. E. B. Du Bois, *The Papers of W. E. B. Du Bois* (New York: Microfilming Corporation of America, 1980), Hugh MacBeth to W. E. B. Du Bois, August 6, 1919, reel 7, frame 1062; E. Burton Ceruti to W. E. B. Du Bois, reel 7, frame 707.

18. *WE*, February 10, 1935, 3; *Baltimore Afro-American*, December 1, 1934, 4. For a discussion of hostility within the black community toward Father Divine, see Weisbrot, *Father Divine*, 176–81; FBI File 62-32932, vol. 1: letters to Bureau dated July 18, 1934; August 4, 1934; September 21, 1934; November 9, 1934; Senator Louis Murphy to J. Edgar Hoover, October 11, 1935. During this period, the Bureau responded to requests for investigation of Father Divine's activities by stating that "the activities of the Reverend Divine do not appear to constitute a violation of any Federal Statute within the investigative jurisdiction of this Bureau, and accordingly, no inquiry is being made into his activities." FBI File 62-32932, vol. 1: letter, John Edgar Hoover to [name censored], November 8, 1935.

19. *NYT*, May 17, 1935, 3; *SCN*, March 8, 1935, 1, 8; March 22, 1935, 1, 3; April 19, 1935, 1, 8; *NYT*, March 6, 1935, 3; March 20, 1935, 9.

20. *SCN*, March 8, 1935, 1, 8; March 22, 1935, 1, 3; April 19, 1935, 1, 8; *NYT*, March 6, 1935, 3; March 8, 1935, 17; March 19, 1935, 13.

21. For a statistical analysis of the growth of Peace Mission extensions, see Charles Samuel Braden, *These Also Believe: A Study of Modern American Cults and Minority Religious Movements* (New York: Macmillan, 1949), 12. The directory of Peace Missions indicates an absence of extensions in rural areas. Although followers in these areas may have existed and neglected to report to the *Spoken Word*, the movement's literature contained no references to activities in agricultural regions. The Peace Mission probably failed to take root in the farming sector because missionaries carrying Father Divine's teachings bypassed rural areas in favor of the more densely populated cities. Furthermore, Father Divine's focus on business and formulas for success within the urban economy may not have appealed to those living in farming regions. For sample directories, see the back cover of the *Spoken Word* or the *New Day*.

22. *Time*, October 14, 1946, 58. Little work has been done on the spread and appeal of the Peace Mission movement abroad, and such a study would

be a fruitful avenue for future research. Eli Diana interview, August 16, 1987, Los Angeles, California. See back cover of *SW*, June 29, 1935.

23. *SW*, August 25, 1935, 24; May 4, 1935, 11; *NYT*, May 2, 1935, 3; May 3, 1935, 18.

24. Robert M. Fogelson and Richard E. Rubenstein, *The Complete Report of Mayor LaGuardia's Commission on the Harlem Riot of March 19, 1935* (New York: Arno Press, New York Times, 1969), 7–18; Harold Orlansky, *The Harlem Riot: A Study in Mass Frustration* (New York: Social Analysis, 1943), 14–15.

25. *SCN*, July 5, 1935, 1, 8; *NYT*, July 2, 1935, 46.

26. *SCN*, August 7, 1935, 1, 8; *NYT*, November 5, 1935, 2; December 8, 1935, pt. 2, 9.

27. *SW*, January 14, 1936, 1–29; *New York Age*, January 18, 1936, 1.

28. The Righteous Government Platform was reprinted many times in Peace Mission literature. The platform appeared for the first time in *SW*, January 14, 1936, 7–16. Weisbrot, *Father Divine*, 152.

29. *SW*, January 14, 1936, 7–11 (quotation appears on p. 7).

30. Ibid., 13.

31. Ibid., 11–14.

32. Ibid., 13.

33. Ibid., 14–16.

34. *SW*, January 14, 1936, 12; *New York Age*, January 18, 1936, 1.

35. *SW*, January 14, 1936, 2.

36. Ibid., 13.

37. Ibid., 4, 5–6, 22.

38. *SW*, January 14, 1936, 4; *New York Age*, January 18, 1936, 1.

39. *SW*, January 14, 1936, 23.

40. Ibid., January 14, 1936, 16; September 5, 1936, 19–21; July 21, 1936, 21.

41. Ibid., September 5, 1936, 19–21.

42. Ibid., September 5, 1936, 19–21; July 21, 1936, 15, 21–22.

43. *SW*, August 1, 1936, 20; December 29, 1936, 24–25.

44. *SW*, April 7, 1936, 5; Weisbrot, *Father Divine*, 125–31.

45. Father Divine believed that Ann Lee manifested God's spirit, but because she had succumbed to sexual indulgence, she did not achieve immortality. The minister also cited the Jesus Christ Church of Latter-Day Saints as another significant religious movement born in upstate New York. *SW*, April 7, 1936, 3–4.

46. John Hoshor, *God in a Rolls-Royce: The Rise of Father Divine, Madman, Menace, or Messiah* (New York: Hillman-Curl, 1936), 30.

47. The editor quoted by Hoshor may have been on the staff of the *New York Amsterdam News*. In his introduction, Hoshor thanked the paper for assistance; and since the *Amsterdam News* had become highly critical of Father Divine, it seems possible that an editor could have made such a statement. Ibid., 187.

48. *SW*, August 18, 1936, 16.

49. *California Eagle*, September 25, 1936, 1, 3.

50. FBI File 62-32932, vol. 2: file on George Baker with aliases "God," Father Divine, Reverend J. Divine, Major J. Devine, M. J. Devine, M. J. Divine, October 3, 1936, 5–7; Mark Naison, *Communists in Harlem during the Depression* (Chicago: University of Illinois Press, 1983), 257, 279–83, 287.

51. Most investigations of Father Divine's participation in the 1936 election portray his order to boycott the polls as an election-eve decision. However, Father Divine had threatened to withhold his support by July of 1936. *SW*, July 21, 1936, 26; August 1, 1936, 13; *NYT*, November 6, 1935, 20.

52. *California Eagle*, July 17, 1936, 1; *SW*, August 1, 1936, 15, 18; September 12, 1936, 21.

53. *SW*, July 21, 1936, 11–12, 16; August 1, 1936, 3, 14, 16; August 18, 1936, 24; *California Eagle*, July 31, 1936, 1.

54. *SW*, August 15, 1936, 15. The proceedings of the convention appeared in *SW*, August 18, 1936, 7–16.

55. *NYT*, September 14, 1936, 28; *SW*, September 5, 1936, 3–4.

56. *NYT*, November 4, 1936, 12; November 8, 1936, pt. 2, 3.

57. Between 1932 and 1936, Father Divine consistently turned out between 2,500 and 3,000 followers to march in parades. Assuming that some angels may have attended the parades as spectators and others may have been prevented from marching by their jobs or other commitments, this roughly places the number of followers in and around Harlem at 3,000 to 4,000. For the *New York Times* estimate, see *NYT*, November 8, 1936, pt. 2, 3; September 14, 1936, 28.

58. The estimate of followers and sympathizers nationwide is derived from the *Spoken Word* circulation figures, which estimated a readership numbering 30,000 in 1936. Taking into consideration the existence of two additional Peace Mission newspapers, the *New Day* and the *World Herald*, the total number of disciples and friends of the Peace Mission movement may have been significantly higher. The number may have been even higher because many of those interested in the movement may have not subscribed to its publications. *SW*, August 25, 1936, 24; *NYT*, November 4, 1936, 12.

59. First spoken December 12, 1936, reprinted in *ND*, December 5, 1987, 1.

CHAPTER EIGHT

1. FBI File 31-46627: Delight Jewett deposition, March 22, 1937, 3–13; Florence Wuest Hunt, File 87-27, March 27, 1937, 2; John Wuest Hunt, File 31-3389, June 17, 1937; interview with Reta Reynolds alias Quiet Devotion, 1–3; John Wuest Hunt, File 31-3418, April 5, 1937; John Wuest Hunt, File 31-3709, April 8, 1937; *California Eagle*, December 19, 1936, 3; *LAT*, June 26, 1937, 1, 2; *LAT*, June 30, 1937, 1, 7; *SW*, January 14, 1936, 6; May 26, 1936,

3, 28; August 1, 1936, 10–11, 13; September 5, 1936, 15; *ND*, May 28, 1936, 2.

2. FBI File 31-46627: letter, John W. Hunt to Alpha Tau Omega Fraternity, February 6, 1936. The Bellevue doctor concluded that Hunt's "letter writing was in the nature of a confession with no other motive than to preach many of his newly acquired principles without any conscious attempt to be obscene. . . . In summary, the patient is a psychopathic personality who has been carried along by a religious movement to the point of being fanatic but not psychotic." John Wuest Hunt, File 31-3389, May 19, 1937, letter, Karl M. Bowman, M.D., to Hon. Mortimer W. Byers, February 24, 1936. A version of Hunt's confession also appeared in *SW*, February 5, 1936, February 15, 1936.

3. *LAT*, June 30, 1937, 1, 7; FBI File 31-46627: Delight Jewett deposition, March 22, 1937, 3–13; *California Eagle*, December 19, 1936, 3; *LAT*, June 26, 1937, 1, 2.

4. *California Eagle*, December 19, 1936, 3; *LAT*, June 26, 1937, 1, 3; June 30, 1937, 1, 7.

5. *California Eagle*, December 19, 1936, 3; *LAT*, June 26, 1937, 1, 3; June 30, 1937, 1, 7.

6. *SW*, December 19, 1936, 3–5; FBI File 31-46627: John Wuest Hunt, File 31-3789, April 8, 1937.

7. Elizabeth "Betty" Peters of Los Angeles listed her occupation as "metaphysicist and fortune teller." She had learned of Father Divine through her friend Florence Hunt. Ben Hur was Elizabeth Peters's son Richard Peters, who returned to his wife and his job as an encyclopedia salesman after the Denver trip. Elizabeth Peters brought Agnes Gardner, another metaphysician, into the movement. Although Gardner claimed to have never been "reborn with the Spirit of Father Divine," she became an active member and worked on the organizing committee for the 1936 California Righteous Government Convention. FBI File 31-46627: John Wuest Hunt, File 31-3418, April 30, 1937, depositions by Elizabeth Peters, 6–9, Agnes Gardner, 3–6; John Wuest Hunt, File 31-37889, April 5, 1937, H. B. Smith deposition, 2–5; John Wuest Hunt, File 31-3418, May 23, 1937, Richard Peters deposition, 2–5; Delight Jewett deposition, March 22, 1937, 3–13; *SW*, August 1, 1936, 15; *LAT*, June 30, 1937, 1, 7; June 26, 1937, 3.

8. FBI File 31-46627: Delight Jewett deposition, March 22, 1937, 3–13.

9. *LAT*, June 24, 1937, 1, 3; FBI File 31-46627: Delight Jewett deposition, March 22, 1937, 5; John Wuest Hunt, File 31-3789, April 8, 1937.

10. *LAT*, June 23, 1937, 3; FBI File 31-46627: Delight Jewett deposition, March 22, 1937, 6.

11. *SW*, December 29, 1936, 7.

12. *LAT*, June 30, 1937, 1, 7; FBI File 31-46627: Delight Jewett deposition, March 22, 1937, 7, 9; Whitley to Director, March 30, 1937, 2.

13. FBI File 31-46627-A: *New York Evening Journal*, April 5, 1937. This file contains newspaper clippings on scandals surrounding the Peace Mission movement in the spring of 1937. The file contains names and dates of

clippings but no page numbers. FBI File 31-46627: Delight Jewett deposition, March 22, 1937, 7.

14. FBI File 31-46627-A: *New York Evening Journal*, April 5, 1937.

15. FBI File 31-46627: John Wuest Hunt, File 31-3418, April 23, 1937, 2–3 (quotation on p. 3); Delight Jewett deposition, March 22, 1937, 9–10; FBI File 31-46627-A: *New York Evening Journal*, April 5, 1937.

16. FBI File 31-46627: Delight Jewett deposition, March 22, 1937, 9–10; John Wuest Hunt, File 31-3418, April 23, 1937, 2–3.

17. The *New York Evening Journal* offered the information on the Hunt-Jewett affair to the FBI in exchange for the Bureau's promise that the Hearst paper would have first priority in publishing the story. Initially, the Bureau hesitated to prosecute Hunt since the Beverly Hills millionaire had not transported the young woman for commercial intent and no evidence existed that he had committed an act of violence. Inexplicably, the Bureau suddenly registered charges against Hunt. The story was leaked through the U.S. attorney's office, and ultimately the *New York Evening Journal* lost its exclusive. FBI File 31-46627: Memorandum from J. Edgar Hoover to E. A. Tamm, March 18, 1937, 11:40 A.M.; memorandum from J. Edgar Hoover to E. A. Tamm, March 18, 1937, 4:25 P.M.; teletype, Hanson to Dir FBI, March 29, 1937; memorandum from E. A. Tamm to Director, March 30, 1937; teletype, Hanson to Director, March 31, 1937; memorandum, E. A. Tamm to Director, March 31, 1937.

18. FBI File 31-46627-A: *New York Evening Journal*, April 5, 1937; *Washington Times Herald*, April 10, 1937; *New York Evening Journal*, April 15, 1937; *Los Angeles Herald-Express*, April 10, 1937; *New York Daily News*, June 24, 1937; *Washington Herald*, June 25, 1937; *Literary Digest*, May 1937, 6–7; *LAT*, June 30, 1937, 1, 7.

19. FBI File 31-46627-A: *Brooklyn Daily Eagle*, June 24, 1937.

20. FBI File 31-46627-A: *Brooklyn Daily Eagle*, June 24, 1937; *New York Post*, June 24, 1937; *LAT*, June 24, 1937, 1, 3.

21. *LAT*, June 30, 1937, 1, 2; July 2, 1937, 3.

22. Ibid., July 2, 1937, 3.

23. Faithful Mary, *"God," He's Just a Natural Man* (New York: Gailliard Press, 1937), 85. Delight Jewett claimed that H. B. Smith, Betty Peters, and Agnes Gardner played instrumental roles in her seduction by convincing her that she was the Virgin Mary and Hunt was Jesus Christ. Smith, Peters, and Gardner denied Jewett's charge. H. B. Smith contended he had nothing to do with the affair and that the women helped Hunt. Betty Peters claimed to remember little of the episode because Hunt had hypnotized her. Agnes Gardner maintained that she had always believed Hunt to be unstable. FBI File 31-46627: Delight Jewett deposition, March 22, 1937, 3–6; John Wuest Hunt, File 31-3418, April 30, 1937; depositions by Elizabeth Peters, 6–9, Agnes Gardner, 3–6; John Wuest Hunt, File 31-3418, April 22, 1937; *LAT*, June 24, 1937, 1, 3; June 25, 1937, 3; *NYT*, July 19, 1937, 2.

24. *NYT*, April 23, 1937, 1; April 25, 1937, 1; April 26, 1937, 38; May 4,

1937, 28; FBI File 31-46627-A: *New York Daily Mirror,* May 4, 1937; *New York American,* May 4, 1937, May 15, 1937; *New York Evening Journal,* June 19, 1937; *New York World Telegram,* June 19, 1937.

25. FBI File 31-46627-A: *New York Post,* April 22, 1937; *Literary Digest,* May 1937, 6–7; *Time,* May 3, 1937, 63.

26. FBI File 31-46627-A: *New York World Telegram,* May 14, 1937; *New York Daily Mirror,* May 15, 1937.

27. *NYT,* April 25, 1937, 1; April 22, 1937, 1; FBI File 31-46627-A: *New York World Telegram,* May 27, 1937; *Washington Times,* April 22, 1937; *New York Evening Journal,* May 27, 1937; Faithful Mary, "God," 81–96, 111; Claude McKay, "Father Divine's Rebel Angel," *American Mercury,* February 1940, 73–80.

28. *Time,* May 3, 1937, 63.

29. *Harlem Heaven's Headman Pinched!* Hearst Metrotone News, April 23, 1937, Newsreel, UCLA Film Archives; *Time,* May 3, 1937, 63.

30. Faithful Mary, "God," 88; FBI File 31-46627-A: *New York Post,* June 18, 1937; *New York Daily Mirror,* June 18, 1937; *NYT,* June 18, 1937, 48; June 19, 1937, 8.

31. Faithful Mary, "God," 17–18, 37–39, 56.

32. Ibid., 23, 24–26.

33. Ibid., 24, 25–26.

34. Ibid., 3, 13, 111.

35. An editor of the *New York Amsterdam News* wrote the preface to Faithful Mary's work, which also contains a picture of an *Amsterdam News* reporter assisting Faithful Mary with her writing. Faithful Mary, "God," xi–xii, 99–110; FBI File 31-46627-A: *New York Evening Journal,* May 27, 1937; *New York Herald-Tribune,* June 2, 1937. Lesselbaum provided Faithful Mary with bodyguards when she testified in court against Father Divine.

36. St. Clair McKelway and A. J. Liebling, "Who Is This King of Glory?" *New Yorker,* pt. 2, June 20, 1936, 22–28; *NYT,* May 7, 1937, 29; FBI File 31-46627-A: *New York Herald-Tribune,* May 25, 1937; *New York Evening News,* May 27, 1937; *New York World Telegram,* May 27, 1937; *New York American,* May 25, 1937.

37. FBI File 31-46627-A: *New York Herald-Tribune,* May 25, 1937; *New York Evening News,* May 27, 1937; *New York World Telegram,* May 27, 1937; *New York American,* May 25, 1937; FBI File 31-46627: report, "Father Divine," June 2, 1937; John Hunt and F. Kirk, "Father Divine: God or Man?" *Our World,* August 1949.

38. Faithful Mary reprinted the court's decision in *"God,"* 47–57; *NYT,* May 29, 1937, 21.

39. The presence of William Lesselbaum at almost all cases against the Peace Mission movement in the late 1930s and his association with the *New York Evening Journal* link Hearst to the ongoing harassment of the organization. St. Clair McKelway and A. J. Liebling, "Who Is This King of Glory?" *New Yorker,* pt. 3, June 27, 1936, 23–32; FBI File 31-46627: Delight Jewett deposition, March 22, 1937, 9–10; John Wuest Hunt, File 31-3418, April 23, 1937, 2–3.

40. For a positive portrayal of Hearst during the 1930s, see Mrs. Fremont Older, *William Randolph Hearst: American* (New York: Books for Library Press, 1936). For a critical analysis that articulates many of the complaints of the liberal sector against Hearst, see Ferdinand Lundberg, *Imperial Hearst: A Social Biography* (1936; reprint, Westport, Conn.: Greenwood Press, 1970); Rodney Carlisle, *Hearst and the New Deal: The Progressive as Reactionary* (New York: Garland, 1979), 86–92, 144–60. Not surprisingly, one of the attacks on Hearst appearing in the *Spoken Word* came from former Utopian John Roine. *SW*, January 14, 1936, 30–31; April 7, 1936, 5.

41. *ND*, July 18, 1938, 39–40.

42. *ND*, November 17, 1938, 100.

43. *NYT*, July 29, 1938, 1; July 30, 1938, 15; *Newsweek*, August 8, 1938, 10–11; *Time*, July 24, 1938, 44; August 8, 1938, 7–8; Robert Weisbrot, *Father Divine and the Struggle for Racial Equality* (Urbana: University of Illinois Press, 1983), 110–11.

44. Spencer's Point was also known as Krum Elbow. *Father Divine and 2,500 Angels Inspect Their New Land at Krum Elbow, New York*, Hearst Metrotone News, August 9, 1938, Newsreel, UCLA Film Archives; Weisbrot, *Father Divine*, 110–11.

45. Weisbrot, *Father Divine*, 110–11; *NYT*, August 7, 1938, pt. 4, 9, 10; August 10, 1938, 3; August 28, 1938, 28.

46. Franklin Delano Roosevelt, *Complete Presidential Press Conferences of Franklin D. Roosevelt*, vol. 12, ed. Johnathan Daniels (New York: Da Capo Press, 1972), 31–33; Weisbrot, *Father Divine*, 110–11.

47. McKay, "Rebel Angel," 73–80. *NYT*, August 30, 1937, 9; *NYT*, February 22, 1938, 23; Carlisle, *Hearst*, 9, 192; Older, *William Randolph Hearst*, 359–62; Daniel Leab, *From Sambo to Superspade: The Black Experience in Motion Pictures* (Boston: Houghton Mifflin, 1976), 180.

48. McKay, "Rebel Angel," 78–79, 80; *ND*, December 29, 1938, A-3–A-6; January 12, 1939, 17–19.

49. *ND*, December 29, 1938, A-3–A-4.

50. Weisbrot, *Father Divine*, 209–10.

51. The first issue of the *New Day* appeared in May 1936, and the editors conceived of the publication as a "commercial" magazine. See *ND*, May 28, 1936, 2; *NYT*, August 21, 1937, 30. By 1937, the *Spoken Word* was reportedly suffering financial difficulties. *ND*, October 20, 1938, 2.

52. The migration east actually began with the editors of the *Spoken Word*; other key followers like John Devoute and his mother, Mary Bird Tree, followed. *ND*, August 27, 1942, 22; Hunt and Kirk, "Father Divine."

53. Followers later organized another order of older and previously married women—Lily-buds. Reverend M. J. Divine, *Rosebuds', Lily-buds', Crusaders' Creeds* (Philadelphia, n.p., n.d.); *ND*, October 10, 1941, 97; February 20, 1941, 1; December 4, 1941, 115–17; Lavere Belstrom interview, October 13, 1986, Philadelphia, Pennsylvania.

54. Reverend M. J. Divine, *Rosebuds', Lily-buds', Crusaders' Creeds*; Mrs. M. J. Divine, *The Peace Mission Movement* (Philadelphia: Imperial Press, 1982), 32.

55. Reverend M. J. Divine, *Rosebuds', Lily-buds', Crusaders' Creeds*. Apparently Priscilla Paul had not only violated Father Divine's restrictions against the intermingling of opposite sexes but had also become involved in several disputes with other followers. His condemnation was harsh: "Now I will let you see and let you know you cannot continue your contemptible acts and ways around ME and I tolerate it or compromise with, neither let it be hid! Now maybe you will be mad but let your madness be to yourself and you better keep your mouth shut and you better not go off and make up any lies, because if you do you are going to get your reward! I know that disposition, I know it; that is all! So the best thing for you to do is to get away from here as quick as you can!" *ND*, January 19, 1939, 64–65.

56. Reverend M. J. Divine, *Rosebuds', Lily-buds', Crusaders' Creeds*.

57. Letter: Mrs. M. J. Divine to Jill Watts, April 14, 1987; Mrs. M. J. Divine, *Peace Mission Movement*, 26–27.

58. Mrs. M. J. Divine, *Peace Mission Movement*, 26–27; Weisbrot, *Father Divine*, 210.

59. *SW*, January 14, 1936, 11; Reverend M. J. Divine, *The Peace Mission Movement As Explained by Father Divine* (Philadelphia: New Day Publishing, n.d.), 72; *ND*, June 2, 1938, 20.

60. Theodore Bilbo, *The Theodore Bilbo Papers*, McCain Library and Archives, The University of Southern Mississippi, Mary Magdelene Heart to Mr. T. G. Bilbow, May 27, 1940. For samples of other letters to the Mississippi senator, see Herald Stedfast to Senator Theodore G. Bilbo, June 2, 1940; Miss Mary Lamb to Hon. Theodore G. Bilbo, April 7, 1940. *ND*, July 25, 1940, 104–5. Bilbo retaliated by reporting to the FBI that Father Divine was allied with Axis powers. However, the Bureau did not act on Bilbo's allegations. FBI File 62-32932, vol. 1: letter: Bilbo to J. Edgar Hoover, June 2, 1940; letter: A Real American (White Girl) to Rep. Bilbo, May 30, 1940; letter: J. Edgar Hoover to Theodore G. Bilbo, June 21, 1940.

61. First spoken March 12, 1937, reprinted in *ND*, March 5, 1983, 8–9; July 25, 1940, 1, 86–93, 114; November 2, 1939, 10; July 25, 1940, 1, 86–93.

62. *ND*, November 5, 1942, 9; FBI File 62-32932, vol. 1: letter: [name censored] to FBI, March 30, 1942; letter: [name censored] to Secretary of War, December 22, 1941. The Bureau seemingly withheld documents pertaining to the investigation of Father Divine's ties to the Axis powers. Memorandums suggest that the FBI conducted a full-scale investigation of the movement during the war years; FBI File 62-32932, vol. 2: confidential report, P. E. Foxworth to Director, January 9, 1943; confidential report, T. J. Donegan to Director, January 23, 1943; report, E. E. Conroy to Director, April 3, 1943; office memorandum, Ladd, September 20, 1946, 3–5; George Baker alias "God," Father Divine, Reverend J. Divine, Major J. Devine, M. J. Devine, M. J. Divine, File 100-81748; FBI File 62-32932, vol. 3: George Baker alias "God," Father Divine, Reverend J. Divine, Major J. Devine, M. J. Devine, M. J. Divine, File 100-4838, 1–2.

63. *ND*, August 27, 1942, 24, 25; May 21, 1942, 13–14. For an account

of the proceedings of Verinda Brown's case, see *NYT,* January 4, 1940, 44; January 9, 1940, 25; January 18, 1940, 14; December 31, 1940, 13; March 1, 1941, 17; May 25, 1942, 25; June 9, 1942, 16; July 30, 1942, 23.

64. *ND,* August 27, 1942, 70; *Washington Times Herald,* July 30, 1942, 17; FBI File 62-32932, vol. 2: George Baker, File 100-81748, October 3, 1946, 5; *NYT,* July 20, 1942, 15; August 14, 1942, 34.

EPILOGUE

1. First spoken on August 7, 1946, reprinted in *ND,* April 25, 1987, 3; July 4, 1987, 9.

2. Mrs. M. J. Divine, *The Peace Mission Movement* (Philadelphia: Imperial Press, 1982), 56; *ND,* October 25, 1986, 7–8; Mrs. M. J. Divine interview, October 15, 1986, Gladwyne, Pennsylvania.

3. Mrs. M. J. Divine, *Peace Mission Movement,* 53–58; *ND,* October 25, 1986, 7–8; Mrs. M. J. Divine interview, October 15, 1986, Gladwyne, Pennsylvania.

4. Mrs. M. J. Divine, *Peace Mission Movement,* 53–58.

5. First spoken August 7, 1946, reprinted in *ND,* April 25, 1987, 1, 3–4; first spoken May 13, 1950, reprinted in *ND,* April 26, 1986, 3. Within certain Pentecostal circles, those who are saved are referred to as the brides of Christ, and the marriage to Christ assures these individuals that they will escape the horrors of the end of the world. The brides of Christ will enjoy eternal life after the Second Coming. For a discussion of this terminology, see James R. Goff, Jr., *Fields White Unto Harvest: Charles T. Parham and the Missionary Origins of Pentecostalism* (Fayetteville: University of Arkansas Press, 1988), 15–45.

6. *Time,* October 14, 1946, 58.

7. Theodore Bilbo, *The Theodore Bilbo Papers,* McCain Library and Archives, The University of Southern Mississippi.

8. See issues of the *New Day,* 1947–1989. Mrs. M. J. Divine, *Peace Mission Movement,* 53–58; *ND,* October 25, 1986, 7–8; Mrs. M. J. Divine interview, October 15, 1986, Gladwyne, Pennsylvania.

9. Bilbo, *Theodore Bilbo Papers;* John Hunt and F. Kirk, "Father Divine: Man or God?" *Our World,* August 1949. Although John Lamb split with the movement, he continued to be highly respected by Father Divine and his followers. Hezekiah Craig and Eli Diana interview, August 16, 1987, Los Angeles, California.

10. Hunt and Kirk, "Father Divine"; FBI File 31-74669: office memorandum, Philadelphia to Director, November 5, 1948; Sara Harris, *Father Divine, Holy Husband* (Garden City, N.Y.: Doubleday, 1953), 112.

11. Hunt and Kirk, "Father Divine."

12. FBI File 31-74669: office memorandum, A. Rosen to D. M. Ladd, November 30, 1949; office memorandum to Director from Philadelphia, November 5, 1948. Although the FBI censored the names of the witnesses and complainants, the testimony reveals that the evidence collected against

Father Divine came from Hunt and his wife. After the Bureau decided against prosecuting Father Divine, Hunt continued to urge the FBI to investigate Father Divine for a variety of alleged crimes. Throughout the fifties, Hunt supplied the Bureau with witnesses claiming to have been seduced by Father Divine, but after the initial investigation, the FBI took no further action.

13. See issues of the *New Day*, 1945–1958. Mrs. M. J. Divine, *Peace Mission Movement*, 143–53.

14. *ND*, December 28, 1957, s.22; September 10, 1955, s.31; Mrs. M. J. Divine, *Peace Mission Movement*, 155–81.

15. *ND*, September 12, 1987, 1, 4–5; December 28, 1957, s.57; *Time*, September 17, 1965, 41; Mrs. M. J. Divine, *Peace Mission Movement*, 59–64.

16. Visits to Woodmont Estate, October 12, 14, 15, 1986; Mrs. M. J. Divine, *Peace Mission Movement*, 59–64.

17. First spoken July 28, 1951, reprinted in Mrs. M. J. Divine, *Peace Mission Movement*, 150.

18. *ND*, December 28, 1957, s.58, s.22.

19. *Time*, September 17, 1965, 41.

20. Mrs. M. J. Divine, *Peace Mission Movement*, 99.

21. Mrs. M. J. Divine, *Peace Mission Movement*, 99; Mrs. M. J. Divine interview, October 12, 1986, Gladwyne, Pennsylvania; Heavenly Rest interview, December 15, 1986, Los Angeles, California.

22. Mrs. M. J. Divine, *Peace Mission Movement*, 51. An in-depth study concentrating on the ministry of Sweet Angel Divine would be an important topic for future research.

23. Mrs. M. J. Divine, *Peace Mission Movement*, 137–41; *NYT*, May 24, 1980, 6; C. Eric Lincoln and Lawrence H. Mamiya, "Daddy Jones and Father Divine: The Cult as Political Religion," *Religion in Life* 49 (Spring 1980): 6–23.

24. Mrs. M. J. Divine, *Peace Mission Movement*, 139.

25. *Guyana Tragedy: The Story of Jim Jones*, CBS movie, April 15, 16, 1980.

26. *National Enquirer*, August 4, 1987, 44.

27. Visits to the Circle Mission Church, 927 Jefferson Avenue, Los Angeles, California, 1983–1991.

28. *ND*, October 8, 1986, 21; Mrs. M. J. Divine interview, October 14, 1986, Gladwyne, Pennsylvania.

29. Visit to the Divine Tracy Hotel, October 12–19, 1986, Philadelphia, Pennsylvania; Mrs. M. J. Divine, *Peace Mission Movement*, 25, 29–31.

30. Visits to Woodmont Estate, October 12, 14, 15, 1986, Gladwyne, Pennsylvania; *ND*, July 15, 1989, 16–18.

31. Visits to Woodmont Estate, October 12, 14, 15, 1986, Gladwyne, Pennsylvania; Mrs. M. J. Divine, *Peace Mission Movement*, 60–61; *Philadelphia Enquirer*, March 13, 1986, 2M–4M; *Wall Street Journal*, May 8, 1985, 1, 16.

32. Mrs. M. J. Divine, *Peace Mission Movement*, 62; visit to Woodmont Estate, October 12, 1986, Gladwyne, Pennsylvania; visits to the Circle Mission Church, 927 Jefferson Avenue, Los Angeles, California, 1983–1991.

Selected Bibliography

PRIMARY SOURCES

INDIVIDUAL CONTRIBUTORS

Lavere Belstrom (Philadelphia, Pennsylvania)
Willie Mae Carey (Rockville, Maryland)
Edna Mae Claybrooke (Gladwyne, Pennsylvania)
George Corey (Los Angeles, California)
Hezekiah Craig (Los Angeles, California)
Eli Diana (Los Angeles, California)
Mrs. M. J. Divine (Gladwyne, Pennsylvania)
Righteous Endeavor (Los Angeles, California)
Mary Gordon Malloy (Rockville, Maryland)
Heavenly Rest (Los Angeles, California)
Eva Slezak (Baltimore, Maryland)
Jane Sween (Rockville, Maryland)

LETTERS

Mrs. M. J. Divine to Jill Watts, April 14, 1987.
Miss Veri Sweete to Jill Watts, March 7, 1983.

LOCAL, STATE, AND GOVERNMENT DOCUMENTS

Land Records, Montgomery County: JA 3; Montgomery County Court
  House, Rockville, Maryland.
Files of the Federal Bureau of Investigation, Father Divine:
  File 5D-2555
  File 9-33785
  File 9-38672
  File 31-46627
  File 31-46627-A
  File 31-74669
  File 62-32932, vol. 1
  File 62-32932, vol. 2
  File 62-32932, vol. 3
  File 62-32932-A

File 62-62736-2-9502
File 63-3583-2
File 100-0-23083
File 100-013773
Freedmen Bureau Records. Series 754, Roll 54.
———. Series 752, Roll 54.
Montgomery County (Slave Statistics) 1867–1868 [MdHR 9876]. Maryland State Archives, Annapolis, Maryland.
Montgomery County Board of Health (Death Records) 1899–1906 [MdHR 20, 213-2]. Maryland State Archives, Annapolis, Maryland.
Prince George's County (Slave Statistics) 1867–1868 [MdHR 6198]. Maryland State Archives, Annapolis, Maryland.
Sanborn Fire Insurance Map: Baltimore, Maryland (Baltimore: Sanborn Fire Insurance Company, 1901, 1910, 1914). Pratt Library, Baltimore, Maryland.
Sheriff, B. R. *R. L. Polk and Company's Baltimore City Directory for 1899.* Baltimore: R. L. Polk, 1899.
———. *R. L. Polk and Company's Baltimore City Directory for 1902.* Baltimore: R. L. Polk, 1902.
———. *R. L. Polk and Company's Baltimore City Directory for 1903.* Baltimore: R. L. Polk, 1903.
———. *R. L. Polk and Company's Baltimore City Directory for 1904.* Baltimore: R. L. Polk, 1904.
———. *R. L. Polk and Company's Baltimore City Directory for 1905.* Baltimore: R. L. Polk, 1905.
———. *R. L. Polk and Company's Baltimore City Directory for 1906.* Baltimore: R. L. Polk, 1906.
———. *R. L. Polk and Company's Baltimore City Directory for 1911.* Baltimore: R. L. Polk, 1911.
———. *R. L. Polk and Company's Baltimore City Directory for 1912.* Baltimore: R. L. Polk, 1912.
U.S. Bureau of the Census. *1850 Slave Census, Montgomery County, Maryland.*
———. *1860 Population Schedules, Prince George's County, Maryland.*
———. *1870 Population Schedules, Montgomery County, Maryland.*
———. *1870 Population Schedules, Prince George's County, Maryland.*
———. *1880 Population Schedules, Montgomery County, Maryland.*
———. *1900 Population Schedules, Montgomery County, Maryland.*
———. *1900 Population Schedules, Baltimore, Maryland.*
———. *1900 Population Schedules, Allegheny City, Pennsylvania.*
———. *1900 Population Schedules, Alexandria, Virginia.*
———. *1910 Population Schedules, Baltimore, Maryland.*

NEWSPAPERS, MAGAZINES, AND PERIODICALS

Baltimore Afro-American (1900–1940)
The Baltimore Sun (1900–1913)
The Black Man (1934–1936)
The California Eagle (1931–1942)
The Light (1933–1935)
Literary Digest (1937)
Los Angeles Herald-Express (1937)
Los Angeles Times (1932–1987)
The Metaphysical News (1929–1934)
Montgomery County Sentinel (1840–1900)
The Nassau Daily Review (1932)
The National Enquirer (1987)
Negro World (1929–1932)
The New Day (1936–1989)
Newsweek Magazine (1934–1965)
New York Age (1926–1936)
New York American (1937)
New York Amsterdam News (1930–1942)
New York Daily Mirror (1937)
New York Daily News (1937)
New York Evening Journal (1937)
New York Herald-Tribune (1937)
New York News (1932–1934)
New York Post (1937)
The New York Times (1919–1942)
New York World Telegram (1937)
Philadelphia Enquirer (1986)
The Reporter (1932)
The Spoken Word (1934–1937)
The Spokesman (1934)
The Suffolk County Citizen (1931)
Suffolk County News (1919–1940)
Time Magazine (1934–1965)
Utopian News (1935–1936)
Valdosta Daily Times (1914)
Wall Street Journal (1985)
Washington Times Herald (1937, 1942)
World Echo (1934)
World Herald (1937)

NEWSREELS, FILM, AND AUDIO

Divine, Reverend M. J. *The Word of God Revealed*. Audiocassette. Philadelphia: Peace Mission Movement, n.d.

Father Divine and 2,500 Angels Inspect Their New Land at Krum Elbow, New York. Hearst Metrotone News, August 9, 1938. Newsreel. UCLA Film Archives.

Guyana Tragedy: The Story of Jim Jones. CBS movie, April 15, 16, 1980.

Harlem Heaven's Headman Pinched! Hearst Metrotone News, April 23, 1937. Newsreel. UCLA Film Archives.

PAPERS

Bilbo, Theodore. *The Theodore Bilbo Papers.* McCain Library and Archives, The University of Southern Mississippi.

Du Bois, W. E. B. *The Papers of W. E. B. Du Bois.* New York: Microfilming Corporation of America, 1980.

Garvey, Marcus. *The Marcus Garvey and Universal Negro Improvement Association Papers.* Vol. 1, *1826–August 1919.* Edited by Robert A. Hill and Carol Rudisell. Berkeley: University of California Press, 1983.

———. *The Marcus Garvey and Universal Negro Improvement Association Papers.* Vol. 2, *27 August 1919–31 August 1920.* Edited by Robert A. Hill, Emory Tolbert, and Deborah Forczek. Berkeley: University of California Press, 1983.

———. *The Marcus Garvey and Universal Negro Improvement Association Papers.* Vol. 5, *September 1922–August 1924.* Edited by Robert A. Hill, Deborah Forczek, and Devra Weber. Berkeley: University of California Press, 1986.

Prettyman, William Forrest. "Remembrances of Rockville, Maryland." (Typewritten), n.d. In Montgomery County Historical Society, Rockville, Maryland.

Roosevelt, Franklin Delano. *Complete Presidential Press Conferences of Franklin D. Roosevelt.* Vol. 12. Edited by Johnathan Daniels. New York: Da Capo Press, 1972.

PAMPHLETS, ARTICLES, AND BOOKS

Baltimore Association. *First Annual Report: Baltimore Association for the Moral and Educational Improvement of Colored People.* Baltimore, 1865.

Bartleman, Frank. *Another Wave of Revival.* 1962. Reprint. Springdale, Pa.: Whitaker House, 1982.

Barton, Bruce. *The Man Nobody Knows: The Discovery of the Real Jesus.* Indianapolis: Bobbs-Merrill, 1925.

———. *The Book Nobody Knows.* New York: Grosset and Dunlap, c. 1926.

Benner, Joseph Sieber. *The Impersonal Life.* San Diego: Sun Publishing, 1916.

Cady, H. Emilie. *Lessons in Truth.* 1894. Reprint. Kansas City, Mo.: Unity School of Christianity, 1926.

Christ in You. New York: Dodd, Mead, 1918.

Collier, Robert. *The Secret of Gold.* New York: Robert Collier, 1927.

DeWaters, Lillian. *The Christ Within.* Stamford, Conn.: Lillian DeWaters, 1925.

Divine, Mrs. M. J. *The Peace Mission Movement*. Philadelphia: Imperial Press, 1982.

Divine, Reverend M. J. *A Treatise on Overpopulation Taken from Interviews, Sermons and Lectures of Father Divine*. Philadelphia: New Day, 1967.

———. *Here's the Answer*. N.p., n.d.

———. *The Peace Mission Movement as Explained by Father Divine*. Philadelphia: New Day, n.d.

———. *Rosebuds', Lily-buds', Crusaders' Creeds*. N.p., n.d.

Douglass, Frederick. *Life and Times of Frederick Douglass*. 1892. Reprint. New York: Collier Books, 1962.

Eddy, Mary Baker. *Science and Health*. Boston: Trustees, Will of Mary Baker G. Eddy, 1906.

Fillmore, Charles. *Jesus Christ Heals*. Kansas City, Mo.: Unity School of Christianity, 1909.

Grier, Albert C., et al. *Father Divine: An Interpretation with Appreciations and Comments*. Santa Barbara, Calif.: Red Rose Press, n.d.

Henson, Josiah. *Father Henson's Story of His Own Life*. Boston: John P. Jewett, 1858.

Krech, Shepard, III, ed. *Praise the Bridge That Carries You Over: The Life of Joseph L. Sutton*. Cambridge: Schenkman, 1981.

Krishnamurti, Jeddu. *The Kingdom of Happiness*. New York: Liverlight, 1927.

Lanyon, Walter Clemow. *The Eyes of the Blind*. Los Angeles: Inspiration House, 1959.

Mary, Faithful. *"God," He's Just a Natural Man*. New York: Gailliard Press, 1936.

Moseley, J. R. *Manifest Victory: A Quest and Testimony*. New York: Harper and Brothers, 1947.

Rawick, George, ed. *The American Slave: A Composite Autobiography*. Vol. 16, *Maryland Narratives*. Westport, Conn.: Greenwood Press, 1972.

Spalding, Baird T. *The Life and Teaching of the Masters of the Far East*. Vol. 1. Los Angeles: Devorss, 1924.

———. *The Life and Teaching of the Masters of the Far East*. Vol. 2. Los Angeles: Devorss, 1927.

Universal Negro Improvement Association. *Official Minutes of the Second Regional Conference*. Toronto: UNIA, 1937.

SECONDARY SOURCES

Anderson, Jervis. *This Was Harlem: A Cultural Portrait*. New York: Farrar Straus Giroux, 1981.

Aptheker, Herbert. *American Negro Slave Revolts*. 1943. Reprint. New York: International Publishers, 1967.

Atlas of Fifteen Miles Around Washington, Including County of Montgomery, Maryland. 1879. Reprint. Rockville, Md.: Montgomery County Historical Society, 1975.

Bach, Marcus. *They Have Found a Faith*. New York: Bobbs-Merrill, 1946.

Baker, Houston. *Modernism and the Harlem Renaissance*. Chicago: University of Chicago Press, 1978.

Baldwin, Lewis V. *"Invisible" Strands in African Methodism: A History of the African Union Methodist Protestant and Union American Methodist Episcopal Churches, 1805–1980*. Metuchen, N.J.: American Theological Library Association, Scarecrow Press, 1983.

Barrett, Leonard D. *The Rastafarians: Sounds of Cultural Dissonance*. Boston: Beacon Press, 1977.

Baur, John E. *The Health Seekers of Southern California, 1870–1900*. San Marino, Calif.: Huntington Library Press, 1959.

Bing, Bart. "Sayville Religious Teaching Draws Big Crowds." *Island News*, October 1, 1931. Reprinted in the *New Day*, June 15, 1974: 18–19.

Blassingame, John. "The Recruitment of Negro Troops in Maryland." *Maryland Historical Magazine* 58 (March 1963): 20–29.

———. *The Slave Community: Plantation Life in the Antebellum South*. New York: Oxford University Press, 1972.

Bloodworth, William. *Upton Sinclair*. Boston: Twayne, 1977.

Boyd, T. H. S. *The History of Montgomery County Maryland, From Its Earliest Settlement in 1650 to 1879*. 1879. Reprint. Baltimore: Regional Publishing, 1968.

Brackett, Jeffrey R. *Notes on the Progress of Colored People of Maryland since the War*. Baltimore: Johns Hopkins University Press, 1890.

Braden, Charles Samuel. *These Also Believe: A Study of Modern American Cults and Minority Religious Movements*. New York: Macmillan, 1949.

———. *Spirits in Rebellion: The Rise and Development of New Thought*. Dallas: Southern Methodist University Press, 1963.

Bromley, David G., and Anson D. Shupe. *Strange Gods: The Great American Cult Scare*. Boston: Beacon Press, 1981.

Brotz, Howard M. *The Black Jews of Harlem: Negro Nationalism and the Dilemmas of Negro Leadership*. London: Free Press of Glencoe, 1964.

Burkett, Randall. *Garveyism as a Religious Movement: The Institutionalization of a Black Civil Religion*. Metuchen, N.J.: American Theological Library Association, Scarecrow Press, 1978.

Burnham, Kenneth E. *God Comes to America: Father Divine*. Boston: Lambeth Press, 1979.

Butchard, Richard. *Northern Schools, Southern Blacks and Reconstruction: Freedmen's Education 1862–1875*. Westport, Conn.: Greenwood Press, 1980.

Callcott, Margaret Law. *The Negro in Maryland Politics: 1870–1912*. Baltimore: Johns Hopkins University Press, 1969.

Cantril, Hadley. *The Psychology of Social Movements*. New York: John Wiley and Sons, 1941.

Carlisle, Rodney. *Hearst and the New Deal: The Progressive as Reactionary*. New York: Garland, 1979.

Carter, Dan T. *Scottsboro: A Tragedy of the American South*. New York: Oxford University Press, 1969.

Carter, Lawrence T. *Eubie Blake: Keys of Memory*. Detroit: Balamp, 1979.

Clarke, Nina, and Lillian Brown. *History of the Black Public Schools of Montgomery County, Maryland, 1872–1961*. New York: Vantage Press, 1978.

Copp, Henry. *Peerless Rockville: What It Offers to Homeseekers and Investors (How to Get Health, Wealth, and Comfort)*. Washington, D.C.: Gibson Brothers, 1890.

Creel, Margaret Washington. *"A Peculiar People": Slave Religion and Community-Culture Among the Gullahs*. New York: New York University Press, 1988.

Cronon, E. David. *Black Moses: The Story of Marcus Garvey and the Universal Negro Improvement Association*. Madison: University of Wisconsin Press, 1955.

Crooks, James B. *Politics and Progress: The Rise of Urban Progressivism in Baltimore, 1895–1911*. Baton Rouge: Louisiana State University Press, 1968.

Daniels, Elam J. *Father Divine: The World's Chief False Christ*. Winter Garden, Fla.: Bible Echo Press, 1937.

Davie, Maurice R. *Negroes in American Society*. New York: McGraw-Hill, 1949.

Davis, Grady Demus. *A Psychological Investigation of Motivational Needs and Their Gratification in the Father Divine Movement*. Madison, Wis.: Microcard Foundation, American Theological Library Association, 1960.

Davis, Kenneth. *FDR, the New Deal Years: 1933–1937*. New York: Random House, 1986.

Dickerson, Charles P. *A History of the Sayville Community*. Sayville, N.Y.: Suffolk County News, 1975.

Dresser, Horatio. *History of the New Thought Movement*. New York: Thomas Y. Crowell, 1919.

Du Bois, W. E. B. *The Souls of Black Folk*. Chicago: A. C. McClurg, 1903.

Farquhar, Roger Brooke. *Old Homes and History of Montgomery County, Maryland*. Baltimore: Monumental, 1952.

Fauset, Arthur Huff. *Black Gods of the Metropolis*. Philadelphia: University of Pennsylvania Press, 1944.

Fields, Barbara Jeanne. *Slavery and Freedom on Middle Ground: Maryland during the Nineteenth Century*. New Haven: Yale University Press, 1985.

———. "Slavery, Race and Ideology in the United States of America." *New Left Review* 181 (May–June 1990): 95–119.

Fogelson, Robert M., and Richard E. Rubinstein. *The Complete Report of Mayor LaGuardia's Commission on the Harlem Riot of March 19, 1935*. New York: Arno Press, New York Times, 1969.

Foner, Philip. *Organized Labor and the Black Worker, 1619–1973*. New York: Praeger, 1979.

Frazier, E. Franklin. *The Negro Church in America*. 1963. Reprint. New York: Schocken Books, 1974.

Genovese, Eugene. *Roll Jordon Roll: The World the Slaves Made*. New York: Vintage Books, 1972.

Goff, James R., Jr. *Fields White Unto Harvest: Charles T. Parham and the Mis-*

sionary Origins of Pentecostalism. Fayetteville: University of Arkansas Press, 1988.

Graham, Leroy. *Baltimore: The Nineteenth Century Black Capital*. Washington, D.C.: University Press of America, c. 1982.

Greene, Suzanne Ellery. *Baltimore: An Illustrated History*. Woodland Hills, Calif.: Windsor, 1980.

Gutman, Herbert. *The Black Family in Slavery and Freedom*. New York: Pantheon, 1976.

Hagood, L. M. *The Colored Man in the Methodist Episcopal Church*. 1890. Reprint. Freeport, N.Y.: Books for Libraries Press, 1971.

Harding, Vincent. *The Other American Revolution*. Los Angeles, Atlanta: Center for Afro-American Studies, University of California, Los Angeles, Institute of the Black World, 1980.

Harlan, Louis. *Booker T. Washington*. Vol. 1, *The Making of a Black Leader*. New York: Oxford University Press, 1972.

———. *Booker T. Washington*. Vol. 2, *The Wizard of Tuskegee, 1910–1915*. New York: Oxford University Press, 1983.

Harris, Sara. *Father Divine: Holy Husband*. Garden City, N.Y.: Doubleday, 1953.

Harris, Sara, and Harriet Crittendon. *The Incredible Father Divine*. London: W. H. Allen, 1954.

Hawkins, Hugh, ed. *Booker T. Washington and His Critics*. Lexington, Mass.: D. C. Heath, 1974.

Henri, Florette. *Black Migration: Movement North, 1900–1920*. Garden City, N.Y.: Anchor Press, 1975.

Hiebert, Ray Eldon, and Richard K. MacMaster. *A Grateful Remembrance: The Story of Montgomery County, Maryland*. Rockville, Md.: Montgomery County Government, Montgomery County Historical Society, 1976.

Hill, Robert A., and Barbara Bair, eds. *Marcus Garvey: Life and Lessons*. Berkeley: University of California Press, 1987.

Hofstadter, Richard. *Age of Reform: From Bryan to FDR*. 12th ed. New York: Alfred A. Knopf, 1977.

Holmes, Ernest Shurtleff. *New Thought Terms and Their Meanings*. New York: Dodd, Mead, 1942.

Holtzman, Abraham. *The Townsend Movement: A Political Study*. New York: Octagon Books, 1975.

Hoshor, John. *God in a Rolls-Royce: The Rise of Father Divine, Madman, Menace, or Messiah*. New York: Hillman-Curl, 1936.

Howell, Clarence. "Father Divine: Another View." *Christian Century*, October 7, 1936, 1332–33.

Huggins, Nathan Irvin. *Harlem Renaissance*. New York: Oxford University Press, 1971.

Hunt, John, and F. Kirk. "Father Divine: God or Man?" *Our World*, August 1949.

Jackson, Carl. *The Oriental Religions and American Thought: Nineteenth-Century Explorations*. Westport, Conn.: Greenwood Press, 1981.

Jackson, Kenneth. *The Ku Klux Klan in the City, 1915–1930.* New York: Oxford University Press, 1967.

Jones, Raymond Julius. *A Comparative Study of Religious Cult Behavior Among Negroes with Special Reference to Emotional Group Conditioning Factors.* Washington, D.C.: Graduate School for Division of the Social Sciences, Howard University, 1939.

Kelley, Hubert. "Heaven Incorporated." *American Magazine,* January 1936, 40–41, 106–8.

Kephart, William. *Extraordinary Groups: The Sociology of Unconventional Life Styles.* New York: St. Martin's Press, 1976.

Koger, Azzie Brisco. *Negro Baptists of Maryland.* Baltimore: Clark Press, 1946.

Kramer, Victor, ed. *The Harlem Renaissance Reexamined.* New York: AMS Press, 1987.

Larson, Martin A. *New Thought or A Modern Religious Approach: The Philosophy of Health, Happiness, and Prosperity.* New York: Philosophical Library, 1985.

Leab, Daniel. *From Sambo to Superspade: The Black Experience in Motion Pictures.* Boston: Houghton Mifflin, 1976.

Leuchtenburg, William E. *Franklin Roosevelt and the New Deal.* New York: Harper Colophon Books, 1963.

Levine, Lawrence. *Black Culture and Black Consciousness.* New York: Oxford University Press, 1977.

LeWarne, Charles P. "Vendovi Island: Father Divine's 'Peaceful Paradise of the Pacific.' " *Pacific Northwest Historical Quarterly* 75 (January 1984): 2–12.

Lewinson, Edwin R. *Black Politics in New York City.* New York: Twayne, 1974.

Lewis, David Levering. *When Harlem Was in Vogue.* New York: Vintage Books, 1982.

Library of Congress. *Newspapers in Microform: United States, 1948–1972.* Washington, D.C.: Library of Congress Catalogue Division, 1973.

Lincoln, C. Eric. *Race, Religion and the Continuing American Dilemma.* New York: Hill and Wang, 1984.

Lincoln, C. Eric, and Lawrence H. Mamiya. "Daddy Jones and Father Divine: The Cult as Political Religion." *Religion in Life* 49 (Spring 1980): 6–23.

———. *The Black Church in the African American Experience.* Durham, N.C.: Duke University Press, 1990.

Litwack, Leon. *Been in the Storm So Long: The Aftermath of Slavery.* New York: Random House, 1979.

Long, Charles J., ed. *Who's Who: Los Angeles County: 1932–1933.* Los Angeles: Who's Who in Los Angeles County Publishing, 1933.

Lowe, W. A. "The Freedmen's Bureau in the Border States." In *Radicalism, Racism, and Party Realignment: The Border States During Reconstruction,* ed. Richard Curry, 245–64. Baltimore: Johns Hopkins University Press, 1969.

Lundberg, Ferdinand. *Imperial Hearst: A Social Biography.* 1936. Reprint. Westport, Conn.: Greenwood Press, 1970.

McDaniel, George W. *Hearth and Home: Preserving a People's Culture.* Philadelphia: Temple University Press, 1982.

McKay, Claude. " 'There Goes God!' The Story of Father Divine and His Angels." *Nation,* February 6, 1935, 151–53.

———. "Father Divine's Rebel Angel." *American Mercury,* February 1940, 73–80.

———. *Harlem: Negro Metropolis.* New York: E. P. Dutton, 1940.

———. *Harlem Glory: A Fragment of Afro-American Life.* Chicago: Charles H. Kerr, 1990.

McKelway, St. Clair, and A. J. Liebling. "Who is This King of Glory?" *New Yorker,* pt. 1, June 13, 1936, 21–28; pt. 2, June 20, 1936, 22–28; pt. 3, June 27, 1936, 22–32.

McMain, Robert, ed. *Historic Saint Mary's.* Washington, D.C.: Moore and Moore, 1963.

McWilliams, Carey. *Southern California, An Island on the Land.* 2d ed. Santa Barbara, Calif.: Peregrine Smith, 1973.

Marquis, Albert Nelson, ed. *Who's Who in America.* Vol. 17, 1932–33. Chicago: Marquis Who's Who, 1932.

Martin, Walter. *The Kingdom of Cults.* Minneapolis: Bethany House, 1985.

Mays, Benjamin, and Joseph W. Nicholson. *The Negro's Church.* New York: Russell and Russell, 1933.

Melton, J. Gordon. *Encyclopedic Handbook of Cults in America.* New York: Garland, 1986.

Mencken, H. L. *Newspaper Days: 1899–1906.* New York: Alfred A. Knopf, 1941.

Mibiti, John S. *African Religions and Philosophies.* New York: Praeger, 1959.

Morris, Robert. *Reading, 'Riting, and Reconstruction: The Education of Freedmen in the South, 1861–1870.* Chicago: University of Chicago Press, 1981.

Muraskin, William. "Harlem Boycott of 1934." *Labor History* 13 (Summer 1972): 361–73.

Naison, Mark. *Communists in Harlem during the Depression.* Chicago: University of Illinois Press, 1983.

"Negro Segregation in the Cities." *Chautauquan,* March 1911, 11–13.

Nelson, Geoffrey K. "The Spiritualist Movement and the Need for a Redefinition of Cult." *Journal for the Scientific Study of Religion* 8 (Spring 1960): 52–60.

———. "The Membership of a Cult: The Spiritualists National Union." *Review of Religious Research* 13 (Spring 1972): 170–77.

Newman, Richard. *Black Power and Black Religion.* Cornwall, Conn.: Locust Hill Press, 1987.

Nugent, John Peer. *The Black Eagle.* New York: Stein and Day, 1971.

Older, Mrs. Fremont. *William Randolph Hearst: American.* New York: Books for Library Press, 1936.

Olson, Sheri H. *Baltimore, The Building of an American City*. Baltimore: Johns Hopkins University Press, 1980.

Orlansky, Harold. *The Harlem Riot: A Study in Mass Frustration*. New York: Social Analysis, 1943.

Ottley, Roi. *'New World A-Coming': Inside Black America*. New York: Houghton Mifflin, 1943.

Parker, Gail Thain. *Mind Cure in New England: From the Civil War to World War I*. Hanover, N.H.: University Press of New England, 1973.

Parker, Robert Allerton. *Incredible Messiah: The Deification of Father Divine*. Boston: Little, Brown, 1937.

Pearson, Fred Lamar, and Joseph Aaron Tomberlin. "John Doe, Alias God: A Note on Father Divine's Georgia Career." *Georgia Historical Quarterly* 60 (1976): 43–48.

Peerless Rockville Historic Preservation. *A Walking Guide to "Peerless Rockville."* Rockville, Md.: Peerless Rockville Historic Preservation, 1975.

Pendleton, Helen B. "Negro Dependence in Baltimore." *Charities: A Review of Local and General Philanthropy* 15 (October 7, 1905): 50–58.

Raboteau, Albert J. *Slave Religion: The "Invisible Institution" in the Antebellum South*. New York: Oxford University Press, 1978.

Ransom, Roger L., and Richard Sutch. *One Kind of Freedom: The Economic Consequences of Emancipation*. New York: Cambridge University Press, 1977.

Rawick, George. *From Sundown to Sunup: The Making of the Black Community*. Westport, Conn.: Greenwood Press, 1972.

Reynolds, Edward. *Stand the Storm: A History of the Atlantic Slave Trade*. New York: Allison and Busby, 1985.

Richardson, Harry V. *Dark Salvation: The Story of Methodism As It Developed Among Blacks in America*. Garden City, N.Y.: Doubleday, Anchor Press, 1976.

Rudin, James A., and Marcia Rudin. *Prison or Paradise?* Philadelphia: Fortress Press, 1980.

Rudwick, Elliott. *W. E. B. Du Bois: A Study in Minority Group Leadership*. Philadelphia: University of Pennsylvania Press, 1960.

Scharf, John Thomas. *History of Western Maryland*. Vol. 1. 1882. Reprint. Baltimore: Regional Publishing, 1968.

Scheiner, Seth. "The Negro Church and the Northern City, 1890–1930." In *Seven on Black: Reflections on the Negro Experience in America*, ed. William G. Shade and Roy C. Herrenkohl, 92–116. Philadelphia: J. B. Lippincott, 1969.

Schroeder, Theodore. "Living Gods." *Azoth: The Occult Magazine of America*, October 1918, 202–5.

———. "Psychology of One Pantheist." *Psychoanalytic Review* 20 (July 1921): 314–25.

———. "A 'Living God' Incarnate." *Psychoanalytic Review* 19 (January 1932): 40–41.

Singleton, Gregory. *Religion in the City of the Angels: American Protestant*

Culture and Urbanization, Los Angeles. Ann Arbor, Mich.: UMI Research Press, 1979.

Sitkoff, Harvard. *A New Deal for Blacks.* New York: Oxford University Press, 1978.

———. "Review of *Father Divine and the Struggle for Racial Equality.*" *American Historical Review* 89 (1984): 542–43.

Spitz, Lewis W. *The Protestant Reformation.* New York: Harper and Row, 1985.

Stampp, Kenneth. *Era of Reconstruction: 1865–1877.* New York: Random House, 1965.

Starr, Kevin. *Inventing the Dream: California through the Progressive Era.* New York: Oxford University Press, 1985.

Stein, Judith. *The World of Marcus Garvey: Race and Class in Modern Society.* Baton Rouge: Louisiana State University Press, 1986.

Stevenson, George John. *The Methodist Hymn-Book.* London: S. W. Partridge Company, 1883.

Strauss, Gerald. *Luther's House of Learning.* Baltimore: Johns Hopkins University Press, 1978.

Susman, Warren. "Piety, Profits and Play." In *Men, Women and Issues in American History,* ed. Howard Quint and Milton Cantor, 202–27. Homewood, Ill.: Dorsey Press, 1980.

Thompson, Noma. *Western Gateway to the National Capital, Rockville, Maryland.* Washington, D.C., 1949.

Tinney, James S. "William J. Seymour: Father of Modern-Day Pentecostalism." In *Black Apostles: Afro-American Clergy Confront the Twentieth Century,* ed. Randall Burkett and Richard Newman. Boston: G. K. Hall, 1978.

Tolbert, Emory. *The UNIA and Black Los Angeles.* Los Angeles: UCLA Afro-American Studies Center, 1980.

Troeltsch, Ernst. *The Social Teachings of Christian Churches.* New York: Macmillan, 1956.

Tuttle, William M., Jr. *Race Riot: Chicago in the Red Summer of 1919.* New York: Atheneum, 1970.

Van Baalen, Jan Karel. *The Chaos of Cults.* 3d ed. Grand Rapids, Mich.: William B. Eerdmans, 1942.

Van Dalsem, Newton. *History of the Utopian Society of America.* Los Angeles: Utopian Society, 1942.

Vincent, Theodore G. *Voices of a Black Nation: Political Journalism in the Harlem Renaissance.* San Francisco: Ramparts Press, 1973.

Waring, J. H. N. "Some Causes of Criminality Among Colored People." *Charities: A Review of Local and General Philanthropy,* October 7, 1905, 45–49.

Warren, Marion E., and Mame Warren. *Baltimore: When She Was What She Used to Be: 1850–1930.* Baltimore: Johns Hopkins University Press, 1983.

Washington, Booker T. "Law and Order and the Negro." *Outlook,* November 6, 1909, 547–51.

Washington, Joseph R., Jr. *Black Sects and Cults: The Power Axis in an Ethnic Ethic.* Garden City, N.Y.: Doubleday, Anchor Press, 1973.

Weisbrot, Robert. *Father Divine and the Struggle for Racial Equality.* Urbana: University of Illinois Press, 1983.

Weiss, Richard. *The American Myth of Success: From Horatio Alger to Norman Vincent Peale.* New York: Basic Books, 1969.

White, Ronald Moran. "New Thought Influences on Father Divine." M.A. thesis, Miami University, 1980.

Wilmore, Gayraud S. *Black Religion and Black Radicalism: An Interpretation of the Religious History of Afro-American People.* 2d ed. Maryknoll, N.Y.: Orbis Books, 1983.

Wilson, Moses. *Black Messiahs and Uncle Toms: Social and Literary Manipulations of a Religious Myth.* University Park: Pennsylvania State University Press, 1982.

Yinger, Milton J. *The Scientific Study of Religion.* New York: Macmillan, 1970.

Index

Compositor: Maple-Vail Book Mfg. Group
Text: 10/13 Palatino
Display: Palatino
Printer: Maple-Vail Book Mfg. Group
Binder: Maple-Vail Book Mfg. Group